Crash Course in Storytime Fundamentals

Recent Titles in
Libraries Unlimited Crash Course Series

Crash Course in Storytime Fundamentals

Second Edition

Penny Peck

Crash Course

AN IMPRINT OF ABC-CLIO, LLC
Santa Barbara, California • Denver, Colorado • Oxford, England

Library of Congress Cataloging-in-Publication Data

Peck, Penny.
    Crash course in storytime fundamentals / Penny Peck. — Second edition.
      pages cm. — (Crash course)
    Includes bibliographical references and index.
    ISBN 978-1-61069-783-5 (pbk.) — ISBN 978-1-61069-784-2 (ebook)   1. Storytelling—
United States.   2. Children's libraries—Activity programs—United States.   3. Libraries and
preschool children—United States.   I. Title.
    Z718.3.P43 2015
    027.62'51—dc23   2014033895

ISBN: 978-1-61069-783-5
EISBN: 978-1-61069-784-2

19 18 17 16 15   1 2 3 4 5

This book is also available on the World Wide Web as an eBook.
Visit www.abc-clio.com for details.

Libraries Unlimited
An Imprint of ABC-CLIO, LLC

ABC-CLIO, LLC
130 Cremona Drive, P.O. Box 1911
Santa Barbara, California 93116-1911

This book is printed on acid-free paper ∞

Manufactured in the United States of America

CONTENTS

INTRODUCTION TO THE SECOND EDITION

Storytime is one of the bedrock services of a public library. Even small one-room libraries will offer a weekly storytime, where parents bring preschoolers to hear stories, sing songs, and check out books. This service has been a part of libraries for more than a century. Large, urban libraries used storytime as a way to convey literature to immigrant children and to help them learn English. It modeled read-aloud techniques to parents, and demonstrated the types of books that were appropriate for children. Even now, in a world where technology has replaced or greatly changed how libraries deliver some of their services, storytime is still an important program. Hearing books read out loud by an adult cannot be replaced by television or the computer; as publisher Dick Jackson once said, preschoolers "need laps, not laptops." Even for libraries that include a story using a tablet device, most of the storytime still involves songs, fingerplays, and books. So if offering storytime at a public library is a new responsibility for you, this Crash Course guide can quickly instruct you on how to perform this service. You may soon learn that doing storytime is the highlight of your week!

Storytime is not just reading stories to a group of children. We incorporate other elements like songs, fingerplays, puppets, movement, arts and crafts, and other visual elements. We also try to convey some preliteracy skills so parents can continue building those skills at home when they read to their children. Techniques like dialogic reading, or other ways to help a child connect the words on the page to reading are modeled during storytime, and parents can copy those techniques. We will cover the five skills parents can see you do during storytime, including playing and singing, so they can continue the preliteracy activities at home. We will also discuss kindergarten readiness, which is covered at many preschool storytimes. Many parents are aware that children are tested upon entering kindergarten and are assessed as to their reading readiness, so offering some kindergarten readiness information can be a great motivator for parents to bring their preschoolers to library storytimes. We will also discuss using volunteers at storytimes, to expand your services to include more storytimes aimed at different ages, and to include bilingual storytime if your community warrants one.

As with other books in the Crash Course series, this book is designed for the novice. It is a starting place; there is a bibliography of other helpful books written on presenting a baby storytime, or a toddler time, or a preschool storytime. It also lists books with ideas for songs and fingerplays, using puppets, arts and crafts ideas, and storytelling techniques, and there are several references to useful websites on many of these same topics. Finally, the book concludes with 100 themed storytime outlines that will be useful to those who already present storytime. These themed outlines include books, songs, activities, and crafts on a topic and are designed for preschool storytime, but of course you can adapt them for toddler or infant storytimes as well. So even well-seasoned storytime presenters should find something useful in this book. Hopefully, it will inspire you to add some new elements to your storytimes, or to start a storytime at your library!

CHAPTER 1

Storytime

Many library employees work at small branches where there may not be a children's librarian on staff. But the community could really benefit from having a weekly library storytime. If you work at such a library, or are a new children's librarian, or have transferred to the Children's Department in a library system, you may be called upon to offer storytime. This "Crash Course" can help you learn how to present storytimes to a wide age group with confidence so it is a rewarding experience for both you and the audience.

WHAT IS STORYTIME?

Thirty years ago when I was a new children's librarian, it was the custom to hold library storytime just for preschoolers. Also, parents were not permitted to come into the story room, and the library registered all attendees with a limit of 20 children. The preschoolers would try to sit quietly and listen to the picture books being read, and songs and fingerplays, and then they would go with their parent to check out books. One of the first changes my supervisor and I made was to allow parents in the room, and dispense with registration. I also wanted to finish each storytime with a simple craft or art project to engage the kinetic learners. Nowadays, librarians under age 40 can't believe that is how it was—and that was the norm! Storytimes have been in libraries for more than 100 years, and they are still a vital and essential service, but they are evolving to emphasize more preliteracy skills, to involve the parents and model read aloud techniques to caregivers, and to add storytimes for infants and toddlers. Sometimes these programs are referred to as "storyhour," even if they last 30 minutes.

1

This chapter will introduce some of the basics of storytime, and as you move through the book we will add other information, such as working with parents and caregivers, or using volunteers. You will discover that storytime doesn't require one to play the guitar or perform but to choose entertaining books and present them in a comfortable manner. Props, storytelling, puppets, and crafts will be covered, as well as publicity and making storytime accessible to a wide audience by reducing red tape. While parents are attending or bringing their children to storytime, you will have an opportunity to talk with them about reading to their children. If you provide a Parent's Bookshelf, you can point out its location and they can look there for other resources, such as books on potty training.

WHY WE DO STORYTIME

Librarians have been conducting storytimes for more than a century; it was the first library program, and we offer storytime because it introduces young children to good books, and conveys the idea that books and reading are valuable. It also models read-aloud techniques for the parents who attend, boosts circulation, and helps preschoolers get ready for kindergarten. They learn skills such as listening to the teacher, sitting quietly, and paying attention. Reading specialists have determined that the one constant in creating a successful reader is a child who is read to on a regular daily basis. Reading ability isn't based on income or class, but on the fact that someone read to that child on a daily basis.

When parents start coming to storytime, they quickly learn that the public library is a major parenting resource center. A big bonus is that the family gets in the habit of coming to the library. When they become regular library users, even as the children grow older, the family will keep coming back for other programming, homework resources, and media. This is especially true if we create a "family-friendly" library, with a section for young children where noise is tolerated, and where toys and other resources are there for very young children to enjoy while the parent selects books to take home or to read in the library.

RESEARCH

Considerable research has been conducted on early brain development, and there has been a lot of media coverage on this. Articles online, and in magazines, newspapers, and the TV news, are telling parents that even babies need to be read to. It shouldn't be too difficult to find some of these articles if you need to include justification for having lapsit or toddler time or if you need to write a proposal for starting these storytimes. Pediatricians are also helping to promote reading to infants and young children with a program called "Reach Out and Read." In this program, doctors give a free book when the child comes for his or her "well baby" visit, which they do about every six months. This includes visits where they get their inoculations and tests for hearing and other developmental testing. The doctors give out free books and remind parents how important it is to read to a child. If you have a flyer available about your library storytimes, pediatricians are a great resource to help you publicize your program.

STORYTIME FORMAT

So, just what is a storytime? There isn't "one best way" of doing a program, but the standard storytime often holds to the following pattern:

Opening song—"Wheels on the Bus"—"It's time to get on the bus and go to storytime!"
Movement song—"Head and Shoulders"—librarian introduces him/herself
Listening song—"Open, Shut Them"
Announce our theme—Stories about Bedtime
Book—*The Napping House* by Don and Audrey Wood, using flannelboard figures
Movement song—"If You're Happy and You Know It"
Counting song with puppet—"Five Little Ducks"
Book—*Llama Llama Red Pajama* by Anna Dewdney
Fingerplay—"Twinkle, Twinkle, Little Star"
Book—*How Do Dinosaurs Say Goodnight?* by Jane Yolen
Song with flannelboard—"Ten in a Bed"
Book—*I Said "Bed!"* by Bruce Degan
Closing song—"Five Little Monkeys Jumping on the Bed"
Craft—Make a simple doorknob hanger that says "Quiet—We Are Reading!"

For the lyrics to the songs and fingerplays listed above, check out the website www.kididdles.com.

Now that we are all on the same page as to what a storytime encompasses, let's talk about what you need to plan and start holding storytimes, and the various types of storytimes. But if you are still unclear on the format of storytime, be sure to visit another library where you can observe one in person; there is no substitute for actually seeing a storytime where parents and children are together.

PHYSICAL ENVIRONMENT

Whether holding the storytime in a meeting room or in the children's area of the library itself, some basic rules of the physical area will work to your advantage. Preschoolers can sit in a semicircle on the carpet, facing the storytime presenter, with parents sitting toward the back of the circle. Some parents like to hold the child on their lap (this is fine), which works if they sit toward the back or sides of the circle so they are not blocking anyone's view. Some parents like to sit in a chair at the back and let their children sit on the carpet by themselves. That is fine too; many grandparents or older caregivers and expectant moms find sitting on the floor uncomfortable. It is not recommended that the children sit in chairs; the carpet works better and you can fit more people. If the floor is not carpeted, see if a local store will donate old carpet sample squares, or have the Friends of the Library purchase a children's carpet available at teacher supply stores (such as www.lakeshorelearning.com). If the storytime is for babies or toddlers, it is preferred that the child and caregiver sit on the floor together, as they will be expected to do several movement songs together.

Think of the area where the reader sits as the stage: you want to be a little higher than the audience who is on the floor, so you will probably want a chair or stool to sit on. Try not to have anything distracting behind you, like a walking area, window, or clock; sit against a blank wall if possible. Try to sit with the entrance door to the back of the circle; that way, latecomers won't distract the audience because the door is not in the line of sight of the audience.

The reader should hold the book with the page facing the audience; do this by grasping the lower edge of the book, with the book's open spine in your hand to hold it open. That way, you can see the book and the audience can as well. Slowly pass the book in front of you from one side to the other, so everyone can see. Turn the page and read, then pass again to the other side.

PREPARATION

Just how much time does it take to prepare for storytime? That depends on how much time you have. If you wear many hats and don't have a lot of preparation time, try to read the book to yourself at least three times and that should be sufficient to have a natural rhythm to your reading. That will be especially helpful with rhyming books, so you can anticipate the beat of the lines of poetry. If you repeat songs, that will also decrease how much preparation time you need. Learning a new song every week is a luxury that few of us can afford, but if you have time, great! Children like songs to be repeated more often than stories, so learning five or six songs to begin with is plenty. Parents also like it when you repeat songs, because it makes it easier for them to join in. You can add a new song approximately once a month if you want to, that should be enough so you don't get bored.

The craft project (if you include one) should take very little prep, maybe just photocopying the coloring sheet or cutouts; if it takes more time than that, see if teen volunteers can do the preparation for you. Most high school students are now required to do volunteer service to graduate and they can be a great help in preparing craft projects that need pre-gluing or pre-cutting.

SCHEDULING

The scheduling of the different types of storytimes will depend on the target audience; it is important that the time of day be convenient for the parent and child, not, for example, at naptime. Of course, you want to schedule the storytimes when it is convenient for staff, but not if it is a time when no one will attend!

Lapsit

Mornings are usually the best time to engage a child under the age of 5 or 6. They are awake and not yet ready for naptime; they have had breakfast and are not yet hungry for lunch. Try holding the lapsit/baby storytime, for infants up to 18 months before the library opens. If the library opens at 10 A.M., begin lapsit at 9:30 A.M., so by the time you have concluded the storytime, the library is open and parents can check out books. The mornings seem to work best as the babies are not as sleepy or cranky. This can also benefit your staff schedule, as the storytime presenter can do the baby storytime, then move on to helping at the public service desk.

Toddler Time

Toddlers range from age 12 months to 3 years of age, so there is some overlap with lapsit and preschool storytimes. Toddler time can be held at 11 A.M. on the same day as the lapsit. Some families stay for both because they have a baby and a toddler. The toddler time runs for about 25 minutes. That time seems to work really well; it isn't nap time, and you can conclude in plenty of time for them to get back home for lunch. If you work at a very small library with just a few staff members, you may want to hold the toddler time on a different day than the baby storytime, but again hold it before the library opens so the presenter is free afterward to help with reference or circulation. Many small libraries have just a few staff members on duty at any time; holding your storytimes a half hour before the library opens can be an easy solution to a staffing shortage, and mornings are best for young children anyway.

Preschool and Family Storytimes

Many libraries will hold two sessions of preschool storytime, which use the same books, on the same day: one at 10:30 A.M. and one at 1:30 P.M., for example. The afternoon storytime attracts many who attend transitional or regular kindergarten, and older preschoolers (4-year-olds) who no longer take naps. The morning session seems to attract more young preschoolers who take naps. You can also hold an evening family storytime, which attracts babies, toddlers, preschoolers, and kids in kindergarten, first, second, and third grades. It is attended by families whose work schedules prevent them from coming to the other storytimes. Depending on your area, the evening storytime can begin at 7 P.M. or 7:30 P.M. Try the earlier time, and if most folks come late, or if you get little turnout, try the later time. If you live in an area where many working parents have a long commute, the later time will be better for them. Saturday mornings can also be a good time for a family storytime, for parents who are working during the weekdays.

GETTING STARTED

If you will be starting to have storytime at your library, either for the first time or after a lapse without any storytimes, start with a weekly preschool storytime in the morning. If that is well attended, branch out to an evening storytime for working parents. If you are in a suburban area, the evening storytime is very likely to be well attended if the word gets out that it is being held. At a downtown city library, evening storytimes may not meet much need unless there is a lot of housing in the area; if it is all office buildings, having an evening storytime at a branch library nearer to family housing may be more popular. If both the morning preschool storytime and the evening family storytime grow to be well attended, add a lapsit on a different morning. Then expand to a toddler time if that will meet a need. This will take time; you may want to add a new storytime just once a year especially if your staff is small or if you are the only fulltime staff member in the children's department.

Some libraries schedule their storytime sessions like college classes; the sessions may last eight to ten weeks, then there is a break. For some of the families who attend, that can be confusing. Holding storytimes on a more regular basis is easier for parents and caregivers to remember, especially if you don't have registration, and you want to include more immigrant families who are still learning English. It is easier to remember that story-time is every Tuesday morning at 10:30 A.M., than to remember which eight-week period is set aside for a storytime session.

MARKETING YOUR STORYTIMES

Publicity is fundamental to the success of any library program, including storytime. A press release with a photo in your local newspaper is a sure way to get the word out. Be sure to have a bulletin board and flyers at your library to notify parents who already come to the library.

Social Media

Many parents are more likely to visit the library's website or Facebook page before they visit the library and notice flyers or bulletin boards. Make sure you promote your storytimes on those websites, as well as on Twitter and other social media. Request that storytime be periodically featured on the main entry page as well as permanently on the children's section of the library's website. Include photos if possible, along with publiciz-ing the themes, arts and crafts, kindergarten readiness activities, or other elements that could motivate the parent or caregiver to attend storytime.

Free Places to Advertise Storytime

Flyers at the local preschools and pediatricians' offices are also an easy way to reach your target audience. Another great way to outreach to parents who are not currently using the library is to put flyers at places they often go to, such as laundromats, children's cloth-ing and toy stores, recreation programs for young children, and places of worship. You can also have your local elementary schools distribute the flyers to primary graders, since many of them will have siblings in the target age group.

Flyers in Other Languages

Many of us live in communities that have large populations who are learning English, and are more likely to speak another language at home. These groups are a target audience for storytime since they may not be aware of the custom of library storytime, and they want to help their children prepare for kindergarten. If there is a dominant foreign language or two spoken in your area, prepare flyers in those languages welcoming parents and young children to your storytime; even if the storytime is in English, they will want to attend as a way to practice English with their children.

LIBRARY TOURS FOR PARENTS AND THEIR YOUNG CHILDREN

Library tours are not just for school classes but for parents and younger children, too. Contact local preschools and daycare centers to see if they can visit the library for a brief tour and a storytime that is just for them. You can also offer tours to parents and children before a storytime in September, or before summer vacation, when you are likely to have new families attending. Another alternative is to offer a special parent and preschooler tour on a Saturday once or twice a year, to give a library orientation to new families in the area.

Because preschoolers have limited attention spans, talk about the things they are most likely to be interested in: checking out books, the children's area and computers, the picture book area, parents' shelf, and media for preschoolers. If parents want to know more about the adult area of the library, give them the schedule for adult tours.

If you give a lot of tours for young children, you can incorporate props. You can do several things to reach the visual, aural, and kinetic learners in a library. Take a free book poster and glue it, using rubber cement, to some tagboard. Then, cut it into a jigsaw puzzle of eight to ten pieces. Have a piece at each major area you are describing: the circulation desk, children's desk, picture books, magazines, DVDs, easy readers, and other areas. The child who can answer a question based on what was just said gets to hold that puzzle piece: "Can you check out books for 1, 2, or 3 weeks?" or "Who wrote *Green Eggs and Ham?*" Then, the children can put the puzzle together to see who is on the poster. This helps them pay attention to what you are saying.

Conclude the tour by reading a fun picture book, usually library related. My favorite for toddlers and preschoolers is *Lola at the Library* by Anna McQuinn (Charlesbridge, 2006). Another fun story set in the library is *Books Always Everywhere* by Jane Blatt (Random House, 2013), which has just two or three words per page; this would even work at a lapsit storytime. One with lots of energy and appeal is *Dinosaur vs. the Library* by Bob Shea (Hyperion, 2011). Then go over what is the same and what is different about your library from the one in the story.

Tours can be a great way to introduce the library to new users, and those families will become regular library visitors if the tour is memorable and fun. They are likely to become regular storytime audience members, too!

WHO CAN DO STORYTIME?

I don't believe you need to be a Children's Librarian with a Master's Degree to be the only one qualified to do storytime. Many of our library assistants have previous experience working at schools, or have other skills that allow them to do storytime. I do believe, however, that the Children's Librarian should do storytime periodically, even if it is to cover those on vacation, because you are the person with the responsibility for the programming. You may have to evaluate the library assistant who does storytime, so you should have experience. You are also the collection development person, so you want to know what are the types of books you should buy that will be successful at storytime. You should also do storytime every once in a while to see behavior issues, see who is coming so you can decide if you need to do outreach, and generally be aware of what it entails and who you are reaching with your storytimes. But library assistants who show interest in doing storytime should be encouraged; with a wider range of staff members to choose from, your library can offer more storytimes, from lapsit and toddler time to bilingual and family storytimes.

Now that we have an overview of storytime, the following chapters will go into more detail on different age groups, ways of enlivening storytime, how to choose books, assisting parents, and other issues. The last section of the book contains outlines for a year's worth of storytimes, which you can adapt to your audience. So there is no excuse for not having storytime at your library! Plus, it is really fun!

CHAPTER 2

Storytime for Babies

Whether it is called lapsit storytime, baby bounce, infant storytime, prewalker storytime, or baby and me storytime, a storytime for children from birth to 18 months is now considered an essential library program. Because there has been so much publicity about brain research and infants, most libraries are expanding the storytime schedule to include at least one weekly program for infants. The American Library Association even has a program called Born to Read, which was started in 1995 to develop partnerships between libraries and healthcare providers to promote reading to babies.

LAPSIT

The storytime for babies, which I will call lapsit, has two main goals. One is to engage babies with great books and songs to promote preliteracy skills. The other goal is to model for parents the types of books, songs, and read-aloud techniques that are developmentally suited to babies and to emphasize how important it is to read to babies. Both the babies and the parents and caregivers are equally important as participants in this storytime. It is essential that the caregivers participate fully by singing the songs, listening to the stories, and doing the movement activities. For a fun look at baby storytime, check out the short picture book *Leo Loves Baby Time* by Anna McQuinn.

Format

The format for lapsit is tailored to the young infants who are not yet confident walkers. These babies may be able to stand and move, or it can be a small baby, but they are not yet ready to sing and dance like a toddler. The format is mellower than the toddler story-time, and contains lots of rhymes, soothing songs, and very short board books and picture books. An average length of a lapsit is 20–25 minutes, beginning with a welcome song, then a rhyme, then a very short book, then another song, rhyme, and book, then a final song, rhyme, book and closing song. Unlike toddler time or preschool storytime, themes are not normally used for lapsit; choosing great books and repeating songs are more impor-tant than themes. You are likely to have time for just three, and maybe four books, but all of the books are very short. Often they will be board books, which average about 12 pages in length. A few picture books are also suitable for this age group, especially books with just a few words per page, and bright, bold illustrations that don't have too much detail. A baby's eyesight cannot discern details, so the deeply saturated colors in a simple picture book is more suitable for this age group. A list of books recommended for lapsit is given at the end of this chapter.

Format for Baby Lapsit Storytime

Opening song: "What'll I do With the Baby-O?"
Song: "Can You Roll Your Hands"
Get ready song: "Pat-a-Cake"
Book: *Tickle Time!* by Sandra Boynton
Fingerplay: "Here Is My Book"
Participation book: *Pete the Cat and his Four Groovy Buttons* by James Dean
Nursery rhyme: "Hey Diddle Diddle"
Song: "Three Little Kittens"
Flannelboard: "Itsy Bitsy Spider"
Book: *Mama Cat Has Three Kittens* by Denise Fleming
Movement rhyme: "I'm a Little Teapot"
Closing song: "Twinkle, Twinkle, Little Star"
Closing activity: Pass out board books to encourage the parents or caregivers to read to
    their babies.

Sign Language

Using sign language at lapsit, even some simple signs used while singing the songs, is very age appropriate. Studies have shown that using simple signs while speaking to a baby encourages the development of their language skills. Sign language can empower young children to communicate, enhancing their language and social skills. Of course, sign language can benefit the children with special needs who are coming to storytime.

Some board books contain diagrams of the signs you can use while reading the story! These include *Five Little Ducks* and *Old MacDonald* (Child's Play, 2013). Another way to learn some simple signs is to view the DVD series *Signing Time!* from Two Little Hands. Since it is recommended to repeat lapsit songs regularly, you can try just learning a few signs to go along with those songs, and then build from there.

Scheduling

Mornings seem to work best for lapsit, even for working parents, because that is when the babies are most alert. Afternoons get into naptime, and evenings are unlikely to be viable since babies often are asleep by then. Try doing lapsit before the library is open, ending around the time the library opens so parents can check out books. Holding lapsit before you open can be really helpful if you do not have a separate space for programming. You can hold the lapsit in the library, but you won't be interrupted by other patrons. Even in families where both parents work, one may have a flexible schedule that will allow them one morning off a week to be with the baby. Or, a grandparent or other caregiver will bring the baby to a morning storytime. It is less likely that parents will bring an infant to an evening lapsit, even if they work all day, because the baby will be asleep by then. If you find mornings are not attracting people, you can also try a lapsit at 6:00 P.M. on a weeknight. If both parents work, they may be able to attend an early evening storytime with the baby, then go home afterward for dinner and to put the baby to bed.

Registration

Registration can be prohibitive to many of the families who need storytime, like English language learners. For a lapsit storytime to be effective, a small group is more desirable than a large group. The maximum that seems to work for lapsit are 15 pairs of baby and parent or caregiver. Ten pairs are even better. A larger group makes it difficult for the baby to see the books and focus on what is happening; but when you first begin holding lapsit, you may not need registration. As word of mouth spreads, you may find the group hitting the desirable attendance limit. At that time you might want to add a second lapsit and require registration for both, allowing the regulars to sign up first, then allowing new parents to register. Since lapsit is about 20 minutes in length, if you have a separate space, you might be able to do two lapsits back to back. That way, the first group can enjoy lapsit, then move into the library to find books, and so the parents can talk to each other and share advice. Then the second group can come into the meeting room for their lapsit. See what works for you; in some smaller towns, you may only get enough babies for one lapsit; in larger towns you may need to have registration and hold two lapsits.

SONGS AND RHYMES

Like all storytimes, songs are as essential as the books you choose. With lapsit, you should repeat the songs regularly. Many of the songs you use at toddler and preschool storytimes will work for lapsit if they are simple and repetitive. We use some special types of rhymes with babies like tickle rhymes that we probably won't use at the other storytimes, so they are listed below. For more on the songs and fingerplays, go to Chapter 5.

Tickle Rhymes

Simple rhymes that involve a soft tickle on the baby are called tickle rhymes. One of the most popular is "Round and Round the Garden," and other rhymes where you tickle the baby's bellybutton. These create a great bonding experience for the baby and caregiver. As the storytime provider, you can use a doll or teddy bear to help you demonstrate the rhyme. Here are some favorites:

"Round and Round the Garden"
Round and round the garden
Goes the teddy bear.

One step, two steps,
Tickle him under there!

"These Are Baby's Fingers"
These are baby's fingers,
These are baby's toes.
This is baby's belly button,
Round and round it goes!

These are baby's eyes,
And this is baby's nose.
This is baby's belly button,
Right where Mommy blows!

"Arabella Miller"
Little Arabella Miller
Found a fuzzy caterpillar.
First it crawled up on her mother.
Then it crawled on baby brother.
Everyone said, "Arabella Miller!
Take away that caterpillar!"

Bouncing Rhymes

Bouncing rhymes are also called knee jogs, since you bounce the baby on your knee as if the baby was going on a pony ride. It is helpful to demonstrate these to show how gentle you should be, and to show how much fun they can be for the baby. Here are some of the most commonly used bouncing rhymes:

"Trot, Trot to Boston"
Trot, trot to Boston,
Trot, trot to Lynn,
Trot, trot to Salem,
Home, home again.

"Bumping Up and Down"
Bumping up and down in my little red wagon,
Bumping up and down in my little red wagon,
Bumping up and down in my little red wagon,
Won't you be my darling?

One wheel's off and the axle's broken,
One wheel's off and the axle's broken,
One wheel's off and the axle's broken,
Won't you be my darling?

"This Is the Way the Farmer Rides"
This is the way the farmer rides,
The farmer rides, the farmer rides.
This is the way the farmer rides
So early in the morning.

This is the way the lady rides,
The lady rides, the lady rides,
This is the way the lady rides
So early in the morning.

This is the way the gentleman rides,
The gentleman rides, the gentleman rides.
This is the way the gentleman rides,
So early in the morning.

Body Rhymes

Probably the best-known rhyme about the body is "Head, Shoulders, Knees, and Toes." Toddlers and even preschoolers love to stand up and do this rhyme, but parent and baby can do this too, with baby lying on his or her back. The rhymes involve pointing to the body part named, which helps a baby and toddler learn vocabulary.

"Head and Shoulders, Knees and Toes"
Head and shoulders, knees and toes,
Knees and toes.
Head and shoulders, knees and toes,
Knees and toes.
Eyes, ears, mouth and nose.
Head, shoulders, knees and toes, knees and toes!

"This Little Piggy"
This little piggy went to market (wiggle the baby's toe)
This little piggy stayed home
This little piggy had roast beef,
This little piggy had none.
And this little piggy went "Wee, wee, wee" all the way home!

"This Is the Way We Wash"
This is the way we wash our hands,
Wash our hands, wash our hands.
This is the way we wash our hands,
So early in the morning.

This is the way we wash our face,
Wash our face, wash our face.
This is the way we wash our face,
So early in the morning.

This is the way we wash our feet,
Wash our feet, wash our feet.
This is the way we wash our feet,
So early in the morning.

This is the way we brush our hair (etc.)
This is the way we brush our teeth (etc.)

Lullabies

If you notice the babies are crying, or squirming, or you get the impression they are out of sorts, a quiet lullaby is a great way to get everyone back in the mood to hear a story or song. Have the caregivers gently rock the baby while we all sing the lullaby; it should bring a calming feeling to the room.

"Twinkle, Twinkle Little Star"
Twinkle, twinkle, little star.
How I wonder what you are.
Up above the world so high,
Like a diamond in the sky.
Twinkle, twinkle, little star.
How I wonder what you are.

"Rock-a-bye Baby"
Rock-a-bye baby, on the treetop.
When the wind blows, the cradle will rock.
When the bough breaks, the cradle will fall.
And down will come baby, cradle and all.

"Hush Little Baby"
Hush little baby, don't say a word.
Mama's (or Papa) gonna buy you a mockingbird.
If that mockingbird don't sing,
Mama's gonna buy you a diamond ring.
If that diamond ring turns brass,
Mama's gonna buy you a looking glass.
If that looking glass gets broke,
Mama's gonna buy you a billy goat.
If that billy goat won't pull,
Mama's gonna buy you a cart and bull.
If that cart and bull turns over,
Mama's gonna buy you a dog named Rover.
If that dog named Rover won't bark,
Mama's gonna buy you a horse and cart.
If that horse and cart fall down,
You'll still be the sweetest little baby in town.

If you would like to learn more tickle songs, knee jogs, or other baby songs, check the books and websites listed at the end of this chapter.

BOOKS FOR VERY YOUNG CHILDREN

Books for babies need to be brief; their attention span only allows for a book that takes just two or three minutes to read. Besides the length of the text, the other aspect to evaluate is the illustration style. The eyesight of a baby cannot see small details, so look for very simple drawings and distinct colors.

Board Books

Board books are usually small, hand-held cardboard books of approximately 8 to 12 pages in length, intended for babies. They can stand up to a toddler's grip, and often have very simple photographs or cartoon illustrations and very little text. Some of the best are the Max the bunny board books created by Rosemary Wells; they have now evolved into longer picture books starring Max and his bossy sister Ruby. But the original Max books were pithy, humorous board books, where Max often spoke in one-word sentences. Some newer board books that work well for storytime include the "Maisy" series by Lucy Cousins, featuring a little white mouse. Also, check out the board books by Leslie Patricelli, many of which include repeated phrases that will appeal to the audience. My favorites are the board books by Sandra Boynton; they are hilarious to an adult, but also very baby/toddler appropriate.

Board books circulated by the library are often chewed, since it is common for a baby to put things in his or her mouth. A few parents may wonder if these books are germ carriers; if so, you can wipe off the books with a baby wipe. Board books usually have a plastic coating on the covers and all the pages, which makes it fine to wipe them off with a moist cloth.

Currently, there is a trend to turn a popular picture book into a board book. This is not usually successful. The shrunken illustrations lose too much detail, or sometimes the text is abridged; it is usually better to find board books that started as board books and are not just "dumbed down" picture books. Bill Martin's *Chicka Chicka Boom Boom* originated as a picture book; the board book version chopped off the ending to fit in the smaller format!

Picture Books

Picture books can appeal to a wide age range; generally speaking, they are made for a parent to read to a child. Some, like Margaret Wise Brown's classic *Goodnight Moon*, are well suited to a baby. Others are better for toddlers, and more are aimed at preschoolers. Some picture books are made for children in kindergarten and even older, so you really have to look at the picture book to see if it will be appropriate for lapsit. Are the pictures simple, in bold colors? If the pictures are too detailed with lots of sketchy ink outlines and shading, they may not be easy for a baby to see. How many words per page? If it is more than a short phrase per page, the book is better suited to toddlers or preschoolers. If you are not sure what type of picture book will work for lapsit, read a few of those listed at the end of this chapter to get a feel for what is recommended. Then, you will have something you can use as a comparison when looking at and evaluating new books.

Mother Goose

Nursery rhymes are common throughout the world; in Western culture, they became known as Mother Goose rhymes in approximately 1700. Some think Mother Goose was based on the English monarch Elizabeth I. But these rhymes, in whatever language, appeal to babies and toddlers for many reasons. They are bouncy, and song-like, and music has a great effect on a baby. The rhymes often have alliteration, and some even have tongue twisters. They feature animals and humor, two topics of great appeal to toddlers. They often involve counting or the alphabet. They are as catchy as advertising jingles, as memorable as TV theme songs, and can build an immediate connection between a baby and caregiver.

Two versions of old Mother Goose rhymes and illustrations are still popular; Kate Greenaway's and Arthur Rackham's illustrations are still in print in Mother Goose collections. They were originally done about 150 years ago. Scholars Peter and Iona Opie compiled several Mother Goose and nursery rhyme collections that are still in print. Randolph Caldecott, for whom the children's book illustration award is named, published *Hey Diddle Diddle Picture Book* in the late 1880s. The two biggest differences in Mother Goose collections are the illustrations and the choice of rhymes. These two factors will influence what choices you make for both your library and for storytimes.

The best-selling contemporary Mother Goose collections are those illustrated by Rosemary Wells; these have a wide age appeal, from babies to even emergent readers, and the rhymes were selected by Iona Opie. The bright colors and animal characters are very eye catching. A few years ago, the equally charming illustrated Mother Goose by Tomie DePaola had many of the same qualities, bright colors and animal characters. A new collection that also includes songs and other material is David McPhail's *My Mother Goose: a Collection of Favorite Rhymes, Songs, and Concepts* (Roaring Brook, 2013).

For a multicultural take on the subject, check out Nina Crews' *The Neighborhood Mother Goose* (Greenwillow, 2004). First published in 1968, Robert Wyndham's *Chinese Mother Goose Rhymes*, illustrated in soft watercolors by Ed Young, is still popular in parts of the United States where many residents speak and read Chinese. Some bilingual English/Spanish nursery rhyme books are now available such as *Tortillitas Para Mama and Other Nursery Rhymes* by Margot C. Griego (Square Fish, 1988), which have the same appeal as Mother Goose rhymes. Or try *Pio Peep: Traditional Spanish Nursery Rhymes* by Alma Flor Ada (Rayo, 2013).

All of these are "gateway" books, leading young children to the love of rhyme and poetry. Mother Goose should be the starting, not stopping point, for this audience to experience rhyming texts. Once they are preschoolers who can recite Mother Goose rhymes from memory, an important kindergarten readiness skill, you can follow up with poetry collections for young children at your preschool storytimes.

RESOURCES FOR BABY STORYTIMES

A wealth of books are suitable for baby storytimes, and many new books for this age group are published each year. Below is a list of great books, suitable for a lapsit. For even more information on how to conduct a lapsit, read *Baby Storytime Magic: Active Early Literacy through Bounces, Rhymes, Tickles, and More* by Kathy MacMillan and Christine Kirker (American Library Association, 2014). They include tips for planning your storytimes as well as songs, flannelboards, American Sign Language activities, and other information. Another great resource is Jane Cobb's *What'll I Do With the Baby—O?* (Black Sheep Press, 2007), which is a collection of rhymes, songs, and fingerplays, with an accompanying CD.

WEBSITES ON BABY STORYTIMES

Kate McDowell's Website
http://katemcdowell.com/laptime/

McDowell started the website as the result of her practicum for her MLIS. She includes ideas for themes, tips on baby storytime, ideas for working with parents, and other practical advice.

Perry Public Library

www.perrypubliclibrary.org/rfb

This Ohio library's website has a great list of baby rhymes, with all the words.

Mel's Desk

http://melissa.depperfamily.net/blog/?page_id=3835

Melissa Depper offers outlines for nearly 50 baby storytimes, including song lyrics, literacy tips, and suggested books.

Born to Read

www.ala.org/alsc/issuesadv/borntoread

The Association of Library Service to Children, a division of the American Library Association, launched this initiative 20 years ago. It offers libraries resources for baby storytimes, and programs to motivate parents to read to their babies.

BOOKS FOR BABIES

Board Books

Bang, Molly. *Ten, Nine, Eight.*
Barrett, Mary Brigid. *All Fall Down.*
Barrett, Mary Brigid. *Pat-a-Cake.*
Beaton, Clare. *Clare Beaton's Garden Rhymes.*
Blair, Karen. *Baby Animal Farm.*
Blake, Michel. *Baby's Day.*
Blake, Michel. *Let's Play.*
Boynton, Sandra. *Barnyard Dance.*
Boynton, Sandra. *But Not the Hippopotamus.*
Boynton, Sandra. *Doggies: A Counting and Barking Book.*
Boynton, Sandra. *Perfect Piggies! A Book! A Song! A Celebration!*
Boynton, Sandra. *Your Personal Penguin.*
Braun, Sebastien. *Growl! Growl! (Can You Say It Too).*
Braun, Sebastien. *Moo! Moo! (Can You Say It Too).*
Braun, Sebastien. *Roar! Roar! (Can You Say It Too).*
Braun, Sebastien. *Woof! Woof! (Can You Say It Too).*
Coat, Janik. *Hippopposites.*
Cousins, Lucy. *Count with Maisy.*
Cuyler, Margery. *The Little Dump Truck.*
Falconer, Ian. *Olivia's Opposites.*
Falconer, Ian. *Olivia Counts*
Franceschelli, Christopher. *Alphablock.*
Global Fund for Children. *American Babies.*

Global Fund for Babies. *Global Babies.*
Global Fund for Babies. *Global Baby Boys.*
Global Fund for Babies. *Global Baby Girls.*
Henkes, Kevin. *Owen's Marshmallow Chick.*
Henkes, Kevin. *Sheila Rae's Peppermint Stick.*
Horacek, Petr. *Honk, Honk! Baa, Baa!*
Hutchins, Hazel. *Cat Comes Too.*
Hutchins, Hazel. *Dog Comes Too.*
Hoban, Tana. *Black on White.*
Hoban, Tana. *White on Black.*
Intrater, Roberta G. *Splash!*
Intrater, Roberta G. *Smile!*
Isadora, Rachel. *Peekaboo Morning.*
Katz, Karen. *Counting Kisses.*
Katz, Karen. *Mommy Hugs.*
Kreloff, Elliot. *Mama, Where Are You?*
Kubler, Annie. *Head, Shoulders, Knees, and Toes.*
Kubler, Annie. *If You're Happy and You Know It.*
Kubler, Annie. *Itsy, Bitsy Spider.*
Kubler, Annie. *Teddy Bear, Teddy Bear.*
Light, Steve. *Planes Go.*
Light, Steve. *Trucks Go.*
Light, Steve. *Trains Go.*
MacDonald, Suse. *Dino Shapes.*
Muldrow, Diane. *Mama, Where Are You?*
Murphy, Mary. *I Kissed the Baby!*
Newman, Lesle'a. *Daddy, Papa, and Me.*
Newman, Lesle'a. *Mommy, Mama, and Me.*
Oxenbury, Helen. *All Fall Down.*
Oxenbury, Helen. *Clap Hands.*
Oxenbury, Helen. *Say Goodnight.*
Oxenbury, Helen. *Tickle, Tickle.*
Page, Stefan. *We're Going to the Farmers' Market.*
Patricelli, Leslie. *Baby Happy Baby Sad.*
Patricelli, Leslie. *Blankie.*
Patricelli, Leslie. *Birthday Box.*
Patricelli, Leslie. *No No Yes Yes.*
Patricelli, Leslie. *Quiet Loud.*
Patricelli, Leslie. *Tickle.*
Patricelli, Leslie. *Tubby.*
Rathmann, Peggy. *Good Night, Gorilla.*
Riggs, Kate. *A Seed Needs Sun.*
Slier, Debby. *Cradle Me.*
Slier, Debby. *Loving Me.*
Star Bright Books. *Carry Me (Babies Everywhere).*
Star Bright Books. *Eating the Rainbow (Babies Everywhere).*
Star Bright Books. *Families (Babies Everywhere).*
Thompson, Carol. *One, Two, Three . . . Climb!*

Thompson, Carol. *One, Two, Three . . . Crawl!*
Thompson, Carol. *One, Two, Three . . . Jump!*
Thompson, Carol. *One, Two, Three . . . Run!*
Uzon, Jorge. *Go, Baby, Go!*
Uzon, Jorge. *Hello, Baby!*
Uzon, Jorge. *Look Around, Baby!*
Wells, Rosemary. *Counting Peas.*
Wells, Rosemary. *Hide-and-Seek.*
Wells, Rosemary. *Love.*
Wells, Rosemary. *Max's Bedtime.*
Wells, Rosemary. *Max's First Word.*
Wells, Rosemary. *Max's New Suit.*
Wells, Rosemary. *Max's Ride.*
Wells, Rosemary. *The Bear Went Over the Mountain.*
Wells, Rosemary. *BINGO.*
Wheeler, Lisa. *Farmer Dale's Red Pickup Truck.*
Wright, Blanche Fisher. *The Real Mother Goose Board Book.*
Yonezu, Yusuke. *Guess What? Food.*
Yonezu, Yusuke. *Guess What? Fruit.*
Zabini, Eleni. *The Best Daddy in the World.*

Picture Books

Adams, Diane. *Two Hands to Love You.*
Allen, Kathryn Madeline. *A Kiss Means I Love You.*
Barton, Byron. *My Bus.*
Barton, Byron. *My Car.*
Blackall, Sophie. *Are You Awake?*
Braun, Sebastien. *I Love My Mommy.*
Braun, Sebastien. *I Love My Daddy.*
Brown, Margaret Wise. *Goodnight Moon.*
Carlstrom, Nancy. *Jesse Bear, What Will You Wear?*
Cousins, Lucy. *Maisy.*
Crum, Shutta. *Mine!*
Degen, Bruce. *Jamberry.*
Dewdney, Anna. *Llama Llama Mad at Mama.*
Fleming, Denise. *In the Small, Small Pond.*
Fox, Mem. *Ten Little Fingers and Ten Little Toes.*
Fox, Mem. *Where Is the Green Sheep?*
Hacohen, Dean. *Tuck Me In!*
Haughton, Chris. *Little Owl Lost.*
Henkes, Kevin. *Little White Rabbit.*
Hill, Eric. *Where's Spot?*
Hudson, Cheryl Willis. *Hands Can.*
Isadora, Rachel. *Uh-Oh!*
Krauss, Ruth. *Goodnight, Goodnight, Sleepyhead.*
Lawrence, John. *This Little Chick.*
Lewis, Anne Margaret. *Fly, Blanky, Fly.*
Long, Sylvia. *Hush Little Baby.*

Markes, Julie. *Shhhhh! Everybody's Sleeping.*
Martin, David. *We've All Got Bellybuttons!*
McQuinn, Anna. *Leo Loves Baby Time.*
Meyers, Susan. *Everywhere Babies.*
O'Connell, Rebecca. *The Baby Goes Beep.*
Palatini, Margie. *No Nap! Yes Nap!*
Parenteau, Shirley. *Bears in the Bath.*
Patricelli, Leslie. *Faster! Faster!*
Patricelli, Leslie. *Higher! Higher!*
Pinkney, Jerry. *Three Little Kittens.*
Reid, Aimee. *Mama's Day with Little Gray.*
Saltzberg, Barney. *Chengdu Could Not, Would Not Fall Asleep.*
Savadier, Elivia. *Time to Get Dressed!*
Sheilds, Carol Diggory. *Baby's Got the Blues.*
Sturges, Philemon. *I Love Trucks!*
Sturges, Philemon. *I Love Planes!*
Sturges, Philemon. *I Love Trains!*
Tafolla, Carmen. *Fiesta Babies.*
Wheeler, Lisa. *Jazz Baby.*
Williams, Vera. *"More, More, More," Said the Baby.*
Wood, Audrey. *Piggies.*
Yolen, Jane. *How Do Dinosaurs Say Good Night?*

Mother Goose

Ada, Alma Flor and Campoy, F. Isabel. *Pio Peep! Traditional Spanish Nursery Rhymes.*
Crews, Nina. *The Neighborhood Mother Goose.*
DePaola, Tomie. *Tomie DePaola's Mother Goose.*
Dillon, Leo and Diane. *Mother Goose: Numbers on the Loose.*
Dyer, Jane. *Animal Crackers: A Delectable Collection of Pictures, Poems, and Lullabies for the Very Young.*
Engelbreit, Mary. *Mary Engelbreit's Mother Goose.*
Griego, Margot C. *Tortillitas Para Mama and Other Nursery Rhymes.*
Long, Sylvia. *Sylvia Long's Mother Goose.*
Mavor, Salley. *Pocketful of Posies: A Treasury of Nursery Rhymes.*
McPhail, David. *My Mother Goose: A Collection of Favorite Rhymes, Songs, and Concepts.*
Marshall, James. *James Marshall's Mother Goose.*
Moses, Will. *Mother Goose.*
Opie, Iona. *My Very First Mother Goose.*
Opie, Iona. *Here Comes Mother Goose.*
Wyndham, Robert. *Chinese Mother Goose Rhymes.*
Yaccarino, Dan. *Mother Goose.*

CHAPTER 3

Toddler Storytime

Because of the movement activity and energy needed to present a toddler storytime, many of us have found it to be our aerobic workout for the day! Songs, fingerplays, action rhymes, and dances are all part of the toddler storytime. And, of course, books! Toddler time is a great way to build preliteracy skills, and can be a highlight of the day for a busy parent, since it allows for parents to talk to others with children the same age and to exchange tips and information about their children. Toddler storytimes can draw big audiences, and parents will check out stacks of books, too. If you don't currently hold a toddler storytime, give it serious consideration as it is a vital resource for parents of young children and well worth the time to do it.

TOTALLY NONSTOP TODDLERS—TNT

Toddler storytimes may have one of several names: walker storytime (as opposed to prewalker or infant storytime), tot time, toddler tales, and my favorite, TNT or totally nonstop toddler storytime. We use this title to help parents know we do not expect their toddlers to sit quietly for the half-hour program; instead, they know this storytime involves lots of movement, singing, and action. Many parents of toddlers are afraid they will be asked to leave the library if their toddler starts with some "Terrible Twos" behavior, but our storytime title clues them in that this storytime is loud and fun!

Format

The format for a toddler storytime has many of the same elements as an infant or preschool storytime: a welcoming song, a closing song, a fingerplay or song before each book, and other visual elements like puppets, flannelboards, or props that will hold the attention of a young child. A main difference between infant and toddler storytimes is the types of songs; we do many movement songs at toddler time, from "Head and Shoulders, Knees and Toes," to "The Hokey Pokey" and "Shake Your Sillies Out." Between each book, there may be a movement song, then another song to help the toddler sit and get ready to listen, such as "Open, Shut Them," or "This Old Man." An average toddler storytime could be outlined as follows:

Format for Toddler Time

Opening song: "Hello Everybody Yes Indeed"
State theme or subject of today's books—Dogs
Get ready song: "Open Shut Them"
Book: *Yip! Snap! Yap!* by Charles Fuge
Fingerplay: "This Old Man"
Participation book: *Bark, George* by Jules Feiffer
Nursery rhyme: "Old Mother Hubbard"
Song: "B-I-N-G-O"
Book: *Stick!* by Andy Pritchett
Movement rhyme: "The Elephant Goes"
Book: *RRRalph* by Lois Ehlert.
App: Felt Board—Mother Goose on the Loose by Software Smoothie
Closing song: "The Alphabet Song"
Closing activity: Stamp participant's hand with a fun rubber stamp and Kid-safe ink.

Altogether, this program will take about 25 to 30 minutes. Each book is very brief, but an essential part of the program, as your choice of books helps parents know what kind of books to look for to take home and read to their toddlers. You can use themes at your toddler time, but it is not essential. It is more common to use themes at a preschool storytime, since themes are used in kindergarten, but not important at toddler time unless you want to use themes. You can also keep the themes very broad, such as all animals, when at preschool storytime they may use a theme like bears.

Scheduling

Just like with lapsit, toddler storytime seems to be most successful in the mornings. Most toddlers still take an afternoon nap, so mornings are better for them. They also go to bed soon after dinnertime, so even if both parents work, a morning storytime can work better for this age group. Maybe a grandparent or other caregiver will bring the toddler, or one of the parents will adapt the work schedule to have one morning off per week for things like storytime, doctor's appointments, and other toddler outings. See what works for your community. If your toddler time is not well attended on a weekday, you could try Saturday mornings instead and see if that is better.

Registration

As we discussed in the earlier chapter on baby storytime, registration for storytime has some pluses and minuses. It can be a barrier to English language learners and adult literacy students who may be the most in need of a storytime to learn how to read to their children. Toddler time can handle more participants than a baby storytime and still be effective; you use so many songs and fingerplays and use larger visuals like Big Books and flannelboards that can be seen by a large group. As was mentioned before in the chapter on baby storytimes, if you get a really big crowd, think about doing two storytimes back to back; the second one doesn't take any extra preparation since it is a repeat of the first with all the same songs, books, and activities. If you feel you must take registration, maybe you can allow a few "guest" spots to stay open for new participants; if the crowd is continually too large for the space, schedule two storytimes on the same morning to accommodate everyone. If your staff is small, you might even consider doing storytime right before you open, so at the end you can move onto the circulation or reference desk, while the parents look for materials to check out.

HOLDING THE ATTENTION OF YOUR AUDIENCE

A few keys can help hold the attention of even the most distracted audience, and toddlers would certainly fit into that group! One is to make sure the audience can see and hear. This means holding the books so the children can see the illustrations, and moving the book from side to side so those on the peripheral edge can see. If the group is larger, it may mean choosing Big Books, or at least picture books that are overall larger in size than average, but not board books that are small in size. Another tip is to move quickly from one element of your storytime to the next: go into the next song right after you have finished reading one of the books. If you allow even a few seconds where nothing is happening, you will lose the attention of some of the audience members. If your transitions are quick, you will have much better control of the crowd.

Rapport with the Audience

Another technique for holding the attention of the audience is to have eye contact with them, which helps create a rapport with the audience. Making eye contact during the songs and fingerplays is natural, but you can also do it when reading a book. During the few seconds when you are showing the illustrations, moving the book from side to side, look at the audience. Another way to create a rapport is to learn the names of the children who attend regularly. Some presenters do this by using nametags, but that is not essential. You can often learn the names of the children by using certain songs, like "Mary Wore Her Red Dress," where you insert the names of the children in attendance.

Age-Appropriate Materials

Sometimes you will lose the attention of your audience when a story is too long for their attention spans. Choosing age-appropriate materials is important during storytime.

There may be times when you plan for a preschool crowd, but a lot of toddlers are in attendance. So prepare more books than you will actually read, and then choose the books that best suit those in attendance. For a family storytime where a wide age range makes up the audience, you can choose toddler-friendly books. The older children will enjoy some of their old favorites, knowing that you are reading them for the younger siblings who are there.

Audience Participation

One sure-fire way to hold the attention of the audience is to use books that allow the group to call out a repeated phrase, or to participate in some way. A wealth of picture books allow for audience participation, from alphabet and counting books, to books with repeated phrases or cumulative passages that the children will repeat. Below we will discuss the various types of participatory picture books.

CHOOSING THE PICTURE BOOKS

When you are choosing the picture books to read to a group, you want to look at the length of the story, as well as the illustrations. Will the pictures carry to a group? Many great picture books work well for one-on-one reading, perfect for a parent and child at bedtime; but these may not work well for a large toddler storytime if the children cannot see the pictures. Large, bold illustrations seem to carry best; those with a lot of small detail, cross-hatching, or very faint watercolors don't carry as well. A few of these are available in Big Book editions, which will allow you to use them at storytime, so think about investing in a few Big Books. You may also prefer books with a brief text; I like books with one sentence, not one paragraph, per page. Preschoolers can appreciate the longer books when they read with a caregiver, but those longer stories are more difficult for a group to listen to without some interruptions.

DIFFERENT TYPES OF STORIES

Some picture books you choose are wonderful stories, but there are others that have an element that allows the audience to participate by shouting out a repeated phrase. Let's cover the different types of interactive or participatory stories that can jazz up your storytimes. These are cumulative, circular stories, participation stories, concept books, creative dramatics, and pop-up books.

Cumulative Stories

Cumulative stories like *The House That Jack Built* by Simms Taback contain reoccurring phrases that are added on, so the listener can chant along. Another very popular cumulative story is *The Napping House* by Don and Audrey Wood, or *The Apple Pie That Papa Baked* by Lauren Thompson. A great multicultural cumulative story is Verna Aardema's *Bringing the Rain to Kapiti Plain.* Some newer cumulative stories include *Give Up Gecko! A Folktale from Uganda* by Margaret Read MacDonald, and *The Sunhat* by Jennifer Ward.

Circular Stories

Circular stories end up where they started. One of the most popular is *If You Give a Mouse a Cookie* by Laura Numeroff, and some of you may have seen her follow up books, *If You Give a Pig a Pancake*, and *If You Give a Mouse a Muffin*. For some new variations, try *And the Cars Go* by William Bee, or *The Deep, Deep Puddle* by Mary Jessie Parker. Circular stories offer listeners the opportunity to predict what will happen in the story, a skill they will later need in kindergarten. Use these at both toddler and preschool storytimes.

Participation Stories

Often called repetitive stories, pattern stories, or call and response stories, these are stories where the listener calls out a repeated phrase. A great example is *The Little Red Hen* by Byron Barton, where listeners call out "Not I!" whenever one of the characters says "Not I!" I try to do at least one participatory story during each storytime. Try *Mama Cat Has Three Kittens* by Denise Fleming, or *Fortunately* by Remy Charlip. Many of you may already know *Go Away, Big Green Monster* by Ed Emberley, and one of my new favorites is *Tiptoe Joe* by Ginger F. Gibson. Another that is especially appropriate for toddlers is *Me Too!* by Valeri Gorbachev. Any book with a repeated phrase can be made interactive. One of the most popular is *Brown Bear, Brown Bear, What Do You See?* by Bill Martin.

Concept Books

Alphabet and counting books are easy to make call and response, because the audience can call out the letter or number on that page of the book. Also, books about shapes, opposites, or colors can invite interaction, with the audience guessing the example of the concept shown in that part of the story. Some of the best concept books actually have a plot, like *Miss Bindergarten Gets Ready for Kindergarten* by Joseph Slate or *Feast for Ten* by Cathryn Falwell. Also try Ashley Wolff's *Baby Bear Sees Blue* and *Baby Bear Counts One*, which are perfect for the toddler audience.

Creative Dramatics

A creative dramatic story is one that can be acted out. These books are found less often than cumulative or participatory stories, but these can be very successful at energizing a storytime. One of the most popular is *We're Going on a Bear Hunt* by Michael Rosen. A newer version of this old story is *We're Going on a Ghost Hunt* by Marcia Vaughan. The audience repeats parts of the text after you read a phrase, and acts out the related movements as they go on the bear hunt by pretending to swim through the river, or ski through the snowstorm. Another old favorite is the Russian folktale *The Enormous Turnip* by Alexis Tolstoy, where children are selected to play the farmer, the dog, the cat, and the bird, who try to pull up the gigantic turnip. A variation that is popular at Halloween is *The Big Pumpkin* by Erica Silverman. Two that are appropriate for toddlers are *Wiggle Waggle* by Jonathan London and *Monkey See, Look at Me!* by Lorena Siminovich.

Pop-Up and Flap Books

Although it can be difficult to offer pop-up, flap, and toy books for circulation (because they fall apart), consider having a few pop-up books to use at storytime as a way to engage your audience. Many children respond to pop-up books because the added three-dimensional element can offer something new. Some of the best for storytime are the pop-up books featuring Maisy, the little white mouse, written by Lucy Cousins. Also try any of the books featuring "Spot the Dog" by Eric Hill, which contain flaps that lift to reveal part of the story. Another great example is Jenny Broom's version of *The Lion and the Mouse*, which contains die-cut holes that are part of the story.

A new type of interactive book doesn't have pop-ups or flaps; instead, it asks the child to touch the pages or shake the book. The first book like this was Herve Tullet's *Press Here*, which asks the reader to press the dots on the pages, emulating the type of action one would do with a touchscreen tablet device. *Press Here* is a landmark book that promotes traditional reading between child and caregiver, while acknowledging the new way people read on a screen. Two other books with similar interactions are *Tap the Magic Tree* by Christie Matheson, and Bill Cotter's *Don't Push the Button*. These are excellent read-alouds for storytimes for all ages; I predict there will be more "faux touchscreen" books like this published in the near future.

USE OF APPS, IPADS, AND OTHER TECHNOLOGY

One of the latest trends in storytime is the use of a tablet device (such as an iPad) with apps (short for applications), and the use of eBooks. The presenter uses the tablet like a pop-up book, walking around the room, allowing the young children to interact with the story. If you have more than 15 pairs of child and parent, you may want to project the tablet on a big screen so everyone can see what is happening. Most presenters will use just one app or eBook during a storytime, often at the conclusion, after doing the regular songs and books we have already discussed.

Apps

Cen Campbell is one of the most knowledgeable librarians on using technology at storytimes. Her website Littleelit.com describes how to use technology at storytime, why it can be appropriate, which apps are the most popular and educational, and other issues. Many of the apps she recommends are based on children's picture books, including *Go Away, Big Green Monster*, and *Five Little Monkeys*. Also recommended are apps based on books by Dr. Seuss, Byron Barton, and Sandra Boynton. Especially useful are apps that provide songs, which you use the way you would a music CD in storytime. Check the websites listed near the end of this chapter for Campbell's list of best apps to use at storytime and other helpful sites.

Before using apps in your storytime, check in with your supervisor. Some preschool educators, parents, and librarians are concerned about the amount of screen time to which young children are exposed. Offer research from Littleelit.com or other resources that explain why using an app in toddler or preschool storytime may be appropriate. Start out with just one app added to the regular books and songs you are using, and see if the audience responds. Since storytime helps children prepare for kindergarten, the use of apps and computers may help in preparing children for the technology that will be used in their classrooms.

eBooks

During storytime, you can model the best way to use eBooks with children when the parent and child engage together to use technology. If you have a large audience for your storytimes, try using an eBook version of a popular picture book. Show the eBook using a projector and a large screen to demonstrate how the eBook version is useful for a large group. You could even use a popular picture book featured on TumbleBooks or BookFlix, two online picture book databases that many libraries license to have on their websites. Using eBooks, TumbleBooks, or BookFlix during storytime is a great way to promote these new resources to interested parents.

The apps and eBooks you choose for your storytime will help parents know which are the best to choose, the way the books you use help parents know the types of books that are best for a child of that age. Your use of apps and eBooks will also demonstrate how to interact with the child, stressing it is important for the parent and child to use the device together, and not use it to keep the child busy.

RESOURCES FOR TODDLER STORYTIMES

Many of the same professional reading books and websites listed in the previous chapter on doing storytime for babies are equally helpful in doing a toddler storytime. You will also find Judy Nichols's book *Storytimes for Two-Year-Olds: 3rd edition* (American Library Association, 2007) a great how-to book. Another thorough book on presenting storytime for parents and toddlers together is by Saroj N. Ghoting and Pamela Martin-Diaz, called *Early Literacy Storytimes @ Your Library* (American Library Association, 2006), which goes into helping parents learn how to take the preliteracy skills home. Also check out Carol Garnett Hopkins's *Artsy Toddler Storytimes: A Year's Worth of Ready-to-Go Programming* (Neal-Schuman, 2013), if you want to add an age-appropriate art project to your storytimes (more on art in Chapter 7).

Toddler storytimes are one of the fastest growing library services, so if you are not currently holding one, give it a try! You will find a very loyal audience, who will "grow into" your preschool storytime, summer reading program, and other services as the children get older. The parents can also be some of the best advocates for your library, since they find toddler time an essential service and a way to network with other parents.

WEBSITES ON TODDLER STORYTIMES

Mother Goose on the Loose
http://www.mgol.org/
The Mother Goose on the Loose program is a library-based storytime for young children and their parents, that encourages lots of singing and rhymes. The website explains why repetition is important for this age group, in getting them ready to learn to read.

Preschool Express Toddler Station

http://www.preschoolexpress.com/toddler_station.shtml

A wealth of activities you can demonstrate for the toddler and parent to repeat at home, from making toys to games and songs.

Little eLit: Early Literacy in the Digital Age

http://littleelit.com

A popular blog on using apps and other Web 2.0 media with younger children; blogger Cen Campbell often discusses how to use apps at storytime.

Very Best App for Young Children

www.alsc.ala.org/blog/2014/03/the-very-best-app-for-young-children/?utm_source=feed burner&utm_medium=email&utm_campaign=Feed%3A+AlscBlog+%28ALSC+Bl og%29

The Association of Library Service to Children lists apps appropriate for storytime planning.

TumbleBooks

www.tumblebooks.com/library/asp/customer_login.asp

An increasing number of libraries are offering online picture books to their patrons. TumbleBooks is one of the main companies that libraries pay so their users can access the books in the online library. You can also offer a picture book from TumbleBooks at a storytime, to demonstrate the proper use for parents.

BookFlix

http://teacher.scholastic.com/products/bookflixfreetrial/

Similar to TumbleBooks, BookFlix offers a collection of online children's books, many paired with video content, to libraries that pay for the service.

Storyline Online

www.storylineonline.net

Storyline Online is a free website that offers something similar to TumbleBooks and Book-Flix. Sponsored by the Screen Actors Guild, this site shows famous actors reading popular picture books, similar to how picture books are read on the Public Broadcasting Service (PBS) series *Reading Rainbow*.

Once Upon an App

www.coloradolibrariesjournal.org/articles/once-upon-app-process-creating-digital-storytimes-preschoolers

Two librarians explain how to incorporate digital content into your storytimes to support early literacy skills and practices.

APPS FOR STORYTIME

Alphabet Animals: A Slide-and-Peek Adventure. Auryn.
Byron Barton Collection. Oceanhouse Media.
Don't Let the Pigeon Run This App. Disney.

Dr. Seuss Beginner Book Collection #1 and #2. Oceanhouse Media.
Drive About: Number Neighborhood. Artgig Studios.
Endless Alphabet. Originator, Inc.
Franklin Frog. Nosy Crow.
Go Away, Big Green Monster! Night & Day Studios.
Hello, Baby Animals! Shortstack.
How Rocket Learned to Read. Random House Digital.
Jack and the Beanstalk. Nosy Crow.
Parker Penguin. Nosy Crow.
Sandra Boynton Collection. Loud Crow.
Simms Taback Children's Book Collection. CJ Educations.
Ten Little Fish. CJ Educations.
Together Time with Song and Rhyme for Parent and Preschooler. Mulberry Media Interactive Inc.
Very Hungry Caterpillar and Friends: Play and Explore. StoryToy.
Wild about Books. Random House Digital.

BOOKS FOR TODDLERS

Cumulative Stories

Aardema, Verna. *Bringing the Rain to Kapiti Plain.*
Ashburn, Boni. *The Fort That Jack Built.*
Aylesworth, Jim. *Mr. McGill Goes to Town.*
Birdseye, Tom. *Soap! Soap! Don't Forget the Soap!*
Bishop, Gavin. *Chicken Licken.*
Brisson, Pat. *Benny's Pennies.*
Brown, Marcia. *The Bun.*
Brown, Ruth. *A Dark, Dark Tale.*
Brown, Ruth. *World That Jack Built.*
Burningham, John. *Mr. Gumpy's Outing.*
Capucilli, Alyssa Satin. *Inside a Barn in the Country.*
Carle, Eric. *Today Is Monday.*
Carlstrom, Nancy. *Baby-O.*
Casanova, Mary. *One-Dog Sleigh.*
Colandro, Lucille. *There Was an Old Lady Who Swallowed Some Books!*
Cole, Henry. *Jack's Garden.*
Cunnane, Kelly. *Chirchir Is Singing.*
Deacon, Alexis. *Cheese Belongs to You!*
Dragonwagon, Crescent. *This Is the Bread I Baked for Ned.*
Duff, Maggie. *Rum Pum Pum.*
Dunrea, Oliver. *Deep Down, Underground.*
Emberley, Barbara. *Drummer Hoff.*
Ericsson, Jennifer. *Whoo Goes There?*
Fleming, Candace. *Oh, No!*
Flood, Nancy Bo. *The Hogan That Great-Grandfather Built.*
Fox, Mem. *Hattie and the Fox.*
Gag, Wanda. *Millions of Cats.*

Galdone, Paul. *Cat Goes Fiddle-I-Fee.*
Galdone, Paul. *The Old Woman and her Pig.*
Gonzales Bertrand, Diane. *The Park Our Town Built/El parquet que nuestro pueblo con-struyo.*
Grimm, The Brothers. *Bremen Town Musicians.*
Hutchins, Pat. *Don't Forget the Bacon.*
Hutchins, Pat. *Little Pink Pig.*
Isadora, Rachel. *There Was a Tree.*
Kalan, Robert. *Jump, Frog, Jump.*
Kellogg, Steven. *Chicken Little.*
Kent, Jack. *The Fat Cat.*
Kimmel, Eric. *The Runaway Tortilla.*
Lobel, Arnold. *The Rose in my Garden.*
MacDonald, Margaret Read. *Give Up Gecko! A Folktale from Uganda.*
Macken, Joann Early. *Baby Says "Moo!"*
Manceau, Edouard. *Windblown.*
Neitzel, Shirley. *The Jacket I Wear In the Snow.*
Norman, Kimberly. *I Know a Wee Piggy.*
Paquette, Ammi-Joan. *Ghost in the House.*
Reidy, Jean. *Light Up the Night.*
Robart, Rose. *The Cake That Mack Ate.*
Sandall, Ellie. *Birdsong.*
Schindler, S. D. *Spike & Ike Take a Hike.*
Simon, Annette. *Robot Zombie Frankenstein*
Sloat, Teri. *There Was an Old Lady Who Swallowed a Trout.*
Sturgis, Brenda Reeves. *The Lake Where Loon Lives.*
Taback, Simms. *There Was an Old Lady Who Swallowed a Fly.*
Thompson, Lauren. *The Apple Pie That Papa Baked.*
Vamos, Samantha R. *The Cazuela That the Farm Maiden Stirred.*
Van Laan, Nancy. *Possum Come A-Knocking.*
Various. *The House That Jack Built.*
Various. *The Gingerbread Boy.*
Verburg, Bonnie. *The Tree House That Jack Built.*
Waddell, Martin. *The Pig in the Pond.*
Walker, Barbara. *I Packed My Trunk.*
Ward, Jennifer. *The Sunhat.*
Wardlaw, Lee. *The Chair Where Bear Sits.*
West, Colin. *"Buzz, Buzz, Buzz," Went Bumblebee.*
West, Colin. *Have You Seen the Crocodile?*
Wolk, Gita. *Gobble You Up.*
Wood, Don and Audrey. *The Napping House.*

Circular Stories

Arnold, Tedd. *Ollie Forgot.*
Becker, John. *Seven Little Rabbits.*
Bee, William. *And the Cars Go.*
Brett, Jan. *The Mitten.*

Brown, Margaret Wise. *The Runaway Bunny.*
Costello, David Hyde. *I Can Help.*
Degman, Lori. *Cock-a-Doodle Oops!*
Dodds, Dayle Ann. *Wheel Away!*
Doyle, Malachy. *The Bold Boy.*
Elkins, Benjamin. *Why the Sun Was Late.*
Feiffer, Jule. *Bark, George.*
Frazee, Marla. *Boot and Shoe.*
Gorbachev, Valeri. *Where Is the Apple Pie?*
Janovitz, Marilyn. *Look Out, Bird!*
Kalan, Robert. *Stop, Thief!*
Kimmel, Eric. *Anansi and the Moss-Covered Rock.*
Lyon, George Ella. *All the Water in the World.*
Munsch, Robert. *Alligator Baby.*
Numeroff, Laura. *If You Give a Moose a Muffin.*
Numeroff, Laura. *If You Give a Mouse a Cookie.*
Numeroff, Laura. *If You Give a Pig a Pancake.*
Parker, Mary Jessie. *The Deep, Deep Puddle.*
Robinson, Michelle. *What to Do If an Elephant Stands on Your Foot.*
Van Laan, Nancy. *Big Fat Worm.*
Van Laan, Nancy. *This Is the Hat.*
Ziefert, Harriet. *It's Time to Say Good Night.*

Creative Dramatic Stories

Bedford, David. *Mole's Babies.*
Domanska, Janina. *The Turnip.*
Freeman, Tor. *Olive and the Big Secret.*
Hoberman, Mary Ann. *Miss Mary Mack.*
London, Jonathan. *Wiggle Waggle.*
Long, Ethan. *The Croaky Pokey!*
Lotz, Karen E. *Can't Sit Still.*
Murray, Alison. *Little Mouse.*
Pearson, Susan. *We're Going on a Ghost Hunt.*
Rosen, Michael. *We're Going on a Bear Hunt.*
Schaefer, Carole Lexa. *The Squiggle.*
Silverman, Erica. *Big Pumpkin.*
Siminovich, Lorena. *Monkey See, Look at Me!*
Smalls-Hector, Irene. *Jonathan and his Mommy.*
Thomas, Jan. *Is Everyone Ready for Fun?*
Thompson, Lauren. *Hop, Hop, Jump!*
Various. *The Farmer in the Dell.*
Williams, Linda. *The Little Old Lady Who Was Not Afraid of Anything.*

Concept Books

Adams, Pam. *This Old Man.*
Austin, Mike. *Monsters Love Colors.*
Aylesworth, Jim. *Little Bitty Mousie.*

Baker, Keith. *1-2-3 Peas.*
Baker, Keith. *Little Green Peas: A Big Book of Colors.*
Barnett, Mac. *Count the Monkeys.*
Beil, Karen. *A Cake All for Me.*
Biggs, Brian. *123 Beep! Beep! Beep! A Counting Book.*
Biggs, Brian. *Stop! Go! A Book of Opposites.*
Brocket, Jane. *Circles, Stars, and Squares: Looking for Shapes.*
Bucknall, Caroline. *One Bear All Alone.*
Carroll, Kathleen S. *One Red Rooster.*
Chernesky, Felicia Sanzari. *Cheers for a Dozen Ears: A Summer Crop of Counting.*
DuBois, Paul. *Count on the Subway.*
Endle, Kate. *Augie to Zebra: an Alphabet Book!*
Falwell, Cathryn. *Feast for Ten.*
Heder, Thyra. *Fraidyzoo.*
Intriago, Patricia. *Dot.*
Lee, Mark. *20 Big Trucks in the Middle of the Street.*
Light, Steve. *Have You Seen My Dragon?*
Long, Ethan. *Soup for One.*
Martin, Bill. *Chicka Chicka Boom Boom.*
Martin, Bill. *Ten Little Caterpillars.*
McGuirk, Leslie. *If Rocks Could Sing: A Discovered Alphabet.*
Murray, Alison. *One Two That's My Shoe!*
Murray, Alison. *Apple Pie ABC.*
Ohmura, Tomoko. *The Long, Long Line.*
Paul, Ann W. *Everything to Spend the Night.*
Peek, Merle. *Mary Wore Her Red Dress, and Henry Wore His Green Sneakers.*
Saul, Carol. *Barn Cat.*
Savage, Stephen. *Ten Orange Pumpkins.*
Sayre, April Pulley. *Go, Go, Grapes! A Fruit Chant.*
Seeger, Laura Vaccaro. *Green.*
Sierra, Judy. *The Sleepy Little Alphabet.*
Slate, Joseph. *Miss Bindergarten Gets Ready for Kindergarten.*
Strickland, Paul. *Ten Terrible Dinosaurs.*
Thong, Roseanne. *One Is a Drummer: A Book of Numbers.*
Thong, Roseanne. *Red Is a Dragon: A Book of Colors.*
Thong, Roseanne. *Round Is a Mooncake: A Book of Shapes.*
Walton, Rick. *So Many Bunnies.*
Wellington, Monica. *Colors for Zena.*
Wilson, Karma. *Bear Sees Colors.*
Wolff, Ashley. *Baby Bear Sees Blue.*
Wolff, Ashley. *Baby Bear Counts One.*
Young, Karen. *There Were Ten in the Bed.*

Participation Stories

Ahlberg, Janet. *Each Peach Pear Plum.*
Alarcon, Karen. *Louella Mae, She's Run Away.*
Alborough, Jez. *Six Little Chicks.*
Allen, Jonathan. *Don't Copy Me!*

Allen, Jonathan. *I'm Not Reading!*
Allenby, Victoria. *Nat the Cat Can Sleep Like That.*
Asch, Frank. *Monkey Face.*
Ashman, Linda. *Peace, Baby!*
Ata, Te. *Baby Rattlesnake.*
Bardhan-Quallen, Sudipta. *Duck, Duck, Moose!*
Bee, William. *Digger Dog.*
Bennett, Jill. *Teeny Tiny.*
Bennett, Kelly. *Vampire Baby.*
Bradman, Tony. *Is That a Coconut? Yuck!*
Brown, Margaret Wise. *Four Fur Feet.*
Buzzeo, Toni. *My Bibi Always Remembers.*
Calmenson, Stephanie. *Ollie's School Day: a Yes and No Book.*
Carle, Eric. *The Very Busy Spider.*
Carle, Eric. *The Very Hungry Caterpillar.*
Chapman, Jan. *I'm Not Sleepy!*
Charlip, Remy. *Fortunately.*
Clark, Leslie Ann. *Peepsqueak!*
Cousins, Lucy. *Peck, Peck, Peck.*
Cowell, Cressida. *What Shall We Do With a Boo-Hoo Baby?*
Cuyler, Margery. *The Little School Bus.*
Cuyler, Margery. *That's Good, That's Bad.*
Czekaj, Jef. *Oink-a-Doodle-Moo.*
Dale, Penny. *Ten Out of Bed.*
Demas, Corinne. *Always in Trouble.*
Denise, Anika. *Baking Day at Grandma's.*
DeRegniers, Beatrice. *May I Bring a Friend?*
Dubuc, Marianne. *Animal Masquerade.*
Dunbar, Joyce. *Four Fierce Kittens.*
Dunbar, Joyce. *Seven Sillies.*
Empson, Jo. *Never Ever.*
Farrell, Darren. *Thank You, Octopus.*
Feiffer, Jules. *Bark, George.*
Fischer, Scott M. *Jump!*
Flack, Marjorie. *Ask Mr. Bear.*
Fleming, Candace. *Oh, No!*
Fleming, Denise. *Mama Cat Has Three Kittens.*
Foreman, Michael. *Oh! If Only . . .*
Fox, Mem. *Shoes from Grandpa.*
Fox, Mem. *Two Little Monkeys.*
Fox, Mem. *Yoo-Hoo, Ladybug!*
Galdone, Paul. *The Three Bears.*
Galdone, Paul. *The Three Billy Goats Gruff.*
Galdone, Paul. *The Three Little Pigs.*
Geringer, Laura. *Boom Boom Go Away!*
Germein, Katrina. *My Dad Thinks He's Funny.*
Gibson, Ginger F. *Tiptoe Joe.*
Gilman, Phoebe. *Something from Nothing.*

Ginsberg, Mirra. *The Chick and the Duckling.*
Gorbachev, Valeri. *Me Too!*
Gorbachev, Valeri. *Shhh!*
Gravett, Emily. *Again!*
Grindley, Sally. *Knock, Knock, Who's There?*
Guarino, Deborah. *Is Your Mama a Llama?*
Hann, Jacquie. *Follow the Leader.*
Harper, Wilhelmina. *The Gunniwolf.*
Heling, Kathryn and Deborah Hembrook. *Clothesline Clues to Jobs People Do.*
Henry, Jed. *Cheer Up, Mouse!*
Himmelman, John. *Duck to the Rescue.*
Hoberman, Mary Ann. *A House Is a House for Me.*
Hoguet, Susan. *I Unpacked My Grandmother's Trunk.*
Horacek, Petr. *Puffin Peter.*
Hulbert, Laura. *Who Has This Tail?*
Hutchins, Pat. *Good Night, Owl!*
Janovitz, Marilyn. *Is It Time?*
Joosse, Barbara M. *Mama, Do You Love Me?*
Joslin, Sesyle. *What Do You Say, Dear?*
Katz, Karen. *Now I'm Big!*
Kraus, Robert. *Come Out and Play, Little Mouse!*
Kraus, Robert. *Whose Mouse Are You?*
Krauss, Ruth. *Big and Little.*
Krauss, Ruth. *The Carrot Seed.*
Landstrom, Lena. *Pom and Pim.*
LaRochelle, David. *It's a Tiger!*
Layne, Steven. *Stay with Sister.*
Lewin, Ted. *Look!*
Lewis, Anne M. *Fly Blanky Fly.*
Lillegard, Dee. *Sitting In My Box.*
London, Jonathan. *Here Comes Doctor Hippo.*
Lum, Kate. *What! Cried Granny: An Almost Bedtime Story.*
Mack, Jeff. *Good News, Bad News.*
Maris, Ron. *Are You There Bear?*
Maris, Ron. *I Wish I Could Fly.*
Martin, Bill. *Brown Bear, Brown Bear, What Do You See?*
Martin, Bill. *Here Are My Hands.*
Martin, Bill. *Panda Bear, Panda Bear, What Do You See?*
Martin, Bill. *Polar Bear, Polar Bear, What Do You Hear?*
Martin, David. *Peep and Ducky.*
Massie, Diane R. *The Baby Beebee Bird.*
McNaughton, Colin. *Suddenly!*
Miyares, Daniel. *Pardon Me!*
Moore, Eva. *Lucky Ducklings.*
Most, Bernard. *The Cow That Went Oink.*
Most, Bernard. *If the Dinosaurs Came Back.*
Nakawaki, Hatsue. *Wait! Wait!*
Nesbitt, Kenn. *More Bears!*

Nichols, Grace. *Whoa, Baby, Whoa!*
O'Byrne, Nicola. *Open Very Carefully: a Book with Bite.*
O'Neill, Gemma. *Oh Dear, Geoffrey!*
Oppenheim, Joanne. *You Can't Catch Me!*
Patricelli, Leslie. *Faster! Faster!*
Patricelli, Leslie. *Higher! Higher!*
Peek, Merle. *The Balancing Act.*
Redeker, Kent. *Don't Squish the Sasquatch!*
Rinker, Sherri D. *Goodnight, Goodnight, Construction Site.*
Rosen, Michael. *Tiny Little Fly.*
Rosenthal, Amy Krouse. *Duck! Rabbit!*
Sattler, Jennifer. *Uh-Oh, Dodo!*
Savage, Stephen. *Little Tug.*
Scott, Ann Herbert. *On Mother's Lap.*
Sendak, Maurice. *Pierre.*
Shannon, George. *Lizard's Song.*
Shannon, George. *Turkey Tot.*
Shaskan, Stephen. *A Dog Is a Dog.*
Shaw, Charles. *It Looked Like Spilt Milk.*
Shields, Carol Diggory. *Baby's Got the Blues.*
Slack, Michael. *Wazdot?*
Stein, David Ezra. *Ol' Mama Squirrel.*
Stileman, Kali. *Snack Time for Confetti.*
Tafuri, Nancy. *Have You Seen My Duckling?*
Thomas, Jan. *Can You Make a Scary Face?*
Timmers, Leo. *Who Is Driving?*
Vaughn, Marcia K. *Wombat Stew.*
Vipont, Elfrida. *The Elephant and the Bad Baby.*
Walton, Rick. *Bunnies on the Go.*
Willems, Mo. *Goldilocks and the Three Dinosaurs.*
Wilson, Karma. *Bear Says Thanks.*
Wood, Audrey. *Silly Sally.*
Yektai, Niki. *What's Silly?*
Yoon, Salina. *Do Cows Meow?*
Yoon, Salina. *Do Crocs Kiss?*
Young, Ed. *Seven Blind Mice.*
Zamorano, Ana. *Let's Eat!*
Zimmerman, Andrea. *Trashy Town.*

Pop-Up and Flap Books

Aliki. *Push Button.*
Bee, William. *Digger Dog.*
Braun, Sebastien. *Who Can Jump?*
Braun, Sebastien. *Who Can Swim?*
Broom, Jenny. *The Lion and the Mouse.*
Carter, David A. *The Happy Little Yellow Box: A Pop-Up Book of Opposites.*
Cousins, Lucy. *Maisy Grows a Garden.*
Cousins, Lucy. *Maisy's World of Animals.*

Cousins, Lucy. *Where Is Maisy? Find Me if You Can!*
Davies, Nicola. *What Happens Next?*
Davies, Nicola. *What Will I Be?*
Davies, Nicola. *Who Lives Here?*
Dubois, Liz Goulet. *What Does a Seed Need?*
Egielski, Richard. *Itsy Bitsy Spider.*
Faulkner, Keith. *The Wide-Mouthed Frog.*
Gershator, Phillis. *Who's In the Farmyard?*
Gore, Leonid. *Mommy, Where Are You?*
Guthrie, Woody. *Riding In My Car.*
Hall, Michael. *It's an Orange Aardvark!*
Hill, Eric. *Where's Spot* series.
Horacek, Petr. *Animal Opposites: A Pop-Up Book.*
Horacek, Petr. *One Spotted Giraffe: A Counting Pop-Up Book.*
Katz, Karen. *Peek-a-Baby.*
Katz, Karen. *Where Is Baby's Puppy?*
Murphy, Mary. *Say Hello Like This!*
Shea, Susan A. *Do You Know Which Ones Will Grow?*
Sirett, Dawn. *Pop-Up Peekaboo! Woof! Woof!*
Tullet, Herve. *The Eyes Game.*
Zelinsky, Paul O. *Knick-Knack Paddy Whack!*
Zelinsky, Paul O. *The Wheels on the Bus.*

CHAPTER 4

Preschool and Family Storytime

Preschool storytime was the first program held in most libraries, often enforcing registration, an age limit, and holding the storytime without the parents in the room. Of course, customs have changed and nearly all libraries have the parent or caregiver in the room during preschool storytime. Many librarians still do not have a craft project at the end of preschool storytime but I am a big advocate of crafts as way to add kindergarten readiness skills to the storytime, plus arts and crafts are fun! So although preschool storytime has always been a traditional public library service, there are new elements we can add to make it more relevant to our audience. These new features can include the use of apps on tablet devices and the use of e-Books as discussed in Chapter 3 on toddler storytime.

FAMILY STORYTIME

Many libraries hold at least one weekly storytime that is for all ages; parents who work and have busy schedules may only be able to attend one storytime yet they have children of various ages, and they need to come in the evening or on the weekend due to their work schedules. Holding a family storytime can fill this need, where the parent brings the baby, the preschooler, and even a school-age sibling who may be 6 or 7 years of age. I conducted an evening storytime like this for 20 years and found that if I choose books, songs, and a craft suitable for the preschooler, everyone else in the family has fun, too. Either the baby or toddler will sit on the parent's lap and participate as best he or she can, or the toddler wants to sit and do everything with the older sibling. And the older child who already goes to school still enjoys the storytime and will help their younger siblings, since they already know the songs and can help do the crafts. So when doing a Family storytime, you can prepare just like you do for preschool storytime.

Format for Family Storytime

Opening song: "We'll All Join in the Circle"
State theme or subject of today's books—Colors
Get ready song: "Shake Your Hands"
Book: *Colors for Zena* by Monica Wellington
Fingerplay: "Hurry, Hurry, Drive the Fire Truck"
Participation book: *Go Away, Big Green Monster* by Ed Emberley
Poetry break: "I Never Saw a Purple Cow" by Gelett Burgess
Song: "Mary Wore Her Red Dress"
Book: *Mouse Paint* by Ellen Stoll Walsh
Movement rhyme: "Johnny Works with One Hammer"
Book: *Monsters Love Colors* by Mike Austin
App: Together Time with Song and Rhyme for Parent and Preschooler Play by Mulberry
    Media Interactive Inc.
Closing song: "The Hokey Pokey"
Closing stay and play activities: Set out various simple toys, such as wooden puzzles,
    stacking toys, Duplo blocks, and puppets. Also have a hands-on art activity: make
    simple monster masks out of green paper plates, curly birthday ribbon for hair, and
    stickers for other features.

Family Stay and Play Storytime

In the outline earlier, you notice we end with a stay and play activity. Basically, this is a free-form play time at the conclusion of storytime, to allow children and parents to interact with each other. Children need to play; it is a key way they learn. Yet many young children do not have as much free time as we did when we were kids, nor do they interact with others as much as school-age children do. Offering a stay and play time will promote the value of play, and it offers parents a nice time to network with each other. This time can be half an hour at most; then announce it is time for cleanup. This is a great opportunity for a retired person to volunteer, to help set out the toys, and then clean up, as well as assist parents, and watch over the space while you are busy helping a parent find books or doing readers' advisory. For suggestions for the types of toys you can offer, check out Chapter 8.

Value of Age-Mixed Play

In his article "The Special Value of Children's Age-Mixed Play," Peter Gray describes his research that concluded that children learn more when their play groups are not seg-regated by age. Families with multiple siblings already know this: younger children learn from the older ones, and older children learn because they are teaching younger children. Family storytimes with stay and play activities can model some of this mixed-age play. Some of the advantages of mixed-age play are:

• Allows younger children to try out play a little too complex for their age group.
• Allows older children to serve as models of social behavior for the younger children.

- Provides younger children care and emotional support in their play.
- Allows older children a chance to be a leader and a teacher.
- Provides opportunities for more creativity in play.

Offering family storytimes with some added playtime can make your library a destination for busy working parents, who have to prioritize what they can fit into their schedules.

PRESCHOOL STORYTIME

Preschool storytime was outlined in the first chapter, showing that you alternate songs, books, and fingerplays. At this age, children can sit for more than one or two books; I often use four or five books at every preschool storytime. If you put a song or fingerplay between each book, it can help the audience focus and listen for the full half hour. Also, with a preschool audience, you may get many younger preschoolers who need more songs and movement so it is not that different from a toddler time or a family storytime. If you offer an afternoon preschool storytime, you may draw older preschoolers who don't take naps, as well as kindergartners, and this group can listen to a longer story. Both older and younger preschoolers enjoy the interactive, participatory books we discussed in the previous chapter on toddler storytime, so try to include at least one of those each time. At preschool storytime, you may have far fewer children who want to sit on a caregiver's lap, but they still enjoy the songs, fingerplays, and movement activities as well as the stories.

Format for Preschool Storytime

Opening song: "Wheels on the Bus"
State theme or subject of today's books—Wind and Weather
Get ready song: "Open Shut Them"
Book: *Tap Tap Boom Boom* by Elizabeth Bluemle
Fingerplay: "Five Little Ducks"
Participation book: *Like a Windy Day* by Frank Asch
Poetry break: "Who Has Seen the Wind?" by Christina Rossetti
Book: *Sneeze, Big Bear, Sneeze!* by Maureen White.
Song: "Ain't Gonna Rain No More"
Book: *Windblown* by Edouard Manceau
Movement rhyme: "Shake Your Sillies Out"
Informational book: *I Face the Wind* by Vicki Cobb
App: Barnyard Dance—Sandra Boynton by Loud Crow Interactive Inc.
Closing song: "If You're Happy and You Know It"
Closing hands-on activity: Make pinwheels.

THEMES

Many librarians use a different theme each week at preschool storytime. I like to start in September with the theme based on the letter "A," like alligators or apples, then follow next week with "B," and so forth. This helps the preschooler practice learning the alphabet, and phonemic awareness by looking for other words that start with that letter. Themes are often used in kindergarten, so it helps preschoolers become accustomed to the concept. But I always try to choose great books, even if they don't fit the theme, rather than read a mediocre book that may fit the weekly topic. Even if your theme is "F is for Food," you can read one book not related to the theme, just by announcing you want to share one new book that you really like and want to show everyone. At the end of this chapter is a list of great websites, each listing hundreds of preschool storytime themes with ideas of suggested books, songs, and arts and crafts projects related to the themes. Also, we have included 100 themed storytime outlines at the end of this book.

Multicultural Themes

Celebrating traditions and holidays from a variety of cultures is a great way to convey inclusiveness at your library. Holding storytimes with multicultural themes can indicate to your community that the library values diversity and has something for everyone. Most schools also celebrate multicultural themes, so having these as themes for preschool storytime helps a child learn about other cultures and prepare of kindergarten. You can have a great storytime focusing on Anansi the Spider and other African folktales during Black History Month, or show the diversity of winter holidays with a variety of crafts in December, including but not limited to Christmas ornaments. Some multicultural themes can be too complex for preschoolers; for example, explaining the historical significance of Cinco de Mayo may be over their heads, but celebrating Mexican culture during that holiday can be done with counting, food, and folktales from Mexico that are appropriate for the preschool audience.

Diversity at All Storytimes

Be aware that diversity at storytime should not just occur during multicultural holidays. Try to include books with diversity during all your themes. For example, you can do the theme of "Snow," and include Ezra Jack Keats' *Snowy Day* which has an African American protagonist. Children are validated when they see themselves in books and other media, so showing children of all cultures at a variety of storytimes can do that. Otherwise, a child may feel marginalized if the only time they see an Asian character in a book at storytime is during Chinese New Year. A storytime on colors can include Roseanne Thong's *Red Is a Dragon*, or one on shapes can include her book, *Round Is a Mooncake*.

Authenticity

Diversity at storytime is easier than it used to be due to the wonderful multicultural picture books being published, although more multicultural characters would be welcome in all books for children. Fortunately for storytime presenters, diversity is far more representative in picture books than it is in easy readers. But you may want to avoid certain books that are archaic, or that bring up discussions that are better suited to parent and child than to preschool storytime. For example, Mary Hoffman's book *Amazing Grace* is a wonderful book that addresses prejudice. In the story, an African American girl is told by a classmate she cannot play Peter Pan in the class play, because the character is a boy and not African American. Grace auditions and wins the part in spite of those discouraging comments. School-age children can understand and discuss the message; preschool storytime may not be the best venue for that book. On the other end of the spectrum are classics like *The Story of Ping* by Marjory Flack. The illustrations offer an Old World depiction of Chinese people that preschoolers may find odd and parents may feel are stereotypical. If you are not of a culture and are unsure if a book will be appropriate for preschool storytime, ask coworkers, volunteers, or other librarians from that culture what they think, or choose another book. If you need more picture books with multicultural characters, check out these resources from publisher Lee & Low Books: http://blog.leeandlow.com/2014/03/21 /where-can-i-find-great-diverse-childrens-books/

YOGA STORYTIMES

In recent years, several libraries have started a yoga-themed storytime, to get the kids moving, focus on their breathing, and allow time to destress. These yoga storytimes have proven quite popular! Others have incorporated simple yoga poses and movements into their regular preschool storytimes rather than start a yoga storytime; survey your parents and see what they might like.

Along with yoga poses and some fun picture books and songs, you can offer some other movement activities using scarves, beanbags, or parachutes. If you would like to offer an art activity to conclude the storytime, make simple pictures based on the yoga poses you use, such as Tree, Dog, Cat, Butterfly, and so forth.

Tips on yoga for kids:

- Use a balloon to demonstrate the concept of full belly breathing.
- Keep poses and games brief (approx. 30 seconds for poses).
- Read a story between every other pose.
- Preschoolers appreciate and learn from repetition; offer some of the same poses each time.
- Be safe; no headstands or other advanced poses.
- Allow for quiet time with simple guided relaxation.
- Involve the parents/caregivers.

If you are starting a yoga storytime, check out *Little Yoga: A Toddler's First Book of Yoga* by Rebecca Whitford and Martina Selway Whitford, and Tae-Eun Yoo's *You Are a Lion! And Other Fun Yoga Poses.* Both books demonstrate yoga poses appropriate for preschoolers. Helpful websites on yoga and preschoolers are Yoga in My School: http:// yogainmyschool.com/yoga-classroom/yoga-games/ and Parents.com: www.parents.com /fun/activities/indoor/yoga-for-kids/

CHOOSING BOOKS FOR PRESCHOOLERS

Storytime presenters have a wonderful and wide selection of picture books that preschoolers will enjoy because you can choose many of the books recommended for toddlers, as well as slightly longer picture books and folktales. I try to include at least one participatory book during preschool storytime, as well as narrative stories, concept books, books based on songs and fingerplays, and even wordless books like Peggy

Rathmann's *Goodnight, Gorilla*, where the children can help tell the story. Just like babies and toddlers, preschoolers appreciate when you repeat old favorites once in a while. Depending on the size of the audience, you may want to pick books with large, clear illustrations like you did for toddlers, just so everyone can see and pick things out of the pictures. Many great preschool books work best one-on-one, like Crockett Johnson's *Harold and the Purple Crayon*, based on the small size of the book, so consider the number in attendance and visibility of the illustrations to the audience when choosing books, as well as story length.

Many picture books are too lengthy for storytime, even if the children are older preschoolers. Dr. Seuss's *How the Grinch Stole Christmas* takes about 15 minutes to read to a group; it works well with children aged 5 and up. But it is too long for most preschool storytimes, and works better at home for most preschoolers. You may find books with just a sentence or two per page work best during storytime, and the longer picture books are better for parents to check out and read at home.

INFORMATIONAL PICTURE BOOKS

Many librarians have noticed new books that walk the line between a picture book story and a nonfiction book: picture books with informational texts. These can be used at storytimes, even with preschoolers, and can help fill the need for more informational books in kindergarten through third grades, where the Common Core asks that half of what is read is informational or nonfiction. Offer one informational picture book at preschool and family storytimes to show parents and caregivers that nonfiction is not just for homework, but it is fun to read aloud to children. Check out the list of informational picture books at the end of this chapter.

PICTURE BOOKS ARRANGED BY TOPIC

A new trend is for libraries to rearrange their picture book collections by topic. Most libraries shelve them by author's last name, but recently, a few libraries divided the books into categories, or "glades." This is more customer friendly for preschoolers and their busy caregivers, and libraries that have made this change noticed a big increase in circulation. The goal was to make it easier for preschoolers and their parents to find what they want—the train books, alphabet books, or other book on their favorite subjects. Librarians who have done this suggest that you limit yourself to nine broad sections:

- Transportation
- Animals and Nature
- Rhymes and Songs
- Folktales
- All about Me
- Favorites/Classics
- Celebrations
- Concept Books
- Stories (meaning everything else)

Within those sections, books are given different colored stickers or dots to divide them further. For example, in Transportation, the train books have one dot color, the truck books another; and shelvers have a very easy time shelving just by the dot color within that category. Or, you could shelve the books in the Transportation category by author's last name, and not use the colored dot system. Librarians who have done this report an increase in the circulation of their picture books, because parents could find what their children want without using the library's online catalog.

POETRY BREAKS

In our formats for family and preschool storytimes discussed earlier, you may have noticed an entry for a poetry break. Offering a Mother Goose rhyme or short poem during storytime can promote your poetry books, as well as offer some key elements of reading readiness. Poetry and rhyme promote phonological awareness, or the ability to pick out sounds and syllables within words. This is especially true when children hear rhyming words, so a short poem can offer that. Of course, most children's poetry and nursery rhymes have humor or other elements that children enjoy. Children exposed to poetry and rhyme will gain skills they will need for kindergarten.

KINDERGARTEN READINESS

In many states, children entering kindergarten are given assessment tests to see how prepared they are. The tests involve a range of skills, from pre-reading skills such as knowing in which direction to turn the pages of a book, to motor skills like holding a pencil properly and hopping on one foot, to content knowledge such as writing your name, saying your phone number, or knowing the alphabet, shapes, and colors. Also, kindergarten nowadays puts a lot more emphasis on learning how to read and write, which is why you hear the phrase "kindergarten is the new 1st grade." So including some kindergarten readiness skills in your preschool storytime can really meet a need, without taking away any of the fun or leaving less time for great books. The goals of storytimes by their very nature feed into kindergarten readiness. Plus, if parents are aware you are covering kindergarten readiness, they will add that to their mental list of why it is important to make time in their busy schedules to bring their children to preschool storytime. Be sure to include the words kindergarten readiness on your flyers and other advertisements about preschool storytime.

Behavior Skills

Preschoolers are tested on kindergarten readiness in four main areas. Behavior is a main component; how will the child act in a classroom setting, and does he or she have the social skills and self-control needed to succeed in kindergarten? These skills include sticking to a schedule, waiting one's turn, controlling anger, and following directions. These skills all can be practiced in preschool storytime. For children who do not attend preschool or a day-care setting, the social interaction of storytime may be the only time they are with a group of other children their age.

Motor Skills

Your child is a genius who can already read and write; who knew he would be tested on skipping at the kindergarten readiness assessment? Of course, children are not kept out of kindergarten if they don't have all the skills needed, but some of the items on the test may seem unusual. Luckily at storytime, we practice skipping, hopping, and jumping in many of our songs such as "The Hokey Pokey" or "Green Grass Grows All Around." Bring some movement songs and circle dances into preschool storytime if you don't already do so; there are songs available on several music CDs from Kimbo.

Other motor skills a child will need are practiced when we do arts and crafts at storytime. Holding a pencil or crayon properly, using a scissors, and other hand/eye coordination skills happen when we do craft projects. This includes putting Cheerios on a shoelace to make a necklace, or putting beads on a pipe cleaner to make a holiday ornament or bracelet.

Factual Knowledge

Many of the books used at storytime will cover some of the factual knowledge a child will need for kindergarten. This includes the alphabet, counting, colors, shapes, and opposites. The names of various animals, foods, body parts, and everyday objects found in most homes are mentioned in many picture books. Most of the songs and fingerplays include these skills, from simple subtraction in "Five Little Monkeys" to naming body parts in "Head and Shoulders." Also, the arts and crafts projects can include some of these factual areas, like writing your name, address, and phone number. Coloring sheets or activity sheets can be distributed for those parents who want to follow up storytime with even more practice of these skills.

Reading Readiness Skills

Storytime is a natural place for many reading readiness skills to be explored; we just have to mention some of these areas when we are presenting a book. Talk about the parts of the book, including the spine, cover, and pages. Name the author and illustrator. Even if the younger preschooler doesn't understand what an author is, maybe the parent will appreciate you saying the author's name so he or she can pick up more books by that author. The dialogic reading technique we will discuss in Chapter 9, where we ask questions about the book, also plays into reading readiness. Point out things in the illustrations, too, and ask the audience to tell you what they see. All of these parts of presenting the book contribute to reading readiness.

Kindergarten Checklist

Make a handout for the parents concerning kindergarten readiness skills, even if the children in your community don't have to take a formal test before entering kindergarten. Parents can practice many of these skills as home, and knowing you cover these skills will help parents make storytime a priority each week. Check with your local schools to see if they have any parent information on kindergarten readiness, and adapt the following list to include any skills not mentioned below:

Basics of Self-Control

Accepting responsibility by doing chores
Sticking to a schedule
Listening to directions
Abiding by the rules
Taming angry feelings
Waiting one's turn
Delaying gratification
Saying please and thank you
Following simple safety rules

Things They Need to Know

Name (first and last)
Age, phone number, address
Names and relations of family members
Point to and name their body parts
Point to and name clothing
Name common animals
Name common foods
Name common shapes and colors
Know some words for how they feel
Opposites and comparisons
How to use the bathroom without help
Count to twenty, pick out individual numbers
Say the alphabet, pick out some individual letters
Write their first names

Motor Skills

Walk, run, and jump
Hop on one foot, balance on one foot
Throw and catch a ball
How to hold a pencil or crayon with thumb and fingers
Open a door by turning the doorknob
Turn water faucets on and off
Cut with a scissors
Lace large beads on a shoelace
Do buttons and zippers on their own clothes
Put simple puzzles together

Reading Readiness

Listen when someone reads aloud
Know which way to turn the pages
Look at the pictures and pick out details
Know common nursery rhymes
Remember parts of a story read to them
Read signs in the store, etc.

Recognize their name in print
Follow directions with three or more steps
Speak in complete sentences
Ask relevant questions

ONLINE STORYTIME OPTIONS

Nothing can replace the wonderful in-person interaction of a live storytime, where children experience the communal aspects of a sing-along, play time, and reading time. But you can augment your live storytimes with some online options for children who cannot get to the library on a regular basis. In no way do these online options replace in-person storytimes, they are an additional resource to assist children who might be home sick, away on vacation, or otherwise unable to attend.

Skype can be used to present a brief storytime, which allows for more interaction than a recorded storytime since it is live. Children can watch you read one or two short books and sing a couple of songs or fingerplays, and you can hear them sing along with you or ask questions. Check with your library's Web master to see if you can set up a Skype storytime for a preschool or day-care group who cannot come to the library.

Recorded storytimes on YouTube can also offer a storytime experience for those unable to attend. Videotape a very brief storytime with a small live audience, and post the storytime to YouTube. Promote the link on your library's Web page to let new families know how storytime works, and they may find time to attend in person. Because these videotaped storytimes are broadcast, you need permission from the publisher of any book you read. So you might want to limit a YouTube storytime to songs and fingerplays in the public domain, and tell some common folktales like *The Three Pigs* just using a flannelboard and not a book.

Finally, be sure to promote if your library's website offers TumbleBooks or BookFlix (mentioned in the previous chapter); if a family is stuck at home during a snowstorm, they may be able to enjoy some online stories using those collections.

RESOURCES FOR PRESCHOOL STORYTIMES

You will find a great number of websites geared for presenters of preschool storytime. These list hundreds of themes, with the books, songs and fingerplays, crafts, and other activities that fit the theme. Most list many books, much more than you would actually use, so even if you only own four or five of the books listed you will have enough for preschool storytime. Also, many list which books are suitable for toddlers, so you can also use these websites to help you plan your toddler storytimes. Many of the professional reading books listed in the chapter on toddler storytimes will also help the novice presenter who is just starting a preschool storytime since we often use many of the same songs and fingerplays at both. One of my favorites is Rob Reid's *Welcome to Storytime! The Art of Program Planning* (Upstart, 2012). If you do themed storytimes, you will find the book *A To Zoo: Subject Access to Children's Picture Books, 9th edition* by Rebecca L. Thomas (Libraries Unlimited, 2014), a very useful resource, since it is a catalog of picture books arranged by theme. Preschool storytime meets an important need in preparing a child for kindergarten, so parents will take the time to come if you promote the kindergarten readiness aspect of the new storytime. So having a preschool storytime as a library program is considered one of the basic services that you want to include, and it can be very fun and rewarding for the presenter!

WEBSITES ON PRESCHOOL STORYTIMES

BayViews/BayNews

www.bayviews.org

This site is from the Association of Children's Librarians of Northern California. It contains a monthly newsletter that also has a column on storytime, with a new theme every month.

West Bloomfield Township Public Library

www.growupreading.org/

This site is a great place to start, to learn why we need to have storytimes, advice for parents, booklists, information on child development, phonemic and print awareness, and other factors important for emergent readers.

Everything Preschool

www.everythingpreschool.com

Also arranged by themes, these lesson plans include books! In fact, the book jackets are shown so you can see which picture books you might have and which may carry well to a group. Under each theme there are also songs, coloring pages, art ideas, recipes, games, and science ideas.

Preschool Express

www.preschoolexpress.com/theme_station.shtml

Thousands of ideas to enliven your storytime, but no books listed. Go to the "Theme Station" for crafts and activities by theme, the "Story Station" for rhymes and stories to tell, the "Toddler Station" for active movement ideas, the "Pattern Station" for craft printables, and more!

Step by Step Theme Pages

http://stepbystepcc.com/themes2.html

Run by a day-care provider named Jana, this is very similar to how most libraries compile their storytime themes. Under each theme, she lists picture books first, then songs and fingerplays, then craft ideas. It appears that she regularly updates this site.

Mid-Hudson Library System Story Hour Page

http://midhudson.org/program/ideas/Story_Hour.htm

Links to sites on flannelboards, music, crafts, and a wealth of other information relating to storytimes is designed for library staff.

Lee & Low Books

http://blog.leeandlow.com/2014/03/21/where-can-i-find-great-diverse-childrens-books/
The publisher Lee & Low Books has a great resource page listing several other publishers as well as lists of multicultural books for children.

KINDERGARTEN READINESS WEBSITES

Poway School District Kindergarten Readiness

http://powayusd.sdcoe.k12.ca.us/news/ebulletin/december03/kindergarten-readiness.htm
From the Poway School District in California, their website lists 26 topics, one of each letter of the alphabet, on kindergarten readiness.

Family Education Kindergarten Readiness Resources

http://school.familyeducation.com/kindergarten/kindergarten-readiness/72117.html
This useful list of articles by various children's education specialists discusses kindergarten readiness and other related issues.

BOOKS FOR PRESCHOOLERS

Many of the books listed at the end of Chapter 3 on toddler storytime work well for preschool storytime, too, especially the participation stories. Also, at the end of this book, there are more than 100 outlines for preschool storytime, listing books, songs, and arts and craft projects by theme. Along with those, here are some great picture books that preschoolers enjoy:

Agell, Charlotte. *Dancing Feet.*
Alborough, Jez. *Some Dogs Do.*
Anderson, Lena. *Tea for Ten.*
Apperley, Dawn. *Good Night, Sleep Tight, Little Bunnies.*
Asch, Frank. *The Sun Is My Favorite Star.*
Baker, Keith. *Little Green.*
Baker, Keith. *Quack and Count.*
Barner, Bob. *Fish Wish.*
Barton, Byron. *I Want to Be an Astronaut.*
Boyd, Lizi. *Black Dog Gets Dressed.*
Bluemle, Elizabeth. *Tap Tap Boom Boom.*
Butler, John. *If You See a Kitten.*
Cabrera, Jane. *Rory and the Lion.*
Carlson, Nancy. *I Like Me.*
Charlip, Remy. *Sleepytime Rhyme.*
Cousins, Lucy. *Maisy Drives a Bus.*
Coy, John. *Vroomaloom Zoom.*
Doyle, Malachy. *Sleepy Pendoodle.*
Edwards, Pamela Duncan. *Slop Goes the Soup.*
Edwards, Pamela Duncan. *Some Smug Slug.*

Ehlert, Lois. *Growing Vegetable Soup.*
Ehlert, Lois. *Snowballs.*
Fox, Mem. *Time for Bed.*
Ginsburg, Mirra. *Across the Stream.*
Hall, Zoe. *The Surprise Garden.*
Harper, Charise Mericle. *So! So! Stop! Stop!*
Henkes, Kevin. *Kitten's First Full Moon.*
Hindley, Judy. *Does a Cow Say Boo?*
Hutchins, Pat. *You'll Soon Grow Into Them, Titch.*
Keats, Ezra Jack. *Snowy Day.*
Klassen, Jon. *I Want My Hat Back.*
Mallat, Kathy. *Seven Stars More!*
Minters, Frances. *Too Big, Too Small, Just Right.*
Mitton, Tony. *Down By the Cool Pool.*
Mockford, Caroline. *Cleo's Alphabet Book.*
Mockford, Caroline. *Cleo's Counting Book.*
Morozumi, Atsuko. *My Friend Gorilla.*
Murphy, Mary. *How Kind!*
Parr, Todd. *It's Okay to Be Different.*
Parr, Todd. *It's Okay to Make Mistakes.*
Pizzoli, Greg. *Number One Sam.*
Pizzoli, Greg. *The Watermelon Seed.*
Rinker, Sherri Duskey. *Goodnight, Goodnight, Construction Site.*
Rockwell, Anne F. *At the Beach*
Rose, Deborah Lee. *Birthday Zoo.*
Sendak, Maurice. *Where the Wild Things Are.*
Spence, Robert. *Clickety Clack.*
Stickland, Paul. *One Bear, One Dog.*
Stojic, Manya. *Rain.*
Surplice, Holly. *Peek-a-boo Bunny.*
Underwood, Deborah. *Bad Bye, Good Bye.*
Waber, Bernard. *Bearsie Bear and the Surprise Sleepover Party.*
Waddell, Martin. *Owl Babies.*
Waddell, Martin. *The Super Hungry Dinosaur.*
Walsh, Ellen Stoll. *Mouse Paint.*
Walter, Virginia. *Hi, Pizza Man!*
Whippo, Walt. *Little White Duck.*
Willems, Mo. *The Pigeon Needs a Bath!*
Zion, Gene. *Harry the Dirty Dog.*

INFORMATION PICTURE BOOKS FOR STORYTIME

Ajmera, Maya, Victoria Dunning, and Cythnia Pon. *Healthy Kids.*
Ajmera, Maya, Elise Hofer Derstine, and Cynthia Pon. *Music Everywhere!*
Arndt, Ingo. *Best Foot Forward: Exploring Feet, Flippers, and Claws.*
Aston, Dianna Hutts. *An Egg Is Quiet.*

Aston, Dianna Hutts. *A Rock Is Lively.*

Aston, Dianna Hutts. *A Seed Is Sleepy.*

Barner, Bob. *Bears! Bears! Bears!*

Berkes, Marianne. *Over In a River: Flowing Out to the Sea.*

Berkes, Marianne. *Over In the Forest: Come and Take a Peek.*

Biggs, Brian. *Everything Goes by Land.*

Biggs, Brian. *Everything Goes by Sea.*

Brocket, Jane. *Cold, Crunchy, Colorful: Using Our Senses.*

Brown, Don. *Henry and the Cannons: an Extraordinary True Story of the American Revolution.*

Bunting, Eve. *The Cart That Carried Martin.*

Butterworth, Chris. *See What a Seal Can Do.*

Campbell, Sarah C. *Wolfsnail: A Backyard Predator.*

DiTerlizzi, Angela. *Some Bugs.*

Floca, Brian. *Moonshot: The Flight of Apollo 11.*

French, Vivian. *Growing Frogs.*

French, Vivian. *Yucky Worms.*

Goodall, Jane. *Doctor White.*

Gray, Rita. *Have You Heard the Nesting Bird?*

Guiberson, Brenda Z. *The Greatest Dinosaur Ever.*

Hopkins, H. Joseph. *The Tree Lady: the True Story of How One Tree-Loving Woman Changed a City Forever.*

Houran, Lori Haskins. *Dig Those Dinosaurs.*

Houran, Lori Haskins. *A Trip into Space: an Adventure to the International Space Station.*

Huber, Raymond. *Flight of the Honeybee.*

Hulbert, Laura. *Who Has These Feet?*

Hulbert, Laura. *Who Has This Tail?*

Jenkins, Steve. *Actual Size* series.

Jenkins, Steve and Robin Page. *Move!*

Jenkins, Steve and Robin Paige. *My First Day: What Animals Do on Day One.*

Judge, Lita. *How Big Were Dinosaurs?*

Krebs, Laurie. *We're Sailing to Galapagos: a Week in the Pacific.*

Levine, Sara. *Bone by Bone: Comparing Animal Skeletons.*

Lewin, Ted. *What Am I? Where Am I?*

Low, William. *Daytime, Nighttime.*

Lunde, Darrin P. *Hello, Baby Beluga.*

Lunde, Darrin P. *Hello, Bumblebee Bat.*

Lunde, Darrin P. *Hello, Mama Wallaroo.*

Lunde, Darrin P. *Meet the Meerkat.*

Lunde, Darrin P. *Monkey Colors.*

Lyon, George Ella. *All the Water in the World.*

Malner, Carol L. *On Kiki's Reef.*

McDonnell, Patrick. *Me . . . Jane.*

Morris, Ann. *Bread, Bread, Bread.*

Morris, Ann. *Families.*

Morris, Ann. *Hats, Hats, Hats.*

Morris, Ann. *Houses and Homes.*

Morris, Ann. *On the Go.*

Morris, Ann. *Tools.*
Prince, April Jones. *What Do Wheels Do All Day?*
Ray, Mary Lyn. *Stars.*
Rockwell, Lizzy. *Plants Feed Me.*
Salas, Laura Purdie. *A Leaf Can Be . . .*
Salas, Laura Purdie. *Water Can Be . . .*
Sayre, April Pulley. *Eat Like a Bear.*
Sayre, April Pulley. *Go, Go, Grapes! A Fruit Chant.*
Sayre, April Pulley. *Let's Go Nuts! Seeds We Eat.*
Sayre, April Pulley. *Rah, Rah, Radishes! A Vegetable Chant.*
Schaefer, Lola M. *Lifetime: the Amazing Numbers.*
Schafer, Kevin. *Penguins 1 2 3.*
Stewart, Melissa. *No Monkeys, No Chocolate.*
Stockdale, Susan. *Bring on the Birds.*
Stockdale, Susan. *Fabulous Fishes.*
Stockdale, Susan. *Stripes of All Types.*
Teitelbaum, Michael. *Baby Penguin Slips and Slides.*
Teitelbaum, Michael. *Baby Polar Bears' Snow-Day.*
Ward, Jennifer. *Mama Built a Little Nest.*
Ward, Jennifer. *What Will Hatch?*

CHAPTER 5

Music, Songs, and Fingerplays

No matter what age group is the target audience for your storytime, songs and fingerplays are an essential part. Songs help signal the audience that it is time to listen, or recaptures those with short attention spans, or helps a distracted child refocus on what is coming next. Plus, songs and fingerplays are fun! Also, most of the songs and fingerplays we do at story-time will be used in kindergarten, so learning common folksongs and nursery rhymes is part of kindergarten readiness. Many of the fingerplays we do involve counting, addition, and subtraction, which also help preschoolers prepare for simple arithmetic. Songs promote the preliteracy skill of phonological awareness, which is the ability to guess rhyming sounds and to pick out syllables within longer words. Rhymes demonstrate the 46 phonemes that are in the English language, the sounds that make up the spoken language. Naturally, songs and fingerplays rhyme, so they easily build phonological awareness in an enjoyable way.

You don't have to be a great singer or play an instrument like a guitar to lead songs at storytime. Experts like Dr. Betsy Diamant-Cohen from "Mother Goose on the Loose" recommend that we repeat songs at storytime, and soon parents and children will drown you out, so don't worry about being a virtuoso. If you are really insecure, you can play a CD or MP3 of the song, to help you stay on key.

I try to keep the welcome song and the closing song the same each time. I also try to do a song in between each book, like "Open, Shut Them," a fingerplay like "Five Little Monkeys Jumping On The Bed," or "Shake Your Hands." These songs signal the children that it is time to "criss-cross applesauce," and listen. I actually do the same songs over and over, even if they don't fit the theme, where other librarians may introduce more songs and repeat them far less often. If you don't know what songs to use, watch "Barney," a PBS television series, which uses most of the songs already mentioned, because the songs they use are in the public domain. Another way to learn storytime songs is to watch a Raffi video, or a Bev Bos video; many of the parents and children will know the songs featured on these videos.

SONGS AS AN ESSENTIAL PART OF STORYTIME

You don't need to play the guitar or be a good singer to include songs in your storytime. You don't have to speak a foreign language to include multicultural songs or fingerplays, either. You can find many CDs and DVDs with children's songs that you can learn from, and lots of picture books that are based on songs. These can include *Who Took the Cookies from the Cookie Jar?* by Jane Manning, *Over in the Meadow* by various authors and illustrators, *The Croaky Pokey* by Ethan Long, *Old MacDonald Had A Farm* by various authors and illustrators, and *The Balancing Act* by Merle Peek, which is the English version of a song also popular in Spanish, "Un Elephante." Many more are listed at the end of this chapter. A good website for songs is www.kididdles.com which allows you to hear the song and to print out the lyrics.

Opening Songs

It is recommended that you open with the same song each week, because it is a signal to the audience that you are ready to begin. Many storytime providers allow the audience into the storytime space 15 minutes ahead of time, so they can settle in, or so parents can talk to each other. When the opening song starts, everyone knows it is time to listen. In fact, many librarians I know use the same opening song for both infant and toddler storytimes. Here are some favorites:

"Hello Everybody, Yes, Indeed"
Hello everybody, yes indeed,
Yes indeed, yes indeed.
Hello everybody, yes indeed.
Yes, indeed everybody.

Wiggle your fingers, yes indeed,
Yes indeed, yes indeed.
Wiggle your fingers, yes indeed,
Yes indeed, everybody.

Clap your hands (etc.).
Let's read a story (etc.).

"Wheels on the Bus"
The wheels on the bus go round and round
Round and round, round and round.
The wheels on the bus go round and round,
All around the town.

Wipers on the bus go swish, swish, swish (etc.).
Money on the bus goes clink, clink, clink (etc.).
Horn on the bus goes beep, beep, beep (etc.).

Baby on the bus goes wah, wah, wah (etc.)
Parents on the bus go shh, shh, shh (etc.).

"We'll All Join in the Circle"
We'll all join in the circle,
We'll all join in the circle,
We'll all join in the circle,
And sing a song or two.

We'll all clap hands together (etc.)
We'll all stand up together (etc.)
We'll all join hands together (etc.)
We'll all turn 'round together (etc.)
We'll all stand still together (etc.)
We'll all sit down together (etc.)

We'll all be quiet together (etc.).
Now singing time is through.

"Mary Wore Her Red Dress"
(each time using the name and clothing item from a child in the audience).

Mary wore her red dress, red dress, red dress,
Mary wore her red dress, all day long.

Carlos wore his blue pants, (etc.)

Closing Songs

Closing songs are a great tradition at storytime, giving everyone closure and signaling your audience that after the song, they are free to get up to find books, or sit for a while so the parents can chat. One favorite you may want to try is "Goodnight Irene," made famous by the folk-singing group The Weavers. For a storytime with the whole family, you could end with the dance "The Hokey Pokey." Here are two traditional closing songs:

"Wave High, Wave Low"
Wave high, wave low.
I think it's time, we gotta go.
Wave your elbows, wave your toes.
Wave your tongue, and wave your nose.
Wave your knees, wave your lips.
Blow a kiss with fingertips.
Wave your ears, wave your hair,
Wave your belly in the air.
Wave your chin, wave your eye,
Wave your hand and say good-bye.

"The More We Get Together"
The more we get together,
Together, together.
The more we get together,

The happier we'll be.
Cause your friends are my friends,
And my friends are your friends.
The more we get together,
The happier we'll be.

"Get Ready to Listen" Songs

Many toddlers will already know "Open, Shut Them" as a song that signals it is time to listen. There are a few others, and it is recommended to repeat them often.

"Open, Shut Them"
Open, shut them,
Open, shut them.
Give a little clap.
Open, shut them,
Open, shut them,
Lay them in your lap.

Creep them, creep them,
Creep them, creep them,
Right up to your chin.
Open up your mouth,
But do not let them in!

"Shake Your Hands"
Shake your hands, shake your hands,
Give a little clap.
Shake your hands, shake your hands,
Lay them in your lap.

Shake your hands, shake your hands,
Hold on to your chair.
Shake your hands, shake your hands,
Wave them in the air.

Shake your hands, shake your hands,
Give a little clap, clap, clap.
Shake your hands, shake your hands,
Lay them in your lap, lap, lap.

Stretch Songs

One of my favorite songs to get the kids up and stretching is Raffi's "Shake Your Sillies Out," available on his CD *Raffi in Concert With the Rise & Shine Band*. Due to copyright law we can't include the lyrics here, but you probably have this CD in your library and it is an easy song to learn. There is also a picture book version! Other songs that are great to get the children up on their feet for a stretch are listed below. These work well to get everyone focused, and then we all sit and are relaxed and ready for the next story.

"Grand Old Duke of York"
The Grand Old Duke of York,
He had ten thousand men.
He marched them up to the top of the hill
And marched them down again.
And when they're up, they're up,
And when they're down, they're down.
And when they're only halfway up,
They're neither up nor down.

"If You're Happy and You Know It"
If you're happy and you know it, clap your hands.
If you're happy and you know it, clap your hands.
If you're happy and you know it,
Then your face will surely show it (smile).
If you're happy and you know it, clap your hands.

If you're happy and you know it stomp your feet (etc.).
If you're happy and you know it turn around (etc.).
If you're happy and you know it do all three (etc.).

"Johnny Works with One Hammer"
Johnny works with one hammer, (hammer one fist lightly on leg)
One hammer, One hammer,
Johnny works with one hammer,
Then he works with two.

Johnny works with two hammers . . .
(hammer both fists on legs)

Johnny works with three hammers . . .
(hammer both fists on legs and stomp one foot)

Johnny works with four hammers . . .
(hammer both fists on legs and stomp both feet)

Johnny works with five hammers . . .
(hammer both fists, stomp both feet, nod head up and down)

Then he goes to sleep! (rest head on hands making snoring sounds)

"The Elephant Goes"
The elephant goes like this and that,
He's terribly big,
And he's terribly fat.
He has no fingers
And has no toes,
But goodness gracious,
What a nose!

"Hurry Hurry, Drive the Firetruck"
Hurry, hurry, drive the firetruck.
Hurry, hurry, drive the firetruck.

Hurry hurry, drive the firetruck.
Ding, ding, ding, ding, ding!

Hurry, hurry, turn the corner (etc.)
Hurry, hurry, climb the ladder (etc.)
Hurry, hurry, squirt the water (etc.)
Hurry, hurry, back to the station (etc.)

FINGERPLAYS

You don't have to be able to carry a tune to sing a fingerplay, because the audience will soon drown you out! Many fingerplays work well for a wide age range, from toddlers to older preschoolers. These include simple movements, and fun action, that are quick for a newcomer to learn since the movement reinforces the lyrics of the fingerplay. Several websites that feature videos of fingerplays being performed are listed at the end of this chapter.

Fingerplays for All Ages

"Where is Thumbkin?"
Where is Thumbkin, where is Thumbkin?
Here I am, (bring out thumb from behind your back).
Here I am (bring out other thumb).
How are you today sir?
Very well I thank you.
Run away, run away (hand go behind your back again).
(Repeat with the rest of your fingers)

Where is Pointer? (etc.)
Where is Tall Man? (etc.)
Where is Ring Man? (etc.)
Where is Pinky? (etc.)

"There Was a Little Turtle"
There was a little turtle
Who lived in a box. (hold hands like a box)
He swam in the puddles (hands make swimming movements)
And he climbed on the rocks. (have two fingers "crawl" on your other hand)

He snapped at the mosquito, (snap your fingers each time)
He snapped at the flea.
He snapped at the minnow,
And he snapped at me.

He caught the mosquito, (clap hands each time)
He caught the flea.
He caught the minnow,
But he didn't catch me! (go to clap your hands but miss!)

"This Old Man"
This old man, he played one, (hold up the number of fingers)
He played knick-knack on my thumb.
With a knick-knack paddy whack,
Give a dog a bone,
This old man came rolling home. (Roll your hands)

This old man, he played two,
He played knick-knack on my shoe (etc.)

This old man, he played three,
He played knick-knack on my knee (etc.)

This old man, he played four,
He played knick-knack on my door (etc.)

This old man, he played five,
He played knick-knack on my hive (etc.)

This old man, he played six,
He played knick-knack on my sticks (etc.)

This old man, he played seven,
He played knick-knack up in heaven (etc.)

This old man, he played eight,
He played knick-knack on my gate (etc.)

This old man, he played nine,
He played knick-knack on my line (etc.)

This old man, he played ten,
He played knick-knack over again (etc.)

Counting Fingerplays

Many of my favorite fingerplays are counting rhymes. They are easy to remember, and of course, help in learning simple arithmetic. Many of the toddlers and preschoolers will know these already, and of course we want to repeat our favorite songs and fingerplays regularly. The motions are easy; you hold up the right number of fingers and count them, then put one finger down as they are subtracted. You basically indicate with simple movements what is happening in the song, like jumping, holding a phone, eating a fly, and so on. Here are some favorites:

"Five Little Monkeys Jumping on the Bed"
Five little monkeys, jumping on the bed.
One fell off and bumped his head.
Mama called the doctor and the doctor said,
"No more monkeys jumping on the bed!"
(Repeat with four little monkeys, then three, etc.)

"Five Little Monkeys Swinging in a Tree"
Five little monkeys, swinging in a tree
Teasing mister alligator, "You can't catch me"
Along comes mister alligator, quiet as can be,
And snapped that monkey right out of that tree!
(Repeat with four monkeys, then three, etc.)

"Five Little Ducks"
Five little ducks went out one day,
Over the hill and far away.
When the mother duck said "Quack, quack, quack, quack,"
Only four little ducks came back.
(Repeat with four ducks, then three, etc.)

No little ducks went out one day,
Over the hill and far away,
When the mother duck said "Quack, quack, quack, quack,"
All the five little ducks came back!

"Five Green and Speckled Frogs"
Five green and speckled frogs,
Sat on a speckled log,
Eating the most delicious bugs, yum!
One jumped into the pool,
Where it was nice and cool,
Then there were four green speckled frogs—Ribbit! Ribbit!
(Repeat until all frogs are in the pool).

"Ten in a Bed"
There were ten in the bed and the little one said
"Roll over, roll over!" (roll your hands)
And they all rolled over and one fell out!

There were nine in the bed (etc.).

There was one in the bed and the little one said
"Alone at last!"

REPETITION

Some storytime presenters will learn new songs every week, to go along with the theme of that week. But learning a core group of songs is more important, because the parents and children who attend will want to sing along. Repetition is important to a young child's learning process; it helps with their phonological awareness and builds vocabulary. Many parents may not originally be from the United States, or may speak English as a second language, so repeating the songs and rhymes helps them learn so they can repeat them at home.

HANDOUTS

Because songs and fingerplays are so important to the storytime experience, it can be very helpful to have handouts for parents containing the lyrics to the regular songs you use. Handouts can help a parent repeat those songs during reading time at home, which will be especially beneficial for those who cannot attend regularly due to work schedules. Also, the handouts can make newcomers feel welcome and part of the group; if everyone can sing the songs except them they will feel left out. Finally, since many of our parents and caregivers may speak English as a second language or may not have grown up in the United States, the handouts can help them familiarize themselves with songs most of us take for granted. Consider making some simple song sheets with just the lyrics (you won't need the sheet music) for the adults who are new storytime attendees.

USING MUSICAL RECORDINGS

Every storytime presenter has his or her own way of performing songs; some prefer to sing a cappella, others like to use a guitar or ukulele, and many like to sing along to a musical recording. In the past, most used CDs, but now the most common method is to use an iPod or other type of MP3 music player, using songs purchased and downloaded from iTunes or another vendor.

Tablet devices with apps can also help you in presenting songs; there are some websites with suggestions for musical apps listed at the end of this chapter. The app plays musical accompaniment with the added feature of displaying the lyrics. This will help you remember the words, but can also be projected on to a large screen to assist parents who are learning the song.

Presenters should use whatever method works for them. I like to sing a cappella, since that allows for more flexibility. You don't have to sing perfectly to present songs at storytime, since the point of it is to get the whole audience to sing along. But if you feel most comfortable singing along with recordings then use them, playing them on whatever device you have available.

DANCE PARTY PROGRAMS

Dance party programs are one of the latest innovations in storytime, encouraging movement and exercise as well as self-expression and the enjoyment of music. Think of a fun name for this special storytime, like "Move and Groove," "Baby Bandstand," or "Toddler Soul Train."

Dance party programs are relatively free form, but you need a leader who is willing to dance and move, similar to an aerobics or Zumba instructor. If you are not that person, hire someone. Along with publicity, room setup, and other basics of any program, you will need:

- Playlist—your list of songs, arranged with some variety between up-tempo and slower songs.
- Recorded songs as well as sing-alongs—have some recorded "free dance" songs along with songs the whole group will sing, such as "Head and Shoulders."

- Props—scarves, beanbags, shakers, hula hoops, pompoms, and other items you may already use in storytimes.
- Sound equipment—make sure the CD or MP3 player has great speakers, and you will also need a microphone for the leader.
- Crowd control—you don't want an uncontrolled "mosh pit" situation where the young children can accidently hurt each other.
- Hydration—be sure to have water and other beverages so participants stay hydrated.
- Quiet reading area for those wanting a break.
- Books to read at the beginning, middle, and end, to give the whole crowd a chance to catch their breath.

Dance party programs are a stand-alone special storytime activity, not a regular weekly event. They can help to attract new audience members for your regular storytimes, or kick-off the summer reading program.

RESOURCES FOR SONGS AND FINGERPLAYS

Concluding this chapter are several handy lists of resources you can access for adding more music to your storytime. The list of books for the adult doing storytime will help in planning your programs, as well as websites that contain songs and fingerplays. I have also listed a selection of children's music CDs/MP3s that contain songs that are perfect to use at storytime, often performed by noted children's performers such as Raffi or Hap Palmer. Finally, there is a list of picture books that contain the text of a song, with illustrations, that can inspire your audience to join in the singing!

Resource Books with Songs and Fingerplays

For those who are too shy to even sing in the shower, check out *Little Hands Fingerplays and Action Songs: Seasonal Activities and Creative Play for 2- to 6-Year-Olds* by Emily Stetson and Vicky Congdon (Williamson Publishing, 2001). Many books are available with fingerplays, including *My First Action Rhymes* by Lynne Cravath and *The Eentsy, Weentsy Spider: Fingerplays and Action Rhymes* by Joanna Cole. You can also find individual picture books based on fingerplays such as *Peanut Butter and Jelly* by Nadine Bernard Westcott, and *Five Little Monkeys Sitting In A Tree* by Eileen Christelow; see our list at the end of this chapter. For multicultural fingerplays, try *Chinese Mother Goose Rhymes* by Robert Wyndham or *Diez Deditos: Ten Little Fingers* by Jose Luis Orozco. *Marc Brown's Playtime Rhymes* by Marc Brown (Little Brown, 2013) was recently revised and contains many popular fingerplays and movement rhymes.

WEBSITES ON SONGS AND FINGERPLAYS

Reading is Fundamental
www.rif.org/kids/leadingtoreading/en/babies-toddlers/finger-plays.htm
The Reading is Fundamental's site contains short videos of a person performing fingerplays for toddlers and babies.

Kididdles

www.kididdles.com/lyrics/allsongs.html

A great resource for song lyrics to popular preschool schools; some of the lyric pages let you hear the music, too.

BusSongs

http://bussongs.com/songs/well-all-join-in-the-circle.php

This site is run by volunteers who wanted to preserve and promote traditional songs used at storytimes and at summer camps. Each entry has lyrics, facts about the song, and some have videos.

Songs for Teaching

www.songsforteaching.com/fingerplays/index.htm

www.songsforteaching.com/movement.htm

The Fingerplays area has a great list of commonly used fingerplays; many come with an audio clip so you can learn the melody. There are also photos of a person doing the fingerplay, so you can copy the movement. There is an area for action songs; many of these also include an audio clip.

Born to Read Songs and Fingerplays

www.ala.org/alsc/issuesadv/borntoread/toddlerrhymesgames

Provided by the American Library Association's "Born to Read" initiative, this site lists several tickle and bouncing rhymes that are perfect for a baby storytime.

CanTeach

www.canteach.ca/elementary/songspoems.html

Poems and songs are listed here by theme. This is intended for teachers but also lists links for school librarians that can be helpful.

Fred Rogers Center for Early Learning and Children's Media

www.fredrogerscenter.org/resources/play-and-learn/

The Fred Rogers Center, named after the renowned television teacher for preschoolers, offers recommendations for apps to use for storytime, many of them featuring music.

Grow a Reader

https://itunes.apple.com/us/app/grow-a-reader/id594398910?mt=8

The Calgary Public Library offers a free app that encourages parents to sing with their children.

King County Library System's Rhymes and Songs

http://wiki.kcls.org/index.php/Category:Rhymes_&_Songs

From the King County Library System in Washington, this site contains hundreds of storytime songs and rhymes, demonstrated with videos featuring staff members performing the songs.

CDs (MANY ALSO AVAILABLE IN MP3 FORMAT)

Arma, Tom. *Animal Songs*. Madacy Entertainment Group, 2004.

Berkner, Laurie. *The Best of the Laurie Berkner Band*. Two Tomatoes, 2010.

Bos, Bev. *We've Been Waiting for You*. Turn-The-Page, 1999.

Boynton, Sandra. *Frog Trouble . . . and Eleven Other Pretty Serious Songs*. Workman, 2013.

Diamant-Cohen, Betsy. *Listen, Like, Learn With Mother Goose on the Loose*. Betsy's Folly Studios, 2006.

Diamant-Cohen, Betsy. *Mother Goose on the Loose: More Nursery Rhymes and Songs*. Betsy's Folly Studios, 2005.

Doherty, Laura. *In a Heartbeat*. CD Baby, 2014.

Feierabend, John M. and Jill Trinka. *There's a Hole in the Bucket*. GIA, 2006.

Gill, Jim. *Jim Gill Sings Do Re Mi on His Toe Leg Knee*. Jim Gill Music, 1999.

Harley, Bill and Keigh Munslow. *It's Not Fair to Me*. Round River, 2013.

Huff, Mary Jo. *Gettin' Loose with Mother Goose*. Storytellin', 2010.

Janiak, William C. *Dances for Little People*. Kimbo Educational, 2004.

Janiak, William C. *It's Fun to Clap*. Kimbo Educational, 2007.

Jenkins, Ella. *And One and Two and Other Songs for Pre-school and Primary Children*. Smithsonian Folkways, 1995.

Jenkins, Ella. *Counting Games and Rhythms for the Little Ones*. Smithsonian Folkways, 1997.

Jenkins, Ella. *Early, Early Childhood Songs*. Smithsonian Folkways, 1990.

Jenkins, Ella. *Multi-Cultural Children's Songs*. Smithsonian Folkways, 1995.

Jenkins, Ella. *123s and ABCs*. Smithsonian Folkways, 2014.

Kisor, David. *Becoming My Own Me: Songs for Developing Toddlers*. Growing Sound, 2011.

Koral, Bari. *Anna and the Cupcakes*. Loopytunes, 2012.

Langstaff, John. *Songs for Singing Children*. Revels Records, 1996.

Lehman, Kim. *All Together Now: Songs to Sing with Children*. Kim Lehman, 2006.

McGrath, Bob. *Bob's Favorite Sing Along Songs*. Bob's Kids Music, 2013.

McGrath, Bob and Katharine Smithrim. *Songs & Games for Toddlers*. Bob's Kids Music, 2000.

Mitchell, Elizabeth. *Little Seed: Songs for Children by Woody Guthrie*. Smithsonian Folkways, 2012.

Muldaur, Maria. *Maria Muldaur's Barnyard Dance: Jug Band Music for Kids*. Kid Rhino, 2010.

Music for Little People. *Apples & Bananas: Songs for Healthy Families*. Music for Little People, 2011.

Music for Little People. *Toddler Favorites*. Music for Little People, 2011.

O'Dell, Dino. *Outer Space*. CD Baby, 2012.

OkeeDokee Brothers. *Can You Canoe?* OkeeDokee Music, 2012.

Orozco, Jose Luis. *De Colores and Other Latin-American Folk Songs for Children*. Arco-iris Records, 1996.

Orozco, Jose Luis. *Fiestas: A Year of Latin-American Songs of Celebration*. Arcoiris Records, 2002.

Palmer, Hap. *Early Childhood Classics: Old Favorites with a New Twist*. Hap-Pal Music, 2000.

Palmer, Hap. *Peekaboo and Other Songs for Very Young Children*. Hap-Pal Music, 1997.

Palmer, Hap. *Sally the Swinging Snake*. Educational Activities, 1994.

Raffi. *Corner Grocery Store.* Shoreline Records, 1979.
Raffi. *Everything Grows.* Shoreline Records, 1987.
Raffi. *More Singable Songs.* Rounder Records, 1977.
Raffi. *Raffi in Concert with the Rise & Shine Band.* Rounder Records, 1996.
Raffi. *Singable Songs for the Very Young.* Rounder Records, 1976.
Roberts, Justin. *Great Big Sun.* Carpet Square, 2001.
Schnitzer, Sue. *Wiggle and Whirl.* CD Baby, 2000.
Smithe, Aaron Nigel. *Everyone Loves to Dance!* Music for Little People, 2011.
Stewart, Georgiana. *Circle Time Activities.* Kimbo Educational, 2004.
Stewart, Georgiana. *Finger Play Fun Fine Motor Exercises.* Kimbo Educational, 2007.
Sweet Honey in the Rock. *I Got Shoes.* Music for Little People, 1994.
Trout Fishing In America. *Rubber Baby Buggy Bumpers.* Trout Records, 2013.
Valeri, Michele. *Little Ditties for Itty Bitties: Songs for Infants and Toddlers.* Community Music, 2010.
Zanes, Dan. *Catch That Train!* Festival Five Records, 2006.
Zanes, Dan. *Family Dance.* Festival Five Records, 2001.
Zanes, Dan. *Turn Turn Turn.* Festival Five Records, 2013.

SONGS DONE AS PICTURE BOOKS

Bateman, Donna M. *Out on the Prairie.*
Bates, Ivan. *Five Little Ducks.*
Bates, Katharine Lee. *America the Beautiful: United We Stand.*
Birdseye, Tom. *She'll Be Comin' Round the Mountain.*
Brown, Marc. *Marc Brown's Playtime Rhymes.*
Cabrera, Jane. *If You're Happy and You Know It.*
Cabrera, Jane. *Row, Row, Row Your Boat.*
Carle, Eric. *Today Is Monday.*
Catrow, David. *Monster Mash.*
Colandro, Lucille. *There Was an Old Lady Who Swallowed a Clover!*
Colato Lainez, Rene. *Señor Pancho Had a Rancho.*
Christelow, Eileen. *Five Little Monkeys Jumping on the Bed.*
Christelow, Eileen. *Five Little Monkeys Swinging in a Tree.*
Dean, James. *Pete the Cat: Old MacDonald Had a Farm.*
Dean, James. *Pete the Cat: Wheels on the Bus.*
Eagle, Kin. *Hey Diddle Diddle.*
Flanders, Michael. *The Hippopotamus Song.*
Frazee, Marla. *Hush Little Baby.*
Galdone, Paul. *Cat Goes Fiddle-I-Fee.*
Galdone, Paul. *Over in the Meadow.*
Galdone, Paul. *Three Little Kittens.*
Garcia, Jerry. *The Teddy Bear's Picnic.*
Geist, Ken. *Who's Who?*
Glazer, Tom. *On Top of Spaghetti.*
Guthrie, Woody. *This Land Is Your Land.*
Hale, Sarah. *Mary Had a Little Lamb.*

Henderson, Kathy. *Hush, Baby, Hush: Lullabies from Around the World.*
Hillenbrand, Will. *Down By the Station.*
Hoberman, Mary Ann. *Miss Mary Mack.*
Hoberman, Mary Ann. *There Once Was a Man Named Michael Finnegan.*
Hort, Lenny. *Seals on the Bus.*
Hughes, Langston. *Lullaby (For a Black Mother).*
Isadora, Rachel. *Old Mikamba Had a Farm.*
Ivimey, John W. *The Complete Story of the Three Blind Mice.*
Jackson, Alison. *I Know an Old Lady Who Swallowed a Pie.*
Koontz, Robin. *This Old Man.*
Jewel. *Sweet Dreams.*
Kovalski, Maryann. *The Wheels on the Bus.*
Kralovansky, Susan Holt. *There Was a Tall Texan Who Swallowed a Flea.*
Langstaff, John M. *Frog Went A-Courtin'*
Langstaff, John M. *Oh, A-Hunting We Will Go.*
Laprise, Larry. *The Hokey Pokey.*
Markell, Denis. *Hush Little Monster.*
Miller, J. Philip. *We All Sing With the Same Voice.*
Norworth, Jack. *Take Me Out to the Ballgame.*
O'Brien, John. *The Farmer in the Dell.*
Owen, Ann. *Ants Go Marching.*
Paxton, Tom. *Going to the Zoo.*
Peek, Merle. *Mary Wore Her Red Dress.*
Peek, Merle. *Roll Over! A Counting Song.*
Raffi. *Five Little Ducks.*
Raffi. *Shake My Sillies Out.*
Raposo, Joe. *Sing.*
Raschka, Chris. *Hip Hop Dog.*
Rees, Mary. *Ten in a Bed.*
Russell, Bill. *A Spider on the Floor.*
Schwartz, Amy. *Old MacDonald.*
Sherman, Allan. *Hello Muddah, Hello Faddah.*
Sierra, Judy. *E-I-E-I-O! How Old MacDonald Got His Farm with a Little Help from a Hen.*
Siomades, Lorianne. *The Itsy Bitsy Spider.*
Siomades, Lorianne. *Three Little Kittens.*
Taback, Simms. *There Was An Old Lady Who Swallowed a Fly.*
Thomas, Jan. *Let's Sing a Lullaby with the Brave Cowboy.*
Trapani, Iza. *The Bear Went Over the Mountain.*
Trapani, Iza. *How Much Is That Doggie In the Window?*
Trapani, Iza. *Row, Row, Row Your Boat.*
Trapani, Iza. *Shoo Fly!*
Westcott, Nadine. *I've Been Working on the Railroad.*
Westcott, Nadine. *The Lady With the Alligator Purse.*
Westcott, Nadine. *Skip to My Lou.*
Whippo, Walt. *Little White Duck.*
Zane, Alex. *The Wheels on the Race Car.*

CHAPTER 6

Bilingual Storytime

Many libraries have found that a sizable percentage of their families with young children speak English as a second language, so offering bilingual storytimes can be one way of attracting those families to the library. In California and Texas, approximately 13 percent of the population speaks only Spanish, so a bilingual storytime will help families prepare their preschoolers with English before they start kindergarten. Let's find out about this type of storytime, which is growing in popularity.

WHAT IS A BILINGUAL STORYTIME?

Bilingual storytime involves reading the books in both English and the other language, and singing songs, enjoying cultural arts and crafts, and doing other activities celebrating the culture of that group. It also helps the group learn English, and to acclimate to songs, nursery rhymes, and books in English so that the children can prepare for kindergarten. For most of this chapter, I will give examples for a Spanish/English bilingual storytime, since that is the type I have conducted. Most of what I know on this topic I learned from Ana Elba Pavon, librarian and coauthor of *Latino Craft Projects* (ALA, 2003).

Need for Bilingual Storytime

Having library programs promotes the library as a "town square," or central meeting place. The library becomes a valuable asset to the community, not just for books but as a cultural center. Good programming draws the community into the library and makes it easier to get the funds to stay open when budget cuts are proposed. Non-English speaking families may not know the library has something for them, but if you hold a program celebrating their culture, they will discover the library has books in their languages, or tutoring. Especially when you feature programming for children, they will learn the library provides homework help for their children. So if your town has a sizable group that speaks something besides English at home, like a large Spanish-speaking community, then a bilingual storytime can serve as a means to demonstrate the library desires that group as customers, and it can help promote kindergarten readiness in that group.

Another need a bilingual storytime can meet is to introduce another language to English speakers. Many preschoolers learn Spanish from their favorite television programs: "Dora the Explorer," "Sesame Street," and other shows. They can also enjoy a bilingual storytime since the stories are read in English, and they can pick up some Spanish vocabulary because the stories are also read in Spanish.

Scheduling

How often you schedule your bilingual storytime will be based on several factors. One may be staffing; you may only have time for a special monthly bilingual storytime, but that would be better than none at all! Some libraries will hold special bilingual holiday programs with stories, songs, crafts, and refreshments; these may be scheduled seasonally like a program for summer, or Cinco de Mayo. The most desirable would be to have a weekly bilingual storytime, one morning or one evening per week. Some librarians try to avoid holding bilingual storytimes on Saturday morning, since Spanish speakers may have Catechism, and Mandarin and Cantonese speakers may have Chinese school. Also, many children have soccer or other sports programs on Saturday mornings, so see what works for your neighborhood. But if a weekly bilingual storytime is just impossible for your staff schedule, a monthly one can draw a consistent audience. If it is just once a month, you can make it extra special if you have refreshments and craft time, so the parents can get to know each other and talk. Make book displays and help encourage book checkout; maybe the monthly storytime is their only trip to the library that month and you want to cover all your services.

NON-ENGLISH STORYTIME

Some librarians will choose to do the entire storytime in the non-English language, but not do a bilingual storytime (English and the other language). Depending on your community needs, library resources, and the model in your local K-12 schools, that may be a suitable choice. If you are not sure, ask some local kindergarten teachers and see which they would recommend; would a bilingual or fully non-English storytime better suit the incoming kindergartners? Or, maybe your community has a tradition of services in that language; a storytime conducted just in Spanish has been a tradition at the branch in the Mission District in San Francisco for many years. Only you and your library director can make the determination of what is a good fit for your library.

BILINGUAL STORYTIME FORMAT

You can use several formats when doing a bilingual storytime. The format you choose may depend on whether or not you have staff that are bilingual and are comfortable reading aloud and singing in the two languages. If you don't have a bilingual staff member who can do the storytime, you can pair with a bilingual volunteer and do the partner-style storytime. Look over the following formats and choose what will work best for you.

Format for Bilingual Spanish/English Storytime

Here is an average format for a Bilingual Spanish/English storytime:

Opening song: "Buenos Dias" by Jose Luis Orozco
State theme or subject of today's books: Animals
Get ready song: "Si Yo Pongo Mis Dos Manos para Arriba"
Book: *Eight Animals on the Town* by Susan M. Elya
Fingerplay: "Cinco Ratoncitos"
Participation book: *Un Gato y un Perro/A Cat and a Dog* by Claire Masurel
Nursery rhyme: A selection from *Uno Dos Tres: My First Spanish Rhymes* by Yanitzia Canetti
Song: "Uno, Dos, Tres Gatitos"
Book: *Es Hora De Dormir/Time for Bed* by Mem Fox
Movement rhyme: "Un Elefante se Balanceaba"
Book: *ABeCedarios: Mexican Folk Art ABCs* by Cynthia Weill
App: Kidztory Classics "The Little Red Hen" or "Three Little Pigs"
Closing song: "Adios Mis Amigos"
Closing hands-on activity: Make simple mouse finger puppets to use with the "Cinco Ratoncitos" fingerplay. You can make them out of work gloves purchased at the dollar store, and add on yarn tails, googly eyes, and felt ears, nose, and teeth.

Partner-Style Storytime

When an English-speaking staff member and a bilingual volunteer or employee pair up to conduct the storytime that is called a partner-style storytime. For this type, both partners learn all the songs and sing them together. But they read in the language they are most comfortable with: one reads in English, the other person reads in the other language. For this style of storytime, you need two copies of the same book. If the book is already bilingual, with the text both in English and the other language, this style of storytime is relatively simple. If a book you want to read only comes in English, then the multilingual partner will have to translate the book ahead of time to prepare for the storytime. Either way, you will need two copies of the book. One advantage of doing the storytime with partners is that one partner is often the children's librarian who may only feel comfortable in English. But since the librarian is a regular presence at the storytimes, the parents and children who attend get to know that person and feel comfortable asking for help. The bilingual partner can be either another staff member, or a volunteer. In fact, you can have a few regular bilingual partners who alternate. If one is on vacation, you have another who is already trained and can fill in.

Using Bilingual Books

More and more picture books are being published in the bilingual format, with English and the other language on the same page. Some of these are translations of popular American picture books, but many are culturally authentic stories from the other language. Piñata Books publishes great Spanish/English bilingual picture books, which work very well in a storytime. You can also find enough bilingual books featuring Chinese and English to have a selection for a regular storytime, if you add in flannelboards and songs. Other languages may be harder to find.

You can use bilingual books a few ways. If you have two storytime presenters, use two copies of the same bilingual book, with one partner reading in English, and one in Spanish, as we discussed earlier. Each partner reads the same page, then turns the page and reads, so you really present the book bilingually. Hearing the same sentence in Spanish, then English, helps children learn the other language. The bilingual children can hear both languages and pick up reading skills so they can learn to read in both. If you have just one storytime presenter who is bilingual, he or she can also read the book alternating the Spanish and English a sentence at the time, which achieves many of the same goals.

Some presenters prefer to read a bilingual book complete in one language, then the other. I think you lose some of the audience this way, and it doesn't serve to help them learn a new language (many of those in attendance will be English language learners). Try different strategies and see what works for you. Also, try to determine the goal of those in attendance: are they English speakers there to learn a new language, or there to help their children learn English before they begin kindergarten? Or are they already fully bilingual, and there to celebrate their culture? You will probably get a mix of people with different abilities, but I am sure you can find some middle ground that helps the group while still being comfortable for the storytime presenter.

Using Two Books

When using two books, one in English and the other in Spanish, you have two methods to choose from. You can read the book in one language all the way through, then repeat the book in the other language. More commonly, the presenter will read one sentence in Spanish (for example), then the same sentence in English, then turn the page. The illustrations are the same, and reading the same sentence in the two languages can help people learn both languages and they will still enjoy the story. To make this work, the picture book should be brief, with one sentence per page, not one paragraph per page which would be too long. You can hold the Spanish copy, then the English copy, but many presenters prefer having a volunteer hold one of the books so you can avoid a juggling act! Have the volunteer sit on one side of you, holding the book so both you and the audience can see it so you can read the words and they can see the illustrations.

Code Switching

Some books will include words in both English and Spanish, using the two interchangeably. The ability to know what is meant when the two languages are mixed is called Code Switching; some folks will use the slang term Spanglish. Many books are written in English with a few Spanish words that are easy to decode because of the context: Pat

Mora's *Uno, Dos, Tres, One Two Three* is a popular choice. Ginger Guy has several very brief picture books that mix English and Spanish, including *Fiesta!* and *Siesta.*

MUSIC, PUPPETS, AND EXTRAS

Just like your regular preschool storytimes, you should include lots of songs and fingerplays in a bilingual storytime. Look for a simple opening song like "Buenos Dias" which is sung to the tune of "Where Is Thumbkin?" There are also counting songs in Spanish. For more song choices in Spanish, listen to the recordings of Jose Luis Orozco, which are listed in our chapter on Songs and Fingerplays. For songs and rhymes in other languages, network with parents who may even volunteer to present the songs in their native languages.

To get started, here are a few simple fingerplays you can use:

"Cinco Ratoncitos"
Cinco ratoncitos
De colita gris
Mueven las orejas
Mueven la nariz
Uno, dos, tres, cuatro, cinco,
Corren al rincon!
Porque viene el gato,
A comer raton.

"Uno Dos Tres Gatitos"
Uno, dos, tres, gatitos
Cuatro, cinco, seis gatitos
Siete, ocho, nueve gatitos
Diez gatitos son.

Uno, dos, tres, perritos
Cuatro, cinco, seis, perritos
Siete, ocho, nueve perritos,
Diez perritos son.

"Manos Arriba"
Manos arriba/hands up
Da un salto/give a jump
Manos abajo/hands down
Da una vuelta/turn around
Un paso para adelante/one step forward
Un paso para atrás/one step back
Brinca, brinca/jump, jump
Ya no mas/no more (shrug shoulders)
A la izquierda/to the left
Andarás/you'll walk
A la derecha/to the right
Volverás/you'll return

Un paso para adelante/one step forward
Un paso para atrás/one step back
Brinca, brinca/jump, jump
Ya no más!/No more (shrug)

OUTREACH TO NON-ENGLISH SPEAKERS

If you start a bilingual storytime, you will need to do publicity and outreach to notify your target audience. As mentioned earlier, many of the people in the target audience may not be aware of what a public library offers, especially if they come from a country that does not have library services except at universities.

Outreach

See if you can schedule some brief visits to places where bilingual parents meet such as clubs at local preschools, elementary schools, churches, or other cultural organizations. Let them know about this new service, speaking in both English and the other language as a way to convey that this is how the storytime will be conducted. You may need to bring your storytime partner who is multilingual if you do not speak the other language.

Publicity

You may need to do more publicity for a new bilingual storytime than you do for regular storytime, since you are reaching a new target audience. Be sure your flyers are in the two languages that will be used at the storytime. Also spell out that the program is free, since many countries do not provide free services in their libraries, and those new to the United States may not be aware that public libraries here offer free programs like storytime. Your flyers and press releases need to reach your target audience, so be sure you have the information at stores, laundromats, churches, or other places frequented by the target group. You can even make door hangers for housing in neighborhoods that have a large amount of the non-English speakers you want to include. Make sure you have a map to the library on the door hanger, and again be sure to specify that the storytime is free.

EL DIA DE LOS NIÑOS/EL DIA DE LOS LIBROS

Many libraries participate in El Dia de los Niños/El Dia de los Libros (Children's Day/Book Day), a celebration promoted by the American Library Association. It is usually celebrated on April 30th, with special bilingual storytimes and Hispanic/Latino entertainment offerings for the whole family. Many libraries have been able to obtain grants to give out one free book per child at these programs. The goal of the program is to promote reading and use of the library by families of all cultural backgrounds. If you are not currently offering bilingual storytimes, you can debut one at "Dia." Check out their website at http://dia.ala.org/ for ways to participate, links to free downloadable materials, corporate partners that offer grants, and more.

RESOURCES FOR BILINGUAL STORYTIMES

Most of the resources concerning bilingual storytime seem to focus on Spanish and English, although there are a few resources listed below for books in Asian languages. If you are doing a bilingual storytime in another language you may have to do extensive research to find books and materials in those languages. You audience may be able to assist you, by letting you know where they buy books or what songs they already know. Even if you do a bilingual storytime in Spanish, there will be songs that are more customary for those from Mexico than those from Puerto Rico, so see what types of stories and songs are common for your audience. You can add new ones after everyone has learned the customary songs. Below is a list of websites helpful in planning a bilingual storytime and finding books in other languages, and a list of popular Spanish/English books you can find to start a bilingual storytime using Spanish.

WEBSITES ON BILINGUAL STORYTIMES

Bibliotecas Para La Gente

www.bibliotecasparalagente.org
This website has a wealth of great ideas for doing storytime in English and Spanish, and is sponsored by the Northern California Chapter of REFORMA.

El Dia de los Niños—Texas State Library

www.tsl.state.tx.us/ld/projects/ninos/songsrhymes.html
Traditional Spanish children's songs and rhymes are listed here, with the words in both English and Spanish, and with sound files.

Lectorum/Scholastic

www.lectorum.com/
Lectorum is the Spanish books division of Scholastic publishers.

Pan Asian Books

www.panap.com/
Located in the San Francisco Bay Area, this book distributor has a website you can use to order children's books in a variety of Asian languages.

Shen's Books

www.shens.com/
Specializing in multicultural children's books, Shen's also has some bilingual books. Their website allows for easy ordering from this Bay Area company.

Children's Book Press

www.childrensbookpress.org/
This unique publisher started as a nonprofit organization, and publishes children's books celebrating world cultures. Now part of Lee & Low Books, many of their picture books feature English and another language.

Washington County Library—Spanish Fingerplays

www.wccls.org/rimas

Videos of popular Spanish fingerplays performed by library staff will help you quickly learn some songs for your storytime.

StoryBlocks—Spanish Songs for Children

www.storyblocks.org/videos/language/espanol/

Provided by Colorado Libraries for Early Literacy, this site contains videos of library staff demonstrating popular children's Spanish songs and fingerplays.

Flannel Fridays—Bilingual Resources

www.pinterest.com/flannelfriday/bilingual/

This Pinterest page has links to flannelboard patterns and lyrics for Spanish fingerplays and songs.

BILINGUAL SPANISH/ENGLISH BOOKS

Ada, Alma Flor. *I Love Saturdays y Domingos.*
Ada, Alma Flor and F. Isabel Campoy. *Pio Peep! Traditional Spanish Nursery Rhymes.*
Ada, Alma Flor and F. Isabel Campoy. *Ten Little Puppies = Diez Perritos.*
Ancona, George. *Mis Aguelos = My Grandparents.*
Ata, Te. *Baby Rattlesnake = Viborita de cascabel.*
Bertrand, Diane Gonzales. *The Party for Papa Luis = La Fiesta para Papa Luis.*
Canetti, Yanitzia. *Uno Dos Tres: My First Spanish Rhymes.*
Chavaria-Chairez, Becky. *Magda's Tortillas = Las Tortillas Para Magda.*
Cisneros, Sandra. *Hairs = Pelitos.*
Colon-Vila, Lillian. *Salsa.*
Crews, Donald. *Freight Train = Tren de Carga.*
Cumpiano, Ina. *Quinito's Neighborhood = El Vecindario de Quinito.*
Delacre, Lulu. *Arroz con Leche: Popular Songs and Rhymes from Latin America.*
Dominguez, Angela. *Maria Had a Little Llama = Maria Tenia Una Llamita.*
Ehlert, Lois. *Cuckoo: A Mexican Folktale = Cucu: Un Quento Folklorico Mexicano.*
Ehlert, Lois. *Moon Rope: A Peruvian Folktale = Un Lazo a la Luna: Una Leyenda Peruana.*
Elias Lujan, Jorge. *Rooster = Gallo.*
Elya, Susan Middleton. *Bebe Goes Shopping.*
Elya, Susan Middleton. *Little Roja Riding Hood.*
Emberley, Rebecca. *My Room = Mi Cuarto.*
Emberley, Rebecca. *Piñata.*
Galindo, Mary Sue. *Icy Watermelon = Sandìa Frìa.*
Gonzalez, Maya Christina. *My Colors, My World = Mis Colores, Mi Mundo.*
Griego, Margot. *Tortillitas Para Mama and Other Nursery Rhymes.*
Guy, Ginger. *Fiesta!*
Guy, Ginger. *My Grandma = Mi Abuelita.*
Guy, Ginger. *Siesta.*

Johnston, Tony. *Day of the Dead.*

Johnston, Tony. *My Abuelita.*

LaCamara, Laura. *Dalia's Wondrous Hair = El Maravilloso Cabello de Dalia.*

Luna, Tom. *I See the World = Yo Veo el Mundo.*

Masurel, Claire. *A Cat and A Dog = Un Gato y Un Perro.*

Membrillas, Sergio. *Good Morning = Buenos Dias.*

Membrillas, Sergio. *Good Night = Buenas Noches.*

Montes, Marisa. *Juan Bobo Goes to Work: A Puerto Rican Folktale.*

Montes, Marisa. *Los Gatos Black on Halloween.*

Mora, Pat. *Book Fiesta! Celebrate Children's Day/Book Day = Celebremos El dia de los niños/El dia de los libros.*

Mora, Pat. *Delicious Hullabaloo = Pachanga Deliciosa.*

Mora, Pat. *Gracias = Thanks.*

Mora, Pat. *Listen to the Desert: Oye al Desierto.*

Mora, Pat. *Uno, Dos, Tres = One, Two, Three.*

Morales, Yuyi. *Just a Minute: A Trickster Tale and Counting Book.*

Morales, Yuyi. *Niño Wrestles the World.*

Orozco, Jose Luis. *Diez Deditos: Ten Little Fingers and Other Play Rhymes and Action Songs from Latin America.*

Orozco, Jose Luis. *De Colores and other Latin-American Folksongs for Children.*

Saldana, Renè Jr. *Dale, Dale, Dale: Una Fiesta de Numeros = Hit It, Hit It, Hit It: A Fiesta of Numbers.*

Soto, Gary. *My Little Car.*

Tafolla, Carmen. *Fiesta Babies.*

Tafolla, Carmen. *What Can You Do with a Paleta?*

Tafolla, Carmen. *What Can You Do with a Rebozo?*

Thong, Roseanne. *Green Is a Chile Pepper: A Book of Colores.*

Thong, Roseanne. *Round Is a Tortilla: A Book of Shapes.*

Vamos, Samantha R. *The Cazuela That the Farm Maiden Stirred.*

Weill, Cynthia. *Count Me In: A Parade of Mexican Folk Art Numbers in English and Spanish.*

Weill, Cynthia. *Mi Familia Calaca = My Skeleton Family.*

CHAPTER 7

Crafts at Preschool Storytime

As we have seen in the earlier chapter on preschool storytime, crafts can be a great way to promote kindergarten readiness skills, such as using a scissors, following directions, identifying colors, holding a crayon and pencil properly, and so forth. Many of the fine motor skills needed by a child entering kindergarten can be developed with arts and crafts projects. Plus, crafts are fun!

WHY WE DO CRAFTS

Crafts are a great way to reinforce what we do at storytime. This includes helping the child remember and retell a story, identifying characters, remembering the book's message, and even recalling a book's author and title. Also, the project or coloring activity can serve as a souvenir of storytime. These are reasons enough to do the arts and crafts projects. Of course, the other main reason is how often crafts help with kindergarten readiness skills.

Crafts and Parents

Many parents of preschoolers already read to their children on a regular basis. They may have attended your lapsit or toddler storytimes, or they have developed the reading habit due to the amount of publicity on how important it is to a child's brain development. They may already have home collections of books. So parents may need an extra motivation to bring their children to preschool storytime, after a long day at work, or with a busy, overscheduled child. Adding a craft project can be that "extra" that makes it worth their time to come. Of course, we know that just the stories and songs are worth their time, but the craft might be the final motivator.

Be sure to publicize your crafts projects if you include them at the end of preschool storytime. Briefly discuss how crafts can help with kindergarten readiness by spelling out what skills are covered by doing craft activities. Also, some of the projects and themes can relate directly to a kindergarten readiness skill, like a child knowing his or her phone number. Read some stories where the characters use the phone, then end with a paper phone cutout with a place for the child to write the phone number.

Another subtle positive aspect of the arts and crafts time at the conclusion of storytime occurs when parents talk to their children and the family works on something together. This time also allows parents to talk to each other; meet a neighbor, ask advice about which dancing school the little girl attends, does the parent like the karate class attended by his or her child? In my experience, parents who have children the same age who have just met will quickly start talking about the children and become friends.

Often at preschool storytime, the parent takes over making the craft. Do everything you can to see that this does not happen. Offer enough supplies so that the parent can make one, and the child can make one. Also, if the craft is too complex for the average preschooler to make without help, then choose an easier project. Making the crafts too complicated just creates frustration on the part of the child, and for the parent, too.

Another reason a parent will take over a craft is that the parent may think a preschooler should not use scissors. You may need to inform some parents that you only use special safety scissors made for preschoolers, and that most kindergarten readiness skills tests measure if a child can use scissors. Once the parents are aware of these two factors, they will relax and let a child use the safety scissors. A related reason a parent may take over the craft is that he or she is afraid their children will make a mess. Assure them that you and the volunteers will clean up the mess, and that you use disposable plastic tablecloths just for that reason.

Crafts and the Child

Early childhood education specialist Bev Bos said it best: "It's the process, not the product." Artwork done by a young child is about the doing, not the result. Children need to explore with paint, try out favorite colors, make collages, and at times the final product will be something the adult would never have thought of and be more complex than the sample made by the teacher. Often this occurs with repetition, so allowing the child to make more than one picture, or cut out more than one stick puppet, can promote creativity and show the child that there is more than one way to accomplish something.

Other skills developed by doing art projects include following directions, fine motor skills demonstrated when holding pencils and crayons, and preliteracy skills like knowing colors, shapes, and other subjects. The art project also allows the child to retell the story using the paper bag puppet to talk about the characters and to act out the plot.

Some art techniques are more age appropriate for preschoolers. Using crayons is more desirable than markers, because a child needs to put pressure on the crayon for the color to be darker. This encourages fine motor skills, where a marker does not. Glue sticks or paste can be easier for a preschooler to control than liquid glue, and they have an easier time putting a glue stick on the right place. Several art books are available for those who work with preschoolers, and they can help you set up your art tables. Look at the list at the end of this chapter.

Crafts and the Storytime Presenter

We want to communicate that we are doing storytime with a craft, not craft time with stories. The books come first. So the craft should be related to one of the books you read that week, even if that means the craft is a simple coloring page. When you have a great craft idea but no story to go along with it, save it for a time when you can match it to a great book. Don't read a mediocre book just because it goes with the craft. Remember, this is storytime with certain preliteracy goals. You can always hold special craft programs if you want to emphasize the crafts, such as a summer reading or a holiday craft program, where older children can attend, too.

SET-UP FOR ARTS AND CRAFTS

Keep the set-up and clean-up of the arts and crafts tables as simple as possible. If you will be working with anything messy, like paint or glue, you can cover the tables with plastic and toss at the end of the program. I usually try to use glue sticks instead of glue, since they are easier for a preschooler to control. A bottle of glue turns into a big puddle on the paper, but a glue stick works more like a crayon and is easier for the preschooler to put the right amount in the right area. If you do use glue, put some on a small paper plate with a few Q-Tips; this allows the child to "paint" a small amount of glue on the paper.

I use small plastic bins with dividers that hold the crayons, scissors, and glue sticks and are ready to use every time. I put one bin per table, along with the paper or other supplies needed for that craft. A tape dispenser is often useful, too, and using tape is something a preschooler needs to practice. I put all the supplies in the middle of the table and let people take what they need; I don't set everything up for each child like a place setting. Also, I believe part of the experience is to share; we don't have enough tape dispensers or glue sticks for each person, although I try to have enough scissors for each person since cutting often takes up a good amount of the time. Learning to share is a kindergarten readiness skill, so start now. I also expect everyone to help clean up their own mess, which is another habit they will need when they get to kindergarten, so encourage the preschoolers to help in picking up paper on the floor, or other clean-up activities they can do.

Crayons

Most of the time, using crayons will be preferable to using markers or paints. Painting is fun but can be a lot of cleanup, and if you hold the storytime in the library itself and not a meeting room, painting can be prohibitively messy. Many parents and young children use markers, but there are studies that explain crayons are developmentally more important than markers for preschoolers. Basically, crayons require the child to put some pressure on the crayon to make the colors come out clearly on the page, and markers do not. So crayons are more helpful in developing fine motor skills in preschoolers. Also, crayons are easier to clean up, and allow for more variation of color and design. They are also less expensive and won't dry out like markers.

Paper Bag and Stick Puppets

One of the easiest, most reliable crafts you can do at storytime is to make a paper bag or stick puppet of the main characters of your featured book. Then, the child can use the puppet to retell the story. You don't need a photocopy master or print out from a website to make a paper bag puppet; the child can draw the face, add yarn or gift wrap ribbon for hair, and other details. To make a stick puppet, you can photocopy an illustration from your featured book, then the children can cut out the character and tape it to a popsicle stick. The children can color the cutout or add other features to make it more lively, but this simple craft will only take a few minutes and needs very little preparation or cleanup. Some popular book characters are featured on the publishers' websites along with print-outs of coloring sheets and other simple crafts, so look for those.

Masks

Masks are also an easy, sure-fire craft that goes with any story. You can use a paper plate for the face of the mask, and add details to show the animal or main character of the featured story. It can be difficult for a young child to cut out the eye holes of a mask, so ask your volunteers to do that ahead of time. The children can get really creative in adding yarn or ribbon hair, adding facial details, and coloring the mask. For safety, it is preferable to attach a craft stick to the mask and have the child hold it up to his or her face, rather than tie it to the face and block his or her vision.

STEM AND STEAM ACTIVITIES

Many elementary schools are seeing a need for more books and activities relating to science, technology, engineering, and math, or STEM. Teachers and librarians suggest adding an A for arts, to make STEAM, since arts and crafts can be a hands-on way of exploring these concepts. Along with the usual coloring, painting, and other art projects, offer simple hands-on science demonstrations. For example, a storytime on wind and weather can conclude with the craft activity of making simple paper windsocks or pinwheels. Expand that by showing how the windsock demonstrates in what direction the wind is blowing. For a storytime on flowers, demonstrate how a flower "drinks" up water by showing a white carnation that has been left in water colored with food coloring; that flower will have streaks of that color after a few days. See the appendix at the end of this book for many science-themed storytimes.

RESOURCES FOR ARTS AND CRAFTS

Several books have very simple craft projects aimed at a preschooler's developmental level and ability. Keeping it simple is the key to doing successful arts and crafts at storytime. If it is simple, the hurried parent can take it home to do, and those that stay are more likely to let the child work on the project instead of the parents doing the entire craft themselves!

RESOURCE BOOKS ON ARTS AND CRAFTS

Bauer, Caroline Feller. *Leading Kids to Books through Crafts* (American Library Association, 2000).

Bos, Bev. *Don't Move the Muffin Tin: A Hands-off Guide to Art for the Young Child* (Turn the Page Press, 1978).

Check, Laura. *Paper Plate Crafts: Creative Fun for 3-to-7-Year-Olds* (Williamson Publishing, 2000).

Cousins, Lucy. *Create with Maisy* (Candlewick, 2012).

Hopkins, Carol Garnett. *Artsy Toddler Storytimes: A Year's Worth of Ready-to-Go Programming* (Neal-Schuman, 2013).

Kohl, MaryAnn F. *Art with Anything: 52 Weeks of Fun Using Everyday Stuff* (Gryphon House, 2010).

Kohl, MaryAnn F. *First Art for Toddlers and Twos: Open-Ended Art Experiences* (Gryphon House, 2012).

Pavon, Ana-Elba and Borrego, Diana. *25 Latino Craft Projects* (American Library Association, 2003).

Press, Judy. *The Little Hands Art Book: Exploring Arts and Crafts with 2-to-6-Year-Olds* (Williamson Publishing, 1994).

Schwake, Susan. *Art Lab for Little Kids: 52 Playful Projects for Preschoolers* (Quarry Books, 2013).

WEBSITES ON ARTS AND CRAFTS

Enchanted Learning

www.enchantedlearning.com

You don't have to be a member to use this site, which contains lots of homework pages, and great craft ideas for storytimes and programs.

The Activity Idea Place: An Early Childhood Educator's Resource

www.123child.com/

Hundreds of themes, with ideas for crafts, games, recipes, songs, and fingerplays (but not books), this is a great secondary source for storytime ideas.

Multicultural Preschool Ideas

www.first-school.ws/theme/places.htm

Lots of easy craft ideas, with printable pages, for preschool storytimes.

Family Crafts

http://familycrafts.about.com/od/craftprojectsbytheme

This has a large selection of free craft projects sorted by theme. Make crafts related to everything from animals to transportation.

A to Z Kids Stuff

www.atozkidsstuff.com

This site has free activities for toddlers, preschoolers, and older children. It also includes links to reviews of children's music, movies, and books.

Child Fun

http://childfun.com/

Provides craft ideas, printable coloring pages, and other activities parents can do with young children.

Coloring Pages

www.coloringpages.net

Choose from hundreds of printable coloring pages for kids. Disney coloring pages include characters like Winnie the Pooh; other characters like Scooby Doo are favorites. They include a large selection of Bible and Christian pages, and many holiday pages.

Crayola Crayons

www.crayola.com

Find rich, hands-on learning experiences that can be searched by subject, theme, grade, media, and completion time.

DLTK Kids

www.dltk-kids.com

Features a variety of fun, printable children's crafts, coloring pages and more including projects for holidays, educational themes, and some of children's favorite cartoon characters.

Spoonful

www.familyfun.go.com

Lots of activities and crafts sorted by theme or age group, Spoonful is a website sponsored by Disney.

Pop Goes the Page

http://blogs.princeton.edu/popgoesthepage

Need ideas for arts and crafts activities for storytime? Check out the blog "Pop Goes the Page," from Dana Sheridan, the Education and Outreach Coordinator of the Cotsen Children's Library at Princeton University.

Learning 4 Kids Science Activities

www.learning4kids.net/category/science-play/

Photos and simple instructions describe science hands-on activities that even a toddler can do!

Thinking Fountain

www.thinkingfountain.org/

From the Science Museum of Minnesota comes this great collection of easy science activities you can do with preschoolers.

CHAPTER 8

Storytelling, Puppets, and Props

Storytime can be much more engaging for the audience, and for you as the presenter, if you add some visual elements along with the books and songs. You don't have to be a professional puppeteer to use puppets, or a trained actor to tell a memorized story. Let's explore a few things you can do that will make your storytime even more exciting.

STORYTELLING

When new staff members hear they may be trained to do storytime, some will think they need to be a storyteller. Technically, a storyteller is one who has memorized and tells stories without the use of a book, the way an actor presents a monologue. Many libraries will hire professional storytellers for special programs, where the storyteller performs stories, often from a specific culture, and from traditional folklore. So it is not mandatory that the storytime presenter be a storyteller. But once you have been doing storytime for a while, you may want to learn some stories you can present from memory, as a way to jazz up storytime.

Several books for the beginning storyteller are listed at the end of this chapter. Storytelling is often more personal than presenting a book at storytime; you may feel more connected to stories from your own culture, and want to learn and perform those. For storytime, the most successful tales told by a storyteller are usually folktales. Young children enjoy Aesop's fables, common folktales such as "The Three Bears" and "The Three Pigs," and ethnic folktales that allow the audience to participate with repeated phrases. The instructional books for the beginning storyteller often include these folktales as the ones most likely to be successful.

Beginning storytellers can also learn stories that involve a prop of some kind. In Nancy Schimmel's book, *Just Enough to Make a Story,* she has some "cut and tell" stories where the storyteller cuts a piece of paper a certain way, to demonstrate part of the story. Also, there are books that show you how to "draw and tell" a story, using a chalkboard or a large piece of paper and marker. The drawing is very simple, but it reinforces parts of the story.

Some storytellers like to write original stories, to tell stories about things that happened in their own families. For the experienced storyteller, these can be a huge hit. But for the novice storyteller in front of young children and parents, traditional folktales and fables are usually the best choices.

If you feel you barely have enough time to prepare for regular storytime, do not feel compelled to memorize and practice storytelling. Many of us work at very small libraries where we have so many responsibilities that adding one more is unreasonable. But for many storytime presenters, the most rewarding part of the experience is to perform a story from memory, holding the rapt attention of the crowd, even without a book to assist you. Many fables and folktales are almost as brief as a song, and just as easy to learn. If you think of learning a story the way you learn a new song, it may seem less intimidating. Also, you don't really have to memorize the story; you can learn the plot and key phrases, but then put it into your own words. So if you feel curious or interested in storytelling, seek out some of the great books mentioned in our bibliography and give it a try!

BIG BOOKS

For the toddler and preschool storytimes that draw a large audience, you may find Big Books a great way to ensure that everyone can see a book's illustrations. Many of the most popular storytime books are available in Big Book editions, including Laura Numeroff's *If You Give a Mouse a Cookie*, or Charles Shaw's *It Looked Like Spilt Milk.* To see which popular picture books are available in Big Book editions, go to the publishers' websites, or a vendor such as Lakeshore Learning (www.lakeshorelearning.com).

MUSICAL INSTRUMENTS

Musical instruments designed for preschool are a great addition to storytime. There are simple shakers, rhythm sticks, and drums you can distribute to the audience to use during certain songs, like Raffi's "Shake Your Sillies Out." Then, you can make a ritual of collecting the instruments. These are also available at the Lakeshore Learning, or you can even make your own shakers if you are crafty.

GAMES AND DANCES

You can enhance storytime with some simple games and dances, especially for toddlers who need to be up and moving most of the time. The best known is probably

"The Hokey Pokey," but there are several others with even simpler movements, like "Ring around the Roses," or "Sally Goes Round the Sun." You can try some of the dances on the CD *Songs & Games for Toddlers* by Bob McGrath and Katharine Smithrim, or *Dances for Little People* by William Janiak, which are listed at the end of the chapter on Music.

Sometimes you can do simple movement activities with toddlers and preschoolers using scarves or beanbags. Hand out a scarf to each child, and then the children use them to wave in the breeze, or put them on their heads, or use them as superhero capes. Lakeshore Learning has both large and small scarves; I prefer the smaller, handkerchief size translucent pastel scarves. The children can use them in several ways; a few of the music and dance CDs listed at www.kimboed.com have scarf or beanbag activity songs. These can help the children improve their coordination and motor skills. Beanbags can also liven up a movement song. Children can put them on their heads, elbows, knees, the small of the back, all of which helps a child with motor skills and coordination.

PUPPETS

Puppets can be a great way to enliven storytime and a way to help your audience focus on what is coming up next. You don't have to do full-blown puppet shows to use puppets, you can just add them as a prop to help sing a song, or to be the "child" that you address, explaining what will be coming next, or how to participate.

Puppet Cohost

Using a puppet as your cohost at storytime can be a fun way to incorporate puppets and accomplish behavior goals at the same time. You can ask your puppet to greet everyone, and the puppet can ask what song are we going to sing next? You can remind the puppet that the next story needs the audience to participate by practicing the repeated phrase they should chant, or remind your puppet that it is time to sit for our next book. Think of the way Shari Lewis used Lampchop as the cohost of her television program.

Puppet Shows

If you are interested in using puppets to tell stories, there are several books that tell you how to do so and even contain scripts of puppet shows. My favorite is Walter Minkel's *How to Do the "Three Bears" with Two Hands: Performing with Puppets* (ALA, 2000). It can be difficult to do a puppet show if you are the only puppeteer, but a few folktales have only two characters, so these are the easiest to turn into puppet shows. One of my favorites is the African tale, "The Crocodile and the Hen," based on the book by Joan Lexau, because you only need the two animal puppets.

Another way to incorporate puppet shows into your storytime is to use your volunteers. Many libraries have high school volunteers helping during the summer. They can perform simple puppet shows based on popular folktales like "The Three Pigs" and "The Three Bears" during your summer preschool storytimes. They can even make the puppets, props, and cardboard scenery. The audience will really enjoy the show and the teen volunteers will feel they are doing something worthwhile and creative!

Puppets during Songs and Rhymes

One of the easiest ways to incorporate puppets into storytime is to use them to help sing songs or perform specific rhymes. You can use a simple duck puppet when singing "Five Little Ducks," or a frog puppet when singing "Five Green and Speckled Frogs." Most storytime providers have a spider puppet we use on rainy days to sing "Eency Weency Spider." Make a list of songs you sing regularly, and see if there is a puppet that could help make the song more visual.

Mitts that come with Velcro figures can be used to help sing a song. These are often called "Monkey Mitts," because the first one was a glove with a monkey attached to each finger to use during the song "Five Little Monkeys Jumping on the Bed." These are available at www.lakeshorelearning.com, the website for the Lakeshore Teachers' Store and are called "Storytelling Gloves." They are similar to a flannelboard but fit on your hand, and the figures are attached to each finger as you sing a song.

Some rhymes use a specific puppet, such as "Three Mice in a Red Box." These puppets can be found at www.folkmanis.com, the website of the Folkmanis puppet company. Many of these are small fingerpuppets, and the rhymes work well for baby or toddler storytimes. These rhymes can be repeated often, so it is worth purchasing a few of these fingerpuppets or puppets you can use during a song, since you will use them nearly every week! Listed below are some of the most popular "Puppet Rhymes":

"Mice in Red Box"
Make a box with your hand.
Open your box.
Let the mice creep out.
The little mice are creeping, creeping.
They don't make a sound as their feet touch the ground.
The little mice are creeping, creeping,
Shhhhh!
Put your mice back in the box.
Put the lid on the box.
And quietly put the box in your lap.

"Here is a Beehive"
Here is a beehive,
But where are the bees?
Hidden away where nobody sees.
Here they come creeping out of the hive,
One, two, three, four, five!
Bzzzzz!

"Two Little Bluebirds"
Two little bluebirds,
Sitting on a hill.
One named Jack, and one named Jill.
Fly away Jack! Fly away Jill!
Come back Jack! Come back Jill!

VISUALS WITH FLANNEL OR VELCRO

Flannelboards are a way to use visuals to reinforce a song, rhyme, or short story. Since many of the young children are visual learners, offering something to look at to go along with the words you are saying can be really helpful. In some ways, flannelboards seem very old fashioned in the computer age, but they are still really effective in showing the words used during a rhyme or song.

Flannelboards

The basic flannelboards can be purchased or made; they are listed at www.lakeshore-learning.com and from other vendors. The material is either flannel or a spongy cloth, which felt figures will naturally stick to without Velcro. Sometimes the figures you purchase will have Velcro on them, especially if the figures have stuffing. But felt cutouts should stick to the flannelboard without Velcro because they are lightweight. These can help your audience see the figures in a large crowd that may not be able to see the illustrations in a board book. The figures can help with songs; for example, put up the next animal in Old MacDonald's farm to cue which verse is coming next. The resource list at the end of this chapter offers some vendors that sell both the flannelboards and the figures. Also books are available that contain patterns if you want to make the flannel figures yourself.

Apron Figures

Very similar to flannelboards, flannel aprons are available to purchase that basically do the same thing. The aprons are more portable since they can be folded and stuffed into your book bag, and the aprons may be more practical for those doing storytimes at various locations. If you do outreach storytimes, try the aprons as a way to bring visuals. Many of the apron figures you can buy are based on popular storytime songs or Mother Goose rhymes, so you will use them repeatedly since you will want to repeat the rhymes and songs. You can also get apron figures based on popular books, including Audrey and Don Woods' *The Napping House.* I use the book and apron figures together, to reinforce what the children are seeing in the illustrations. As each character jumps out of bed at the end of the book, I pop the apron figure off and it flies into the air. The audience loves the action and it really brings the book to life.

TOYS AND PLAY AT STORYTIME

A popular trend is to conclude a storytime by putting out toys to use. The parents really appreciate this playtime, as it extends the storytime and allows a time and place for the parents to share information and talk about their children. The American Library Association has a special initiative called "Read! Build! Play!" It encourages librarians to incorporate play into their storytimes and other services for young children. They have a website with a free downloadable toolkit to help: http://readbuildplay.com/. Plenty of vendors offer developmentally appropriate toys, such as blocks, stacking toys, very simple puzzles, and musical instruments. These vendors are listed at the end of this chapter.

Stay and Play Storytimes

In Chapter 4, in our discussion on family storytimes, we introduced the subject of stay and play storytimes. Many librarians are adopting the concept of stay and play at the conclusion of storytime. After the formal presentation of books and songs, the librarian will bring out simple toys for the child and caregiver to use. This allows parents to see developmentally appropriate toys, and to encourage parent–child playtime. It also gives a time for parents to talk to each other about all types of issues, from recommending a local pediatrician to talking about upcoming dance classes or sports programs for preschoolers.

At some libraries, the stay and play time is monitored by a trained volunteer, who sets out the toys, watches out for safety issues, and then cleans up. Often these are retired people who are grandparents or former teachers, who enjoy interacting with the parents and children. This also allows the storytime presenter to leave the storytime room and go to the picture book area of the library to assist families looking for books to check out.

One real concern is that too many young children are not offered enough time to play; they are often overscheduled, or plopped in front of a television. So offering a play time with toys and other children their own age can really benefit many toddlers and preschoolers. Some libraries are even creating toy-lending libraries, to offer items to children who may not have many toys at home.

Some libraries are able to purchase learning toys using grant money; see if your state offers funds to encourage literacy storytimes, Early Learning for Families, or Play Places in libraries. If not, the Friends of the Library could be approached for funds to purchase toys. Often these learning toys include Duplo blocks, trains and trucks, stacking toys, stuffed animals, and wooden toys and puzzles from Melissa and Doug: www.melissaanddoug.com. It is also helpful to have a few "adaptive" toys for those with special needs; often these light up or offer other sensory embellishments that make them fun for all children.

Sanitizing Toys

Babies and toddlers often put board books and toys in their mouths, so librarians have an obligation to periodically clean those items. The first step is to wash them with soap and warm water, before sanitizing, since dirt can hide in grease and grime. To sanitize, wipe down the toy with a solution of 1/2 cup of bleach mixed in a gallon of water. Many state childcare regulations recommend this method.

COMMERCIAL-FREE STORYTIMES

Another consideration when selecting toys, books, and other media is whether or not that item promotes certain large media corporations. For example, some librarians try to avoid choosing items from television programs that are not appropriate due to violence or crass humor. Instead, they try to choose traditional toys like wooden blocks and puzzles. A nonprofit movement called Campaign for a Commercial-Free Childhood (CCFC) promotes this effort, www.commercialfreechildhood.org/. Founded in 2000, this organization points out the negative impact of advertising on children, so part of their mission is for educational environments (like libraries and storytimes) to avoid the use of characters from television and films. Instead, the CCFC recommends using items based on book characters, or generic toys, puppets, and dolls. The Association of Library Service to Children has hosted CCFC cofounder Susan Linn as a speaker at their conferences.

The efforts by the CCFC have made librarians more conscientious about the items they choose to use at storytimes. For example, instead of using a puppet that is a character on a Saturday morning commercial television show, you might choose a generic puppet character. This helps to avoid certain expectations from the audience, who think the TV character acts or speaks a certain way, where the generic puppet allows for more creativity. If some parents don't allow their children to watch commercial television, then it makes sense that the librarian doesn't use toys with those characters at its stay and play storytimes. There are so many other educational and creativity-promoting toys that you should have plenty of noncommercial items from which to choose.

DVDs

Showing DVDs at storytime always seemed like an odd fit to me, but there may be rare circumstances when you want to add a DVD showing on the end of storytime. If you are having a large crowd at preschool storytime, you could show a DVD for some kids to watch while others do the craft, and then switch. In the summer, there may be several older children, usually primary-grade siblings of the preschoolers, who come to storytime. They finish the craft quickly, and can watch a DVD while waiting for the rest of the family. The DVDs I use contain songs for the kids to sing-along and move with, or contain a book being read. These types of DVDs extend the storytime experience; I avoid the movie and television show DVDs. Here is a list of DVDs recommended for storytime:

All around the Kitchen with Dan Zanes and Friends, Festival Five, 2005.
> Dan Zanes, former rock musician, now leads a popular music group for all ages, from toddlers to parents! This live concert recording is augmented with music videos that originally appeared on Sesame Street and Noggin.

Baby Babble series, Talking Child, 2004–2007.
> Speech enhancement is one of the skills toddlers can learn from these interactive DVDs, which encourages repetition of sounds, facial expressions, and includes sign language. Good for all toddlers, include children with autism.

Braincandy series, ThinkFilm, 2004–2007.
> Puppets representing the five senses interact with babies and toddlers in this live action series of educational DVDs. Titles include *Hear My World, See My World, Smell My World, Taste My World, Touch My World, Eyecandy,* and *My 5 Senses.*

Cantamos y Aprendemos con Jose Luis Orozco, Arcoiris, 2003.
> The noted Hispanic-American children's singer and songwriter Jose Luis Orzoco appears in this live concert DVD, leading a family audience in a sing-along.

Goldy Luck and the Three Pandas, Dreamscape, 2014.
> In this Chinese-American take on the classic "Three Bears" tale, a girl brings a turnip cake to her panda neighbors. Based on the book by Natasha Yim, this contains some Chinese phrases.

Goodnight Moon and Other Sleepytime Tales, Home Box Office, 2005.
> Notable celebrities narrate or sing children's classics, including Susan Sarandon reading the title book, Billy Crystal reading *There's a Nightmare in My Closet*, and Tony Bennett singing "Hit the Road to Dreamland." The visuals are animated from the original book illustrations.

Guess How Much I Love You: Hidden Treasure, Entertainment One, 2011.
> Seven new adventures featuring the father and child nutbrown hare from Sam McBratney's popular picture books are collected into one DVD.

Here Come the ABCs, Universal Music, 2005.

Alternative rock band They Might Be Giants created this award-winning DVD, which uses puppets, animation, and live action to teach the alphabet.

Live Oak Media DVDs, Live Oak Media, 2003–2014.

Live Oak Media (www.liveoakmedia.com/) produces recorded picture books and DVDs based on picture books, using iconography so that the movie version uses the same illustrations as the book. Books by Eric Kimmel, Don Freeman, Thacher Hurd, Sarah Stewart, and Bernard Weber are featured in their collections.

Max and Ruby Series, Nick Jr./Paramount, 2004–2014.

Beloved sibling bunnies Max and Ruby star in this animated series based on the picture books by Rosemary Wells. Each DVD contains six 15-minute animated episodes.

Party Day (The Laurie Berkner Band), Two Tomatoes/Razor & Tie, 2011.

An audio CD is included in the DVD, which contains both concert footage and interviews with Berkner and her band.

Puppies! Puppies! Puppies! (Martha Speaks! Series), PBS Kids, 2013.

Six 15-minute episodes of the popular PBS animated series "Martha Speaks!" are collected in this DVD. Based on Susan Meddaugh's picture books featuring the talking dog, the episodes help children build vocabulary, and will inspire them to check out the books.

Raffi: Young Children's Concert, Universal Music, 2005.

Raffi stars in this live concert DVD with songs aimed at the toddler audience. Raffi's style and lyrics have a gentle quality that is still energetic and fun, but not frenetic.

Scholastic Story Collections on DVD, Weston Woods, 2003–2014.

Weston Woods and Scholastic have partnered to create a series of DVDs that bring award-winning picture books alive. Narrated by noted actors, backed by original music, and with graphics taken directly from each book to preserve the illustration style, this series is the closest thing on DVD to having a book read out loud. The series includes *Bear Snores On, Bark George, Chicka Chicka Boom Boom, Corduroy, How Do Dinosaurs Say Goodnight, Harold and the Purple Crayon, Noisy Nora, Snowy Day, Lucky Ducklings, Don't Let the Pigeon Drive the Bus, Duck on a Bike, This Is Not My Hat,* and *Where the Wild Things Are* (westonwoods.scholastic.com /products/westonwoods/).

Secret Pizza Party, Dreamscape, 2014.

A raccoon is obsessed with obtaining pizza in this uproarious adaptation of the picture book by Adam Rubin.

Sesame Beginnings series, Children's Television Workshop, 2006–2007.

From the makers of "Sesame Street" come four DVDs aimed at toddlers, starring the classic characters Big Bird, Cookie Monster, Elmo, and Prairie Dawn as babies, singing and moving and encouraging the viewer to join in the fun.

Signing Time! Series, Two Little Hands, 2004–2007.

A multivolume set of DVDs that teach parents (and children's librarians) basic sign language. The volumes have themes, like "Family, Feelings, and Fun," or "Time to Eat." Many child development experts recommend librarians use some basic signs when conducting lapsit or toddler storytimes, especially during the songs.

So Smart Series, Big Kid Productions, 2001–2007.

Simple concepts are taught using bold graphics and sounds, including the alphabet, numbers, shapes, colors, and even an introductory Spanish DVD.

Toddworld Series, Discovery Kids, 2005–2012.
Picture book author/illustrator Todd Parr's books are brought to life in this animated series. His bold, brightly colored simple cartoons are well suited to babies and toddlers, with episodes including *Being an Individual* and *It's Okay to be You.*

We Are the Laurie Berkner Band, Sony Music, 2006.
With vocals similar to those of Sheryl Crow, Berkner and her band sing songs for a wide age group; even parents will enjoy this live concert. Includes a bonus CD.

RESOURCES FOR PUPPETS AND PROPS

A wealth of information is available for the storytime provider on using puppets or flannelboards to make your storytime more engaging for the squirmy toddlers. With the Internet, it is easier to purchase these materials, too. Even with small donations from your Friends of the Library, you can add some visual elements to storytime, such as a frog puppet to help you sing "Five Green and Specked Frogs," or a flannelboard of a favorite nursery rhyme. And, as we learned in the chapter on songs and fingerplays, it is desirable to repeat these elements so you will find yourself using the puppets or felt figures on a regular basis, which makes them worth the money. So give it a try!

BOOKS ON STORYTELLING AND PUPPETRY

Bauer, Caroline Feller. *Leading Kids to Books through Puppets* (American Library Association, 1997).

Bauer, Caroline Feller. *New Handbook for Storytellers* (American Library Association, 1995).

Champlin, Connie. *Storytelling with Puppets: Second Edition* (American Library Association, 1997).

Crepeau, Ingrid M. and Ann M. Richards. *A Show of Hands: Using Puppets with Young Children* (Redleaf Press, 2003).

Del Negro, Janice M. *Folktales Aloud: Practical Advice for Playful Storytelling* (American Library Association, 2014).

Haven, Kendall and MaryGay Ducey. *Crash Course in Storytelling* (Libraries Unlimited, 2006).

Isbell, Rebecca and Shirley C. Raines. *Tell It Again! 2: Easy to Tell Stories with Activities for Young Children* (Gryphon House, 2000).

MacDonald, Margaret Read. *Look Back and See: Twenty Lively Tales for Gentle Tellers* (H.W. Wilson, 1991).

MacDonald, Margaret Read. *The Storytellers's Start-Up Book: Finding, Learning, Performing, and Using Folktales* (August House, 1993).

Minkel, Walter. *How to Do "The Three Bears" With Two Hands: Performing with Puppets* (American Library Association, 2000).

Schimmel, Nancy. *Just Enough to Make a Story: A Sourcebook for Storytelling* (Sisters' Choice, 1992).

Sierra, Judy. *Mother Goose's Playhouse: Toddler Tales and Nursery Rhymes, with Patterns for Puppets and Feltboards* (Bob Kaminsky Media Arts, 1994).

WEBSITES ON FLANNELBOARDS AND PUPPETRY

Lakeshore Learning

www.lakeshorelearning.com
A resource for a wide variety of storytime props, including puppets, Big Books, flannelboards, storytelling aprons and figures, musical instruments and shakers, and more.

Folkmanis Puppets

www.folkmanis.com
This small company carries the finest puppets sold commercially; check out their selection of realistic animal puppets.

Melissa and Doug

www.melissaanddoug.com
Melissa and Doug sell traditional toys such as wooden blocks and puzzles that are great for a stay and play storytime.

Read! Build! Play!

http://readbuildplay.com/
The American Library Association has a special initiative called "Read! Build! Play!" which encourages libraries to incorporate play into their storytimes and other services for young children. Check their website for a free downloadable toolkit.

Campaign for a Commercial-Free Childhood

www.commercialfreechildhood.org/
The CCFC is an advocacy group with the goal of eliminating corporate influences in educational environments (such as schools and libraries); they suggest libraries use non-commercial toys and puppets at storytime.

Beyond the Book Storytimes

http://btbstorytimes.blogspot.com/search/label/Program%20Summary
Children's librarian Steven Englefried offers tips on using puppets and music at library programs.

Mid-Hudson Library System Resource Page

http://midhudson.org/program/support/Flannel_kits.htm
A comprehensive listing by a public library in New York, describing sources for purchasing flannelboards and other storytelling props.

Kimbo Education

www.kimboed.com/
Kimbo Education is well known for their award-winning music recordings for children. They also sell accessories such as scarves and beanbags to go along with some of their dance CDs for young children.

Fat Brain Toys

www.fatbraintoys.com/special_needs/
There are several great resources for toys for children, but Fat Brain offers adaptive toys for children with special needs.

CHAPTER 9

Special Issues at Storytime

Storytime is often the most rewarding part of the library employee's day, but sometimes issues come up that can be challenging, such as disruptions at storytime. These will be addressed below. Other issues occur because of the changes happening in storytime; so, long-time storytime presenters have to change their routines. In the earlier chapters we discussed the new trend of adding some technology to storytime in the form of apps on tablet devices. Another new common practice is to include literacy tips for parents during storytime, so parents can continue the learning process at home with their children. It is not that the librarian is offering tips on how to parent, but offering tips to parents on getting their young children ready to learn to read. Some of these preliteracy skills will be discussed in this chapter. Another challenge can occur when your storytime becomes so popular you have to deal with large crowds; success brings its own challenges!

BEHAVIOR

New storytime presenters often are concerned about having a child who won't sit still, or one that won't listen during the storytime. Don't worry too much if the younger babies and toddlers don't seem to be paying attention; you will be surprised how much they will retain. For example, if a toddler sits with his back to you, or is wandering around the perimeter, he will still remember much of what you said. So long as a child's behavior isn't hurting the experience for others, don't let it bother you. However, that doesn't mean you have to put up with noisy kids or talking parents. I often will ask, "Could the parent help me with this child, I am not sure everyone can hear (or see)?" That often will lead the parent to hold the child on his or her lap so the noise or distraction will stop, yet it doesn't embarrass the parent. I try to phrase things in a positive say so it doesn't come across as a list of don'ts. For example, instead of a rule saying "No toys or food allowed," you could say "Save toys and snacks until after storytime because you need your hands free for the fingerplays." You may also have to state the obvious: "No cell phones" and "Stay in the library" are two rules parents need spelled out for them even though many of us would take those rules for granted. Also, singing a song between each story allows for latecomers to grab a seat, or for people to reposition themselves to a more comfortable seat. Having a volunteer can also be a great help at storytime; they can usher latecomers to their seats or help with children who cannot find their caregivers.

ASSISTING PARENTS

When parents bring their children to the library, you are given a great opportunity to talk with them about reading to their children. It also provides you with an opportunity to suggest materials they may need to help them be good parents.

Allowing parents to participate in storytime is a great way to model read-aloud techniques for parents. It also allows parents to see the types of books you are choosing for young children, so they can conclude their visit by choosing similar books to take home and read at bedtime or other times. Having parents at storytime also gives you a contact with them, so later when they are finding homework or recreational reading books, they will remember when you were the storytime person and know you are a friendly face at the library.

During storytime, you can mention how a certain book or song is helping a child with preliteracy skills. That may encourage the parent to repeat the activity at home; it becomes more than just a story but something that is developmentally important for the child's growth. For example, you can mention how a rhyming story is helping a child build vocabulary and phonological awareness. You can keep it as brief as that, but then the parent is aware of what your goal was. Having a simple handout of some of the preliteracy skills covered at storytime can help a parent follow up at home with similar stories and activities, without taking up too much time, or making storytime become a parenting class.

Because of the changing dynamics of families, and because most young children live in a household where both parents work, you can expect that the person who brings a young child to storytime is not always going to be the mother. Fathers attend storytime, too, so it is helpful if you don't call your storytimes Mommy and Me or variations that label it for moms. It can be just as likely that a grandparent, nanny, aunt or uncle, or other caregiver is the one bringing the child, so an inclusive title for your storytime is more inviting. Some libraries that have enough staff may even offer a special storytime for fathers if there is enough demand.

Many public libraries now have a parents' shelf in the children's room. This area will have books on child development, behavior and discipline, baby names, traveling with children, decorating a child's room, and more. Some parents will bring their children to the library but never venture into the adult book area. If this is true, your parent's shelf can demonstrate there are great books for them. The parents' shelf can also hold the interest of parents of young children who must stay in the same room as their children. They will now have something to read while their preschoolers are looking for picture books or playing a computer-learning game.

EVERY CHILD READY TO READ PROGRAM

Every Child Ready to Read is a parent education initiative from the Association of Library Service to Children (ALSC), a division of the American Library Association. The main focus is to encourage library storytimes and other programs to provide education for parents as well as education for the young child, so the parent or caregiver can continue the practices at home. Their website (http://everychildreadytoread.org/) offers training materials, posters, brochures, and other items for sale, to help libraries promote reading readiness skills for young children. Every Child Ready to Read promotes the five parent practices we will discuss in the next section.

FIVE PARENT PRACTICES

As part of your storytime, encourage parents to continue the five simple practices of reading, writing, singing, talking, and playing at home, which help a child develop into a reader. Here are some reasons you can use to explain the importance of these five practices:

Reading

An essential method of helping a child learn to read and to enjoy books includes how the pages turn to how a story develops. Plus, picture books often have a more advanced vocabulary than conversation, and books also help children learn the names of things such as animals.

Writing

Writing simple words helps a child learn the alphabet and the sound each letter represents. Scribbling is an important step in learning to write; it allows a child practice in holding a pencil, and lets them develop fine motor skills. Writing can be practiced by tracing, coloring in a coloring book, and using sidewalk chalk.

Singing

Songs help children learn sounds in words and phonological awareness. Parents should not be self-conscious about singing with their children; there is no one to judge you. Sing along with the car radio, sing while making dinner, setting the table, or when giving baths. Feel free to repeat songs; repetition is very important to learning.

Talking

Talking helps children learn oral language, a keystone of early literacy. Books offer a far larger vocabulary than the average spoken word household, but talking with children is fundamental to them learning basic vocabulary. Children need to learn the names of things. Talking to your child during car trips can be one easy way to find time to talk with your child. Encourage parents to narrate what they are doing so the child can learn to explain things, and encourage parents to use their regular vocabulary and not baby talk!

Playing

Playing helps a child reenact a story and learn new words. Play also encourages communication, problem solving, confidence, purpose, self-control, cooperation, curiosity, and the managing of emotions. Many child development experts will say that "play is the work of children."

These are five important things, playing, singing, talking, reading, and writing, that a caregiver or parent can do with a young child to help prepare them for school and learning to read. To help demonstrate the importance of these five practices, include some of the books listed at the end of this chapter that focus on playing, singing, talking, reading, and writing in your storytime.

DIALOGIC READING

Dialogic reading is the technique of reading aloud to a child and asking open-ended questions about the book being read, to create a dialogue about book. Instead of a child being asked to be quiet, the child is encouraged to talk about what is happening in the story, or what he or she sees in the illustrations. Eventually the child will have actively listened to the story in such a way that he or she can retell the story. According to Saroj Ghoting and Pamela Martin-Diaz in their book, *Early Literacy Storytimes @ Your Library* (American Library Association, 2006), dialogic reading can help a child in language development and other emergent literacy skills. With dialogic reading techniques, the child is actively listening and engaging with the book.

Some of the skills that dialogic reading can build include print awareness, vocabulary, letter knowledge, and phonological awareness such as guessing rhyming words. You can also cover some of the skills that are part of early literacy and kindergarten readiness, such as the parts of the book, showing in which direction a sentence runs, and in which direction pages turn. Having a child talk about what he or she notices in the illustrations also helps build visual literacy skills.

But how can we do dialogic reading with a room filled with children? This was a common concern when longtime librarians and storytime presenters first heard about dialogic reading. It is quite understandable that a parent could practice this technique with a child, while reading a story at bedtime. But we need to try to model dialogic reading for the parents and caregivers who attend storytime, even if it is with just one of the stories we read each session. If we demonstrate the techniques of asking open-ended questions about the story and illustrations, the parents will grasp the concept and repeat it during read-aloud time at home. If we have a handout with some tips on dialogic reading, they are even more likely to give it a try. Dialogic reading is not the natural way most parents read to their children; many still feel that the child fidgets too much, or that interrupting the story is distracting, so it is important to model the technique and let parents know how important it is.

Even if you know what to do for dialogic reading, it can be daunting to try it at a large storytime. You will get so much discussion about the book it can be difficult to finish the story! So try it on your last story of the session, where you can allow more talking and don't have to worry about getting the audience to settle down. Try some of the conversational questions about the last story you read, and then go onto the closing song. Any child who still wants to talk about the book can do so while others have moved on to the art project, or while you clean up.

RESEARCH

Read any parenting book, or book on preschoolers and literacy, and it will talk about the importance of reading to very young children. Many quote studies and reports that explain the one key to preparing a child to learn to read, is that the child be read to on a regular basis. Many studies even spell out that a child should be read to for 20 minutes per day, minimum. This research appears in many media reports, like the nightly news, so most parents are aware of it. That is why so many of them start using the public library to borrow books, and to attend storytime. So be sure to include some information on the importance of reading to very young children on all your handouts and flyers relating to storytime. This will reinforce to the parent that storytime relates to this brain research, and remind parents storytime is valuable.

PRELITERACY SKILLS

Many of the newer books and workshops on doing storytime suggest offering parenting skills or parenting tips. I prefer to use the term preliteracy tips, since it is logical for the librarian to offer advice on literacy more than on parenting. If the librarian is offering parenting skills, it can sound condescending or patronizing, but it makes much more sense for us to offer skills on helping your child prepare to learn to read. During storytime, you can give a brief tip to parents that a certain book or activity will help with preliteracy skills, so the parent can repeat the activity at home, or find more books like the one you are reading aloud to reinforce what the child has experienced at storytime.

Six basic preliteracy skills (not to be confused with the five parent practices we discussed earlier) are listed below. You can demonstrate all six at storytime. You can even have a handout or bookmark that describes the skill and explains how parents can practice the skill at home. Free downloadable handouts on early literacy can be found at the American Library Association's Born to Read website at www.ala.org/alsc/issuesadv/borntoread. More websites on child development are listed at the end of this chapter.

Print Motivation

Print motivation means a child has interest in and enjoys books. Bringing children to library storytime is a great way to instill the skill of print motivation, and parents should be congratulated for making the time to come to the library! Parents can also promote print motivation by reading books at home, by letting their children see them reading, and by visiting the library regularly.

Phonological Awareness

A child's ability to hear the smaller sounds within words, like rhyming syllables, is phonological awareness. Singing songs and reciting rhymes is a key to building phonological awareness, and repeating songs and rhymes is also very helpful. Fingerplays and sign language help breakdown songs and rhymes into the individual words, which will help a young child pick out sounds within a word.

Vocabulary

Reading allows a child to learn many new words and the names of various things, which builds the child's vocabulary. The words used in books have more variety than the words we use in conversation. For example, many children's books name all types of animals. We wouldn't mention the names of those animals unless we took the child to the zoo or a farm, but a book helps a child learn all types of new words. When doing their daily read aloud at home, parents can point to the illustrations in a book and have the child name what is being shown in the picture. During storytime, you can also point to the pictures in a book and have the children shout out what they see. If a book has an unusual word, stop and see if anyone knows what the word means and define it, then move on with the story. Most preschoolers haven't eaten porridge, but while reading "The Three Bears," you can mention that porridge is similar to oatmeal, a food many of them have tried!

Narrative Skills

Many young children will practice their narrative skills by telling you what they did that morning, or what happened at preschool that day. Reading books helps a child understand how to tell a story, that a story has a beginning, middle, and end, and that when they tell about something they saw or heard they can do the same. Reading favorite books more than once helps a child memorize the story, so they can retell it in their own words, which also builds narrative skills.

Print Awareness

Our world is surrounded by print: signs, billboards, food packaging, and of course books. A child who is read to on a regular basis can identify letters of the alphabet, and that a sign is telling them something even if they cannot read the sign yet. Print awareness is promoted when a parent reads signs while driving, reads packaging in the grocery store, and reads books on a daily basis. Children will soon identify letters of the alphabet and know how to hold and turn the pages of a book, which are fundamental preliteracy skills.

Letter Knowledge

While reading road signs to a child, or reading food packaging, point out letters of the alphabet as well. What letter does that sign start with? These activities promote letter knowledge, and help a child understand that words are made up of letters. Demonstrate this activity during storytime, by letting the children yell out the first letter of the book's title, or by reading lots of alphabet books. This will demonstrate letter knowledge techniques for parents to use later with their children, at home, in the car, or at the store.

DEALING WITH DISRUPTIONS

We all know that there will be disruptions at storytime no matter how we try to be proactive and prevent them from occurring. So don't let intermittent disruptions bother you too much. Also, there is no one best way to take care of disruptions at storytime, but we will address some common storytime issues and possible ways to address them.

Disruptions by Parents

When I ask other librarians what disruptions bother them the most, the majority of behaviors named are things parents do (or don't do)! For example, a ringing cell phone, talking on the cell phone, parents talking to each other and not participating, or coming in late and seating their children in front of others. It is important not to embarrass the parent, but to state what you need: "I don't think everyone can hear, can you all help me out by singing along?" If the parents don't take your cues, you can speak to them after storytime and let them know it is a program for a parent and child to participate together, and not for the parents to sit in the back.

Disruptions by Children

Many of the disruptions caused by a child, such as standing up and talking to you during the story, actually demonstrate that the child is involved and paying attention. So you don't want to be negative; try to ask the parent to sit with the child, or say "I am glad you like the story, let's all sit flat on our bottoms so everyone can see." Often the interruptions by a child occur when parents are not sure if they should intervene, like a child walking in front of everyone. Again, just ask for what you need: "I could use a parent's help with this child so he (or she) can find a seat."

Positive Steps

Because we want to be welcoming and gracious, stating our needs in a positive way can be more effective than being negative. You should still be able to have rules, and explain to parents what you need from them, but stating it in a positive way can make all the difference in whether that parent and child return. I like to briefly explain why we have a rule, since that seems to get quicker buy-in from the parents. For example, I can ask, "the children's hands need to be free for the songs and fingerplays, so put away any toys or snacks you brought and save them for the end of storytime." In our list of rules in the next section, nearly all of them are stated in a positive, not negative manner. The way you say something gives the parents an indication that you understand child behavior and really want them to be there.

Set Expectations

One of the biggest ways to avoid future disruptions is to set expectations for the parents. Maybe they did not attend storytime as a child; how do they know what the "rules" are? You should announce the rules at every storytime; you can do that with flyers, or a poster at the entrance with the main points. Common expectations to list include:

- Sit and participate with your child
- Everyone's hands need to be free for the songs—leave toys and food in your bag
- Don't leave your child unattended
- Try to be on time, but if you are late, please sit at the back
- If your child is crying, take a break outside the room
- No cell phones

By letting parents know what your expectations are, you are making them partners in the success of storytime. They may not realize it is less disruptive to leave storytime with a crying child, than it is to try and calm the child down right in the center of your reading circle.

Volunteers Can Help

Many storytime disruptions can be taken care of by volunteers. A volunteer can help seat latecomers so they don't walk in front of others during the story. They can also take a parent aside to quietly ask them to turn off their cell phone, so the person is not embarrassed. They can help a parent take a crying child out of the room. Many of our storytime volunteers are grandparents, who are tactful but clear, and are respected by the parents in attendance.

DEALING WITH SUCCESS

Some challenges occur at storytime because it is so popular! You may want to avoid registration to be more inclusive, but that means you may need to deal with large groups. Using Big Books, puppets, flannelboards, apps shown on a big screen, and other visuals and props can help hold the attention of a large group.

Crowd Control

If you have a large group attending storytime, your volunteers can be essential in helping with crowd control. A volunteer usher can help seat a latecomer in a way that doesn't disturb everyone else. Having special stroller parking outside the storytime room can make more room for the audience. Or, limit the use of chairs to only expectant moms or older caregivers who cannot sit on the floor.

Adding More Sessions

If you want to limit the size of the group, one way is to hold two sessions back-to-back. Two sessions of the same storytime do not require more prep time, and you really only have one setup and one cleanup if you do two sessions, one right after the other. The one new challenge you face if you hold two sessions is moving the first group out of the space so the next group can enter. If you hold storytime in a meeting room, you can simply announce at the end of the first that it is time to go into the library and look for books. If you are holding storytime in the children's area of the library, this can be more difficult.

Limiting the Size of the Group

Another way to limit the size of your preschool storytime is to have latecomers start with the craft in a different room or area, and then repeat storytime for that group while the first one goes into the craft area. Basically, it is like doing two storytimes back-to-back, with some children doing the craft first and some doing it after storytime, as a way to divide a large crowd in half. I have done this in the summer, when I have teen volunteers available to monitor the craft area, and when we have larger crowds due to older siblings attending.

SERVICES TO CHILDREN WITH SPECIAL NEEDS

It is vitally important that children with special needs have access to your regular storytimes. Research proves that both the special needs child and those without special needs benefit from inclusion. Also, legally the library needs to accommodate individuals with special needs, including children. This can occur by offering room for wheelchairs, sign language interpreters, and other accommodations. Staff training can also be quite beneficial to making the library a welcoming place to those with special needs. For more on this subject, be sure to check out *Including Families of Children with Special Needs* by Carrie Scott Banks (Neal-Schuman, 2014).

In our chapter on baby storytimes, we briefly discussed using sign language during parts of the storytime; this doesn't just assist deaf families, but can help with all young children. Sign language can engage children with autism, or those with attention deficit disorder, as well as those with speech delays or emotional issues. Using sign language for the songs and fingerplays is relatively easy to learn to do, and can make your storytime more welcoming for special needs children.

Another way to accommodate those with disabilities is to use some technology to help all attendees see the books. Use a projector and screen to show the pictures for the books you are presenting; this can help at storytimes with more than 20 children, as well as assist those with vision disabilities. Some children may also need to hold a manipulative toy during storytime, to calm them and help them to focus, so have some available. Many children with special needs appreciate consistency and repetition; since we repeat so many songs and fingerplays at our storytimes, and often have a set format, this should help those with autism who appreciate predictability.

SENSORY STORYTIMES

Some librarians have found that there is a large enough group of special needs children that they will offer a sensory storytime, which is sensitive to children (especially those with autism) who can suffer from sensory overload. Although this is open to all children, those with special needs may find it especially helpful. A sensory storytime incorporates some of the elements used in occupational therapy, including stretching activities, art projects, use of scarves and beanbags during songs, and other adaptive techniques to help children self-regulate their behavior. For example, allow children who cannot sit for a story stand or walk along a designated area of the storytime where they won't prevent others from seeing the presenter and book.

To find out more about presenting a sensory storytime, check out the information from Barbara Klipper of the Ferguson Library in Stamford, Connecticut. She offers detailed plans on constructing a sensory storytime, on the website of the Association of Library Service to Children: www.ala.org/alsc/sensory-story-tots.

EVALUATING YOUR STORYTIMES

Periodically, you should evaluate what you are doing at storytime. This doesn't need to be overly critical, but it is important to see if you are adding new families and reaching those in your community who can benefit from storytime. You can also ask someone from a branch library to observe your storytime and ask for any advice:

- Are you loud enough?
- Can the audience see the book and illustrations?
- Are your expectations for behavior clear?
- Do you have a handout with lyrics for new parents?
- Are interruptions handled effectively without alienating the person?

Another important concern is that the books you choose reflect our multicultural world; do you choose books with nonwhite characters?

Sometimes we notice a decline in attendance; sometimes this is temporary due to bad weather or other causes. But often this is due to the need to continually outreach to families: regular revision of publicity on storytime, outreach to those who do not speak much English, targeting new library card holders who may not know about your children's programs, and so forth. It is important to do a yearly evaluation of what you offer at storytime, as well as assess who is attending and if you are including all cultures represented in your community.

PARENTS AN IMPORTANT AUDIENCE

Parents and caregivers are an important part of your storytime audience. They are there to learn some preliteracy skills like dialogic reading, and to hear about new resources in your community geared to young children. They want to help their children prepare for kindergarten, and are interested in hearing what will be expected of their children and what they can practice at home to be ready. They can assist in making storytime go smoothly if you let them know how to help, by clearly communicating your expectations. The adults who bring their children to storytime can be the library's biggest cheerleaders when it is time to request a budget increase or when funding legislation is up for a vote, since they come to your library regularly and see what great things are happening there. So inform your parents; they are a child's first teacher. If they are coming to the library, you can count on their interest; and they can become lifelong library patrons as their children get older, too.

RESOURCES FOR PARENTS AND PRELITERACY

Our libraries have a wealth of great books for parents on all types of subjects, from potty training to helping a child learn to read. I will only list a few resources on literacy here since most libraries have a parenting section, but I have also listed some websites that have great resources including handouts, booklists, and other information you can distribute to the parents and caregivers who attend storytime.

PARENTING BOOKS ON LITERACY

Banks, Carrie Scott. *Including Families of Children with Special Needs* (Neal-Schuman, 2014).

Fox, Mem. *Reading Magic: Why Reading Aloud to Our Children Will Change Their Lives Forever—Second Edition* (Mariner, 2008).

Ghoting, Saroj Nadkarni and Pamela Martin-Diaz. *Early Literacy Storytimes @ Your Library* (American Library Association, 2006).

Ghoting, Saroj. *Storytimes for Everyone! Developing Young Children's Language & Literacy* (American Library Association, 2013).

McNeil, Heather. *Read, Rhyme and Romp: Early Literacy Skills and Activities for Librarians, Teachers, and Parents* (Libraries Unlimited, 2012).

Silberg, Jackie. *Reading Games for Young Children* (Gryphon House, 2005).

Straub, Susan and K. J. Dell'Antonia. *Reading with Babies, Toddlers, and Twos: A Guide to Laughing, Learning, and Growing Together Through Books* (Sourcebooks, Inc., 2013).

Trelease, Jim. *The Read-Aloud Handbook: Seventh Edition* (Penguin, 2013).

WEBSITES ON PRELITERACY AND PARENTING

Every Child Ready to Read @ Your Library

http://everychildreadytoread.org/

Every Child Ready to Read is a program sponsored by the American Library Association. The website lists suggestions on incorporating preliteracy tips for parents into your storytimes, and has printable handouts including booklists for different age groups.

Born to Read

http://www.ala.org/alsc/issuesadv/borntoread

Another program sponsored by the American Library Association, Born to Read offers free materials to motivate parents to read to their children.

Storytime Share

www.earlylit.net/storytimeshare

If you would like to add simple advice for parents on how a book relates to literacy, the "Storytime Share" blog is a great resource. Saroj Ghoting is a noted expert on early literacy, and her blog shares songs and books, with tips on how they can help children acquire preliteracy skills.

Kent Library District—Five Early Literacy Practices.

www.kdl.org/kids/go/pgr_five_practices

Kent Library has a clear explanation of the five literacy practices you can encourage parents to do at home by demonstrating them in your storytimes.

Linda Lucas Walling Collection

http://faculty.libsci.sc.edu/walling/bestfolder.htm

Linda Lucas Walling was a professor of Library and Information Science at the University of South Carolina. Walling's website offers guidelines for evaluating children's books that depict disabilities, and contains lists of recommended children's books that show the disabled.

Zero to Three

http://www.zerotothree.org/site/PageServer?pagename = homepage

Zero to Three is a national nonprofit organization that promotes education for babies and toddlers. Their website has a wealth of printable handouts on a variety of topics, including brain development in babies and building bridges to literacy.

National Association for the Education of Young Children

http://www.naeyc.org/

From knowing what toys are recommended for which age groups, to advice on using singing as a teaching tool, to brain research in young children, this website has a wealth of concise and clear information for parents, caregivers, and preschool teachers.

BOOKS THAT EMPHASIZE THE FIVE PARENT PRACTICES

Read

Allen, Jonathan. *I'm Not Reading!*
Benton, Jim. *The End (Almost).*
Blatt, Jane. *Books Always Everywhere.*
Bruss, Deborah. *Book! Book! Book!*
Burk, Rachelle. *Don't Turn the Page!*
Gravett, Emily. *Again!*
Freedman, Deborah. *The Story of Fish and Snail.*
Kohara, Kazuno. *The Midnight Library.*
Watt, Melanie. *Have I Got a Book for You!*

Write

Austin, Mike. *Monsters Love Colors.*
Bossio, Paula. *The Line.*
Daly, Cathleen. *Emily's Blue Period.*
Johnson, Crockett. *Harold and the Purple Crayon.*
Light, Kelly. *Louise Loves Art.*
Lionni, Leo. *The Alphabet Tree.*
Mack, Jeff. *The Things I Can Do.*
Rosenthal, Amy Krouse. *Exclamation Mark.*
Russell, Natalie. *Lost for Words.*
Schubert, Leda. *Reading to Peanut.*
Watt, Melanie. *Chester's Masterpiece.*
Winter, Jeanette. *Henri's Scissors.*

Sing

Craig, Lindsay. *Farmyard Beat.*
Davenier, Christine. *It's Raining, It's Pouring!*
Hillenbrand, Will. *Down By the Barn.*
Hughes, Langston. *Lullaby (for a Black Mother).*
Ketteman, Helen. *There Once Was a Cowpoke Who Swallowed an Ant.*
Lies, Brian. *Bats in the Band.*
Lithgow, John. *Never Play Music Right Next to the Zoo.*
Litwin, Eric. *Pete the Cat: I Love My White Shoes.*
Marino, Gianna. *Following Papa's Song.*
Marley, Ziggy. *I Love You, Too!*
Murray, Alison. *Hickory Dickory Dog.*
Norman, Kim. *If It's Snowy and You Know It, Clap Your Paws!*
Numeroff, Laura. *Nighty-Night, Cooper.*
Sierra, Judy. *E-I-E-I-O: How Old MacDonald Got His Farm (with a little help from a hen).*
Shields, Carol Diggory. *Baby's Got the Blues.*
Wissinger, Tamera Will. *This Old Band.*

Talk

Adderson, Caroline. *Norman, Speak!*
Ashman, Linda. *Rain.*
Fleming, Denise. *Shout! Shout it Out!*
Fox, Mem. *Tell Me About Your Day Today.*
Gay, Marie-Louise. *Any Questions?*
LaRochelle, David. *Moo!*
Light, Steve. *Diggers Go.*
Meddaugh, Susan. *Martha Speaks.*
Most, Bernard. *The Cow That Went Oink.*
Murphy, Mary. *Say Hello Like This.*
Sitomer, Alan Lawrence. *Daddy's Zigzagging Bedtime Story.*
Stein, David Ezra. *Interrupting Chicken.*
Watt, Melanie. *You're Finally Here!*

Play

Andreae, Giles. *Giraffes Can't Dance.*
Cronin, Doreen. *Wiggle.*
Garland, Sally Anne. *Share.*
Gravett, Emily. *Matilda's Cat.*
Heder, Thyra. *Fraidyzoo.*
Joosse, Barbara M. *Hooray Parade.*
Martin, Emily. *Day Dreamers.*
Morales, Yuyi. *Niño Wrestles the World.*
Murguia, Bethanie Deeney. *Zoe's Jungle.*
Portis, Antoinette. *Not a Box.*
Spires, Ashley. *The Most Magnificent Thing.*
Yoon, Salina. *Found.*

BOOKS THAT HELP DEMONSTRATE THE SIX PRELITERACY SKILLS

Print Motivation—All books

Print Awareness

Cotter, Bill. *Don't Push the Button!*
Greene, Rhonda. *No Pirates Allowed! Said Library Lou.*
Krilanovich, Nadia. *Chicken, Chicken, Duck.*
LaRochelle, David. *Moo!*
Marsalis, Wynton. *Squeak, Rumble, Whomp! Whomp! Whomp!*
Matheson, Christie. *Tap the Magic Tree.*
Springman, I. C. *More.*
Sutton, Sally. *Demolition.*
Tullet, Herve. *Mix It Up.*
Tullet, Herve. *Press Here.*
Van Lieshout, Maria. *Backseat A-B-See.*
Viva, Frank. *A Long Way Away: A Two-Way Story.*

Phonological Awareness

Anderson, Airlie. *Momo and Snap Are Not Friends!*
Arndt, Michael. *Cat Says Meow and Other Animalopoeia.*
Aylesworth, Jim. *Cock-a-doodle-doo, Creak, Pop-pop-, Moo.*
Bee, William. *Digger Dog.*
Bryant, Megan E. *Alphasaurus.*
Carle, Eric. *Slowly, Slowly, Slowly, Said the Sloth.*
Crum, Shutta. *Thunder-Boomer!*
Dale, Penny. *Dinosaur Rescue!*
DePalma, Mary N. *Bow-Wow, Wiggle-Waggle.*
Dragonwagon, Crescent. *All the Awake Animals Are Almost Asleep.*
Fleming, Denise. *Tippy-Tippy-Tippy, Splash!*

Fleming, Denise. *Under Ground.*
Gibson, Amy. *Split! Splat!*
Gibson, Ginger F. *Tiptoe Joe.*
Janovitz, Marilyn. *Play Baby Play!*
Johnston, Tony. *Laugh-Out-Loud Baby.*
Jonas, Ann. *Watch William Walk.*
Joosse, Barbara. *Old Robert and the Sea-Silly Cats.*
Kennedy, Anne Vittur. *The Farmer's Away! Baa! Neigh!*
Lewin, Betsy. *Thumpy Feet.*
Lickens, Alice V. *Can You Dance to the Boogaloo?*
Mahy, Margaret. *The Man from the Land of Fandango.*
McDonnell, Patrick. *The Monsters' Monster.*
Meadows, Michelle. *Piggies in Pajamas.*
Pinder, Eric. *If All the Animals Came Inside.*
Smith, Maggie. *Pigs in Pajamas.*
Steggall, Susan. *The Diggers are Coming!*
Stevens, Janet. *Find a Cow Now!*
Sutton, Sally. *Demolition.*
Swenson, Jamie A. *Big Rig.*
Viau, Nancy. *Storm Song.*

Vocabulary

Aston, Dianna Hutts. *A Rock Is Lively.*
Baker, Ken. *Old MacDonald Had a Dragon.*
Barton, Byron. *The Three Bears.*
Helakoski, Leslie. *Big Pigs.*
Sendak, Maurice. *Where the Wild Things Are.*
Stockdale, Susan. *Bring on the Birds.*
Ward, Helen. *The Town Mouse and the Country Mouse.*
Yuly, Toni. *Early Bird.*

Narrative Skills

Allen, Kathryn M. *A Kiss Means I Love You.*
Barton, Byron. *The Little Red Hen.*
Bloom, C. P. *The Monkey Goes Bananas.*
Boyd, Lizi. *Inside Outside.*
Burningham, John. *Picnic.*
Colon, Raul. *Draw!*
Fox, Mem. *Tell Me About Your Day Today.*
Gordon, Domenica. *Archie.*
Hills, Tad. *Rocket Writes a Story.*
Idle, Molly. *Flora and the Flamingo.*
Jay, Alison. *Out of the Blue.*
Judge, Lita. *Red Hat.*
Kasza, Keiko. *Silly Goose's Big Story.*
Klassen, Jon. *This Is Not My Hat.*
Lamb, Albert. *Tell Me the Day Backwards.*

LaRochelle, David. *Moo!*
Mack, Jeff. *Ah Ha!*
Pett, Mark. *The Boy and the Airplane.*
Pett, Mark. *The Girl and the Bicycle.*
Stead, Philip C. *Bear Has a Story To Tell.*
Willems, Mo. *Goldilocks and the Three Dinosaurs.*

Letter Knowledge

Bingham, Kelly. *Z Is for Moose.*
Kontis, Alethea. *Alpha Oops! The Day Z Went First.*
Lichtenheld, Tom. *E-mergency!*
Maccarone, Grace. *The Three Bears ABC: An Alphabet Book.*
Martin, Bill. *Chicka Chicka Boom Boom.*
Schaefer, Carole Lexa. *ABCers.*
Sierra, Judy. *The Sleepy Little Alphabet.*
Slate, Joseph. *Miss Bindergarten Gets Ready for Kindergarten.*
Vamos, Samantha. *Alphabet Trucks.*

CHAPTER 10

Using Volunteers at Storytimes

Storytime is such an effective program in promoting literacy that many libraries use volunteers as a way to increase the amount of storytimes, or to take storytimes out to the community. We have seen that you don't need to be a librarian to perform storytimes, although a children's librarian often plans and coordinates the storytimes at a library. Library support staff can be excellent storytime practitioners. Volunteers can also be trained to perform storytimes, allowing the library to extend storytime to more children and to more places. One of the most effective uses of volunteers doing storytime is outside of the library, taking storytime to day cares, preschools, classrooms, doctor's offices, Headstart programs, and other places visited by young children on a regular basis. To have a successful volunteer storytime program, you need do some training and screening.

RECRUITING VOLUNTEERS

Many libraries already have a volunteer coordinator, and a method of recruiting volunteers. If not, you may still experience folks asking about volunteering, and specifically asking about reading to children. If you need to recruit volunteers, there are several ways to do so which are not time consuming. A press release to the local papers could be effective, especially if you include a photo of someone reading to children. This same press release should go to the local homeowners associations' newsletters; these are more likely to reach your target audience. Also publicize your need for storytime volunteers on the library's website, Facebook page, and through other social media venues. Often the most reliable and well-suited storytime volunteers are retirees; you are likely to get volunteers who may be retired teachers or others who worked with children in the past. Teen volunteers can also be helpful for some storytime volunteer tasks, so recruiting volunteers through the high school can be effective. Most high schools have chapters of national service clubs such as Key Club, Octagon, and Interact, so contacting the school to notify those clubs works quite well.

SCREENING VOLUNTEERS

Most government agencies like libraries and schools have a screening process for volunteers. Often it is more rigorous if the volunteers will be working with children. So check with your supervisors on how volunteers are screened; or you may need to check with your city or county human resources or personnel department. It is not uncommon for adult volunteers who work with youth to go through a fingerprinting process and not begin until they have been cleared. There may be other screenings, like a tuberculosis test, that may be required, so be sure to get all the information before you proceed. You want to have some sort of application for each volunteer, on file at you library, with the person's contact information just in case they become ill while at the volunteer job.

TRAINING VOLUNTEERS

Usually there are two clear reasons volunteers are successful: they were placed in a job suited to their talents and one they enjoy, and they received adequate (or better) training. Be sure to interview each volunteer and really hear what each person would like to do and what he or she is good at. Have them watch you do a storytime so they have a feel for what will be expected of them.

Next, be sure to have a solid orientation and training process. Storytime readers will need more training than those who help as ushers or those who help with arts and crafts setup and cleanup. This book can help in training them. If they are retired teachers they may need less training than someone who hasn't worked with children. Make sure the volunteers know what they are getting into, how much time each week they will be asked to commit to, and spend time with them the first few sessions where they read stories before you have them work on their own. The time you invest interviewing and training them will be rewarded with volunteers who are consistent, and who stay around for the long run.

OUTREACH

Outreach is the term used for services that are performed outside of the library—where we take a library program or service to where the customer is. This is especially important for those who may not be able to visit the library like the homebound, small children in all-day day care or preschool, or families who may not be aware of what the library can do for them. Many libraries train volunteers to do outreach storytimes at Headstart, preschools, transitional kindergarten, and larger day-care facilities. They may come weekly or even just once a month, bringing handouts about the library, card applications, and of course they read books, sing songs, and bring some visual elements like a flannelboard, puppet, scarves, or musical instruments.

Headstart Programs

A popular form of outreach occurs when a volunteer goes to a Headstart preschool once a month, to read to the children and give them all a free paperback picture book. This partnership between Headstart and the library is often run through the literacy division of the library. Grants are usually the source of funding for the giveaway books, or a program like Reading is Fundamental or First Book can sometimes provide the books. This service can be a great way to publicize the library, and to demonstrate the importance of reading and owning books to the parents of those children. Include your library flyers and library card applications with the free books, and the parents will become library users.

Reach Out and Read

Many pediatricians and hospitals participate in the Reach Out and Read program, which involves doctors giving free books to their patients who come for annual visits, regular inoculations, and other visits to the doctor by very young children. Doctors have found that reading to children is so important to a child's preliteracy skills that they want to encourage all parents to read to their children, the way doctors encourage good nutrition habits, hygiene, and other things that contribute to the health and well-being of a child. Some libraries will partner with a hospital or doctor to help choose the books that are purchased for the program. Some libraries will send a volunteer reader to doctors' waiting rooms, to read to the children, or to hospitals, to read to children who are staying at the hospital or just visiting the hospital for an appointment. The library volunteers are trained to choose age-appropriate books and add songs, fingerplays, puppets, or other elements to make the read-aloud experience exciting for children with a variety of learning styles.

Storytimes at Day-Care Centers and Preschools

Preschools and day-care centers may not be able to bring their children to the library for your storytimes for several reasons. Recent changes in the laws on car seats make it very difficult to bring more than a few children in one vehicle; in the past, some preschools had vans and buses that could bring the children to storytime. Now, that is nearly impossible since it is so difficult to fit the buses with car seats. Also, it is not unusual in many communities to find most preschoolers in day care all day since both parents work; there are few stay-at-home parents in many towns and cities. So going to the preschoolers is one alternative to reach those children. Finally, if a preschool or day-care group is able to get to your library storytime, it could be difficult to fit everyone in the room if large groups are in attendance. So doing an outreach storytime at the day care or preschool can be a win-win for everyone. Due to cutbacks and budget woes, it is likely the library staff may not have time to visit these day-care centers or preschools, but volunteers could be trained to give this service.

Many library volunteers will enjoy visiting a group, and it only takes an hour or so each week for these visits. Many volunteers will find it most convenient to visit the day care or preschool near their homes. Weekly visits are the most desirable, to really convey the importance of reading and to help the children get familiar with popular books and songs that will help them later when they get to kindergarten. The library staff can even help the volunteer by pulling the books for these weekly visits, and have them ready to go if the volunteer is in a hurry. Of course, many of the volunteers will enjoy choosing books, so it can be a collaborative process between the librarian and the volunteer.

The preschool or day-care center is likely to already include reading as part of their daily activities, and the library's volunteer storytime does not replace that. It is just one more opportunity for the children to hear great books read out loud, and is a way to promote the library. It can also be a welcome break for the day-care provider or preschool teacher, to have a weekly special guest come in to read to the children. But it in no way implies that day-care centers or preschools are not already reading with the children.

Storytimes at Schools

Some libraries work out a partnership with local schools to send storytime volunteers to read to the younger grades, such as kindergarten. These volunteers may need to go through a screening or registration process with the school district, but since they represent the library, you also want to register and train them. You may want to help choose the books, especially if the teachers ask for books to go along with the curriculum. Many school schedules are greatly impacted by standardized testing so they may not have time for even a weekly reading time with a library volunteer, so check out what will work for the school before you recruit or train any volunteers.

Serving Transitional Kindergarten Classes

Many states are instituting transitional kindergarten in public schools. These classes are for children approximately age 4 and a half, who are not yet 5 and ready for kindergarten, but they are ready for classes to prepare them to attend kindergarten next year. Much of the curriculum offered to transitional kindergarten incorporates preschool activities as well as emergent reader education and socialization offered in kindergarten. Transitional kindergarten offers a daily circle time with songs and read-alouds, just like a library's storytime. Be sure to connect with all your local transitional kindergarten teachers and let them know about your library's resources of great picture books, music recordings, and online picture book offerings on TumbleBooks or BookFlix. Let them know they can phone ahead to request books on the subject for that week: planting, weather, community helpers, and so forth, so you can pull books they can pick up after school.

STORYTIME BAGS

One method of making it easier for volunteer readers is to have storytime bags ready for them to borrow to take to the Headstart, preschool, doctor's office, or wherever they are doing the outreach storytime. The bags contain books, song lyrics, a puppet or flannelboard figures, and a laminated instruction sheet, so that the volunteer will have everything he or she needs for the visit. Often the items in the bag focus on a theme that is interesting for preschoolers: holidays, food, seasons, animals, or other topic that will make the storytime a teachable moment and encouraging the children to talk about that topic and learn more about it. If the storytime is at a preschool or Headstart, the staff at the school may extend the storytime with crafts, art projects, or other activities on the same topic. Of course, the staff may read to the children every day, and may want to borrow more books on the theme so it lasts all week.

To fund the storytime bags, many libraries will obtain minigrants that help in purchasing the tote bags, the extra copies of the books, and the puppets or other storytime props. Many large businesses, like Target stores, offer minigrants of $500 or more that can be obtained with a minimum of forms and paperwork, so are worth the time to apply. You can also seek donations, or obtain funds from the Friends of the Library, to fund the bags.

1,000 BOOKS BEFORE KINDERGARTEN

One way of extending the benefits of library storytime is to encourage reading at home. Librarians are doing this with a new reading incentive program called 1,000 Books before Kindergarten. In some ways, it is like a summer reading program for preschoolers, but offered all year long. The parent or caregiver and child pick up a reading log from the library, and keep track of the books they read at home. The concept is to insure that children have had 1,000 books read to each of them by the time they enter kindergarten, so they are ready to learn to read.

For this program, the rewards can be very simple, such as a sticker for every 100 books read. Some libraries have received grants, so they can give one new paperback picture book for every 100 books read, or a canvas book bag after the first 100 books read, as an incentive to continue. What is just as valuable is the diploma celebrating the completion of the program, which a child can show to his or her kindergarten teacher the first week of class.

For more on offering this program, check out the materials offered by its originator, Sandy Krost of the Bremen Public Library, Indiana: www.cde.state.co.us/cdelib /LibraryDevelopment/YouthServices/1000Books.htm. Also, librarian Marge Loch-Wouters of La Crosse, Wisconsin, collected materials from various programs at: www.pinterest .com/lochwouters/let-1000-books-bloom/

THERAPY DOG READING PROGRAMS

For young children learning how to read, practicing their reading skills can be stressful. Although not technically a storytime, libraries offer a program where trained dogs sit with a child while the child reads out loud. The trained dog gives the child a nonjudgmental audience and helps the child feel at ease. Often these programs are called Paws to Read, Barks for Books, or other fun name to attract interest.

Therapy dog reading programs can be relatively easy to run. First, make contact with a therapy dog group in your area; most are already aware of this program. Arrange for the best day/time on a weekly basis, such as Wednesday afternoons, or Saturday mornings or whatever time will be good for a few dogs and when children are out of school. Have an orientation for the dog handlers in the library, in the room or space where the program will take place. Go over the expectations and procedures of the program, so the dog handlers know they are not tutors. They don't need to correct the child or teach reading; they are mainly there to accompany and control the dog, answer questions, and explain the program.

Children learning to read are the target audience for this program (kindergarten through second grade), although you will want to allow older children with learning or reading disabilities. Publicize the program with flyers and posters in the library, and also send flyers to schools, targeting the teachers of kindergarten to second graders. Those teachers may know of a child who would benefit from the program, and they can recommend it to parents. That way, you are likely to get the children who really need the program, not just parents and children looking for something to do.

Once you have the publicity and dogs in place, be sure you have a quiet meeting room and a registration list. Any child in this program should have parental permission to attend, so you want registration of some kind. In fact, you may even want the parents to stay in the library so they can pick up the child at the end of the reading session, which is usually 20–30 minutes in length. Also, since you are likely to have a limited number of dogs, you want each child to have a reservation with the time they are assigned to read with a dog. At 20-minute increments, one dog can only read with three children in an hour, so each child needs to know the assigned time.

You should also have a display of easy reader books from which to choose. Hopefully children will check out the books they read to their dog buddy. Books in the *Biscuit* series by Alyssa Satin Capucilli or *Clifford the Big Red Dog* series by Norman Bridwell are perfect for this program, but you don't need to choose just dog-themed books; anything on the easy reading level will work.

Many librarians give children a reading record to keep track of how often they read with their dog buddies. They receive a sticker for each 20-minute session. After a set number of sessions, the child receives a free book to keep. Often you can purchase these with money donated by the Friends of the Library. You can also give out bookmarks and other prizes to reward children for their efforts. Once the program is in place, the dog handlers do a lot of the work. They enjoy giving out bookmarks and other rewards. A volunteer can be assigned to check in the children, make sure they are assigned to a dog, and generally moderate the activity. Once you have the volunteers and dog handlers accustomed to the program, you may not need to be there for the whole program, as long as the volunteers know where to find you if they have a question.

TEEN VOLUNTEERS

Teen volunteers can also be a great storytime resource, especially if you recruit and train those suited to the task. Many high schools have programs that require students to perform community service, so you may already have teens volunteering at your library. Sometimes a parent is compelling a teen to volunteer and sometimes this works well; but sometimes the teen is just not suited to the organizational culture of a library. Interview the teens just like you would the adults who want to volunteer, to see where they would be the best fit.

Helping at Storytime

For storytime, teens can help as ushers, and setup and cleanup the craft tables. Teens can also do any preparation for the crafts, like cutting out the eye holes in masks. Teen volunteers are usually available for evening and weekend storytimes, but what about morning or early afternoon storytimes? It is more likely a retired person will be able to volunteer at those times.

It may be more difficult to schedule teens to volunteer during the school day, but check with your local high school. Some students may have independent study projects that allow them a more flexible schedule. Also, during winter and spring breaks, and summer vacation, teens will be out of school and willing to help at morning storytimes. Teens know that volunteer service looks good on their college applications, so they are eager to find interesting and challenging volunteer work. Many may be thinking about become teachers or librarians, and may want to volunteer to get experience.

Can teens be trained to be volunteer readers? Of course! Many of them will remember going to storytime at the library, and enjoy working with younger children. With training, older high school students can become a great resource as story readers, and can do outreach storytimes in their neighborhoods. Many teens are bilingual, and can read in both English and another language; if that is a need at some local preschools and day-care centers, a teen volunteer could be the perfect person for that volunteer job!

Reading Buddies

Some libraries already have a Saturday morning reading time, or afterschool reading time, where high school volunteers read to young children at the public library. Some of these programs are called Reading Buddies, but you can come up with a catchier name if you like! Usually these programs are relatively informal, where the young children just drop in for reading time. The volunteers are trained and scheduled of course, but Reading Buddies is not as formally structured as your regular preschool storytime. At Reading Buddies, usually the teen reads with a child one-on-one. Sometimes you will have kindergarten and first graders come to Reading Buddies, to practice reading out loud to the teen volunteer, who is available to assist with words the child cannot sound out yet. It isn't really tutoring, but a more relaxed, casual reading time where a child is in a safe environment with a teen who can help with new vocabulary and make reading fun. You can add arts and crafts projects, too, to follow up the books that have been read, so it really becomes a fun event.

The Reading Buddies volunteers will need some basic training in read-aloud techniques, such as how to hold the book so the children can see the illustrations. Let the teens know that it is fine if a child asks questions, or if you ask the child simple questions about the book, so that some dialogic reading skills are taking place. You may want to go over things like being a role model, and a dress code, since the Reading Buddies represent the library, and the parents will want the teens to be a good influence on the children. You also want the teens to have some accountability, so they should wear nametags, and sign in and out like at a regular job. You should spell out some procedural issues, like finding the parent if a child needs the restroom, and not to take a child to the restroom yourself.

You should choose both picture books and easy readers for the Reading Buddies to use, to make sure they are for the target audience. Some picture books will be too long and are better to read at home, or in class. You probably want some of the simpler easy readers, too. The Reading Buddies can help choose books but you or another children's staff member should approve them all. Some picture books address issues like divorce, violence, or other social issues that are not appropriate for the Reading Buddies setting but better for the parent to read.

I often grouped books into theme boxes, with at least three different picture books and one easy reader on the theme, along with a very simple craft project or coloring sheet. The themes were often seasonal: in May we would have a Mother's Day theme, Cinco de Mayo theme, Spring, and flowers.

Reading Buddies can be a program that takes place just once a month or every week, depending on how many reliable volunteers you can schedule. You don't want it to conflict with other library programs; if you have a magic show scheduled for a Saturday morning, you don't want to have the Reading Buddies compete for the same audience. Some libraries have enough teen volunteers to have Reading Buddies after school on a daily basis; some will just have it once a month on a weekend. Find what your community need is, and see what seems practical. You don't want to schedule Reading Buddies and have no teen volunteers show up; that would create a negative impression on the library and really disappoint the children who came for the program.

RESOURCES ON USING VOLUNTEERS

One of the first resources you need to access is your governing body's policy on using volunteers. Your city or county may have a volunteer coordinator, check with Personnel or Human Resources. They are likely to have a procedure for screening volunteers, such as fingerprinting volunteers who work with children. They may also have forms to fill out and other paperwork so volunteers are covered in case of an accident. Once you know how to process volunteers, you can recruit them by contacting senior centers, sending press releases to the local newspapers, and notifying local high schools that you take volunteers. You will want to have some training for your volunteers, which could include a tour of the library, an outline of what their duties are, a printed schedule of when they work, timesheets, dress code, and any employee rules they should follow. Below are a few other sources on working with volunteers:

BOOKS ON USING VOLUNTEERS IN THE LIBRARY

Driggers, Preston and Eileen Dumas. *Managing Library Volunteers: ALA Guides for the Busy Librarian—Second Edition* (American Library Association, 2011).
Gillespie, Kellie M. *Teen Volunteer Services in Libraries: A VOYA Guide from Voice of Youth Advocates* (VOYA Books, 2004).

WEBSITES ON LIBRARY VOLUNTEERS

Reach Out and Read
www.reachoutandread.com
Reach Out and Read was developed in 1989 by two doctors in Boston. Doctors and other healthcare practitioners encourage parents to read aloud to their young children, distribute free children's books, and create literacy-rich environments in their waiting rooms.

1,000 Books before Kindergarten

www.cde.state.co.us/cdelib/LibraryDevelopment/YouthServices/1000Books.htm
For more on starting this program, check out the materials offered by its originator Sandy
Krost of the Bremen Public Library, Indiana.

Let 1,000 Books Bloom

www.pinterest.com/lochwouters/let-1000-books-bloom/
Another great resource for starting a 1,000 Books before Kindergarten is this Pinterest site
maintained by librarian Marge Loch-Wouters of La Crosse, Wisconsin.

Intermountain Therapy Animals

www.therapyanimals.org
Therapy Animals is the organization that promotes the use of animals for several different therapy causes, including literacy. The site includes lots of helpful information
including a training guide.

Youth Service America

http://ysa.org/
Youth Service America is a nonprofit organization dedicated to helping youth contribute
volunteer service. Their website has great tip sheets on working with teen volunteers,
and information on grants and other partnerships.

CONCLUSION

As you have read through our *Crash Course on Storytime Fundamentals*, we have
tried to build on basic storytime outlines and procedures. You may be taking over a storytime schedule already in place, or just starting one storytime per week. If you are starting
storytimes at a library that has not had them for a while, you may want to assess the community need, and then choose your target age group. Maybe a toddler time will draw the
most people, or perhaps a preschool storytime is more important due to the kindergarten
readiness element. Start small, then add more songs, or add some new elements like puppets once you are comfortable. As we said at the very beginning, one of the best ways to
familiarize yourself with storytime if you have never done it before, is to observe one at a
neighboring library. Of course, there is not "one best way" to do storytime; you have to do
what is comfortable for you. But once you have done it for a few weeks, you are likely to
find it is one of the most enjoyable parts of your work week! So take the plunge, and jump
into storytime!

APPENDIX

Themed Preschool Storytime Outlines

In this section, there are outlines for 100 preschool storytimes (arranged alphabetically); enough to last you a two years if you do storytime once a week! Books and craft ideas are listed, with an occasional song or app that fits the topic. But remember, you don't need to change the songs every week; it is actually a plus to repeat songs. Many of the craft ideas will have Web links, but of course with the Web, these links may have expired by the time you read this.

Even though these themed storytimes are aimed at preschoolers, you can easily adapt them for a toddler storytime. I list more than the average four or five books you might do at a storytime; some of the books I list will work for toddlers. I also list several books per topic since no library will own all the books, giving you plenty of choices. As always, you want to read each book to yourself before presenting it at storytime, so you can decide if it is good for your audience.

Besides the themes listed here, check out the websites mentioned at the end of the chapter on preschool storytime. Many of those websites list hundreds of preschool storytime themes! Also, you may want to write in other new books that fit the themes listed here, and update these outlines with other books you have at your library. You may also find it beneficial to keep a file of past craft projects, since you can repeat those from year to year as you welcome new preschoolers to your storytimes.

Themes by Topic

Animals:

Alligators and Crocodiles
Ants
Bees
Birds
Butterflies
Cats
Chickens
Crickets
Dinosaurs
Dogs
Dragons
Fleas
Flies
Foxes
Frogs
Hamsters and Gerbils
Horses
Ladybugs
Lizards
Penguins
Pets
Snakes
Turtles and Tortoises
Zoos

Everyday Things:

Beach
Bedtime
Camping
Circus
Cooking
Days of the Week
Hats
Helping
Houses and Homes
Names
Noises
Pizza
Potatoes
Strawberries
Telephones
Treehouses

Multicultural:

Africa
Alaska
Australia
Canada
Caribbean
China
Hawaii
India
Japan
Mexico
South America
United Kingdom

People:

Astronauts
Baby
Crime Fighters
Firefighters
Knights
Magicians
Mail Carriers
Monsters
Mother Goose
Pirates
Prince and Princess
Queens and Kings

Science:

Body Parts
Bubbles
Building and Construction
Chemistry
Colors
Eggs
Five Senses
Gardening
Grossology
Habitats
Healthy Eating
Hibernation
Leaves and Trees

Math
Migration
Movement
Music
Ocean Life
Outer Space
Photosynthesis
Rain
Shadows
Shapes
Snow
Solve It
Sun and Moon
Teeth

Wind
Weather

Special Days:

Birthdays
Earth Day
Father's Day
Fourth of July
Halloween
Mother's Day
Thanksgiving
Valentine's Day
Weddings

AFRICA

Aardema, Verna. *Bringing the Rain to Kapiti Plain.*
In this cumulative tale, a boy shoots an arrow into the clouds to start the rain.

Aardema, Verna. *Why Mosquitoes Buzz in People's Ears.*
Animal sound effects will inspire the audience to participate in this folktale about gossip.

Feelings, Tom and Muriel. *Moja Means One.*
A counting book that celebrates Swahili.

Isadora, Rachel. *Old Mikamba Had a Farm.*
This take-off on "Old MacDonald" features an African game preserve and the various
    animals there.

Joosse, Barbara. *Papa Do You Love Me?*
A Masai father reassures his young son that he loves him.

Knight, Margy Burns. *Africa Is Not a Country.*
In this factual picture book, listeners will learn that Africa has a variety of people, coun-
    tries, and habitats.

Lexau, Joan. *Crocodile and Hen.*
Hen reminds crocodile they are cousins, because they both lay eggs. It can be easily adapted
    into a puppet show.

MacDonald, Margaret Read. *Give Up Gecko! A Folktale from Uganda.*
In this cumulative tale, various animals try to stomp on the ground to create a pool of water.

MacDonald, Margaret Read. *Mabela the Clever.*
A mouse uses all her senses to outwit a cat, in this story with repetition that engages
    listeners.

McDermott, Gerald. *Zomo the Rabbit.*
A Nigerian folktale about the trickster rabbit that must perform three acts to gain wisdom.

Craft: Make a drum using two paper cups, gluing the two bottoms together. Cover the two open ends and the outsides with small lengths of beige masking tape. Dab brown shoe polish on the masking tape to give the whole thing the look of wood. Draw designs on the sides of the drum.

App: *Simms Taback Children's Book Collection.* CJ Educations.

ALASKA

Brown, Tricia. *Charlie and the Blanket Toss.*
Charlie wants to participate in the annual Inupiat blanket toss, but he is afraid.

George, Jean Craighead. *Snow Bear.*
Bessie finds a baby polar bear while exploring the tundra.

Gerber, Carole. *Arctic Dreams.*
A mother lulls her child to sleep by describing the Arctic animals.

Joosse, Barbara M. *Mama, Do You Love Me?*
A mother in the Arctic describes how much she loves her daughter.

Kroll, Virginia. *The Seasons and Someone.*
A girl witnesses the changing seasons in Alaska.

Rogers, Jean. *Runaway Mittens.*
Pica loses his mittens, about the same time his dog is having puppies.

Scott, Ann Herbert. *On Mother's Lap.*
Showing an Inuit mother and her toddler and baby, listeners will rock back and forth during this story of sibling rivalry.

Craft: Have the children trace their hands on red construction paper, and cut out the tracings to make red mittens. Tape each of the mittens to the ends of a string or piece of yarn, and the children can wear the mittens around their necks.

ALLIGATORS AND CROCODILES

Aliki. *Use Your Head, Dear.*
Charles the alligator forgets to do his chores, makes a mess, and his mother reminds him repeatedly to "Use your head, dear."

Berkes, Marianne Collins. *The Swamp Where Gator Hides.*
In this cumulative rhyming book, listeners will learn the various animals in the Florida Everglades.

Christelow, Eileen. *Five Little Monkeys Sitting in a Tree.*
The fingerplay done as a picture book, where the monkeys tease an alligator.

Galdone, Paul. *The Monkey and the Crocodile.*
In this brief folktale from India, a croc tries to trick a monkey into being his dinner.

Gomi, Taro. *The Crocodile and the Dentist.*
Both the dentist and his croc patient are afraid in this brief, repetitive text that humorously reminds kids to brush their teeth.

Gralley, Jean. *Very Boring Alligator.*
A little red haired girl can't get the alligator to leave in this delightful rhythmic story, with lots of repetition.

Hurd, Thacher. *Mama Don't Allow.*
Miles and his band play at the Alligator Ball in this Reading Rainbow selection.

Lionni, Leo. *Cornelius.*
A croc is hatched from an egg, and walks upright.

Wilson, Karma. *A Frog in a Bog.*
A frog grows larger and larger until he attracts the attention of an alligator.

Yoon, Salina. *Do Crocs Kiss?*
In this book with flaps, various animals are shown with their mouths open, to demonstrate the sounds they make.

Craft: Make a simple alligator paper bag puppet.
Song: "Five Little Monkeys Swinging in a Tree."
App: *Alphabet Animals: A Slide-and-Peek Adventure.* Auryn.

ANTS

Climo, Shirley. *The Little Red Ant and the Great Big Crumb.*
In this Mexican fable, an ant thinks he needs help lifting a crumb of cake, so he asks various animals to assist him.

Edwards, Pamela Duncan. *The Wacky Wedding: A Book of Alphabet Antics.*
At the wedding of two ants, various animals in attendance experience several accidents at the reception.

Emberley, Rebecca. *The Ant and the Grasshopper.*
In this colorful variation on the Aesop's fable, an ant works to the sound of grasshopper's band.

Heap, Sue. *Ants in Your Pants.*
In this rhyming counting book with flaps, ants in pants end the simple story.

Ketteman, Helen. *There Once Was a Cowpoke Who Swallowed an Ant.*
In this cumulative tale based on "There Was an Old Woman Who Swallowed a Fly," a cowboy swallows various critters to find the ant he has swallowed.

McDonald, Megan. *Ant and Honeybee—What a Pair.*
Ant and Bee dress up for a costume party.

Mizumura, Kazue. *The Way of an Ant.*
An ant tries to climb a hill as high as the sky.

Nickle, John. *The Ant Bully.*
After squirting ants with his water gun, Lucas shrinks to the size of an ant to feel what it is like to be bullied. This book was made into an animated film in 2006.

Pinczes, Elinor. *One Hundred Hungry Ants*.
While marching to a picnic, the 100 ants form different groups to show readers how to count by tens, or twenties, etc.

Poole, Amy. *The Ant and the Grasshopper*.
This retelling of Aesop's fable is set in China, and tells of a hardworking group of ants who prepare for the winter, while Grasshopper does nothing to get ready.

Prince, Joshua. *I Saw an Ant on the Railroad Track*.
The engineer tries to stop the train before it runs over an ant.

Van Allsburg, Chris. *Two Bad Ants*.
After they venture out on their own, two ants realize they need to return to the safety of the colony.

Wells, Rosemary. *Max's ABC*.
Escaping from the ant farm, Max's ants crawl over everything in this alphabet book.

Craft: Make an egg carton ant, using three sections of the egg carton to reflect the three sections of an ant's body. Add eyes and antenna, and paint or color the egg carton.
Song: "The Ants Go Marching."

ASTRONAUTS

Barton, Byron. *I Want to be an Astronaut*.
Using simple brightly colored paintings, Barton describes what an astronaut does.

Bartram, Simon. *Man on the Moon*.
We see Bob and his typical day out in space as the astronaut who takes care of the moon.

Corwin, Oliver J. *Hare and Tortoise Race to the Moon*.
This fable spin-off features the two friends racing to the moon.

Floca, Brian. *Moonshot: The Flight of Apollo 11*.
A brief narrative and stunning illustrations make this informational book on the Apollo 11 moon landing appropriate for preschool storytime.

Houran, Lori Haskins. *A Trip into Space: An Adventure to the International Space Station*.
In this informational picture book, two astronauts go to the International Space Station.

Jenkins, Steve. *Looking Down*.
Dramatic collages show earth from space.

Johnson, Crockett. *Harold's Trip to the Sky*.
With help from his purple crayon, Harold explores outer space.

Loomis, Christine. *Astro Bunnies*.
In this fun picture book, bunnies take rocket ships and explore space.

Mayo, Margaret. *Zoom, Rocket, Zoom!*
Repeated action verbs and deeply saturated collage art combine for a great story on astronauts and rockets.

Reiser, Lynn. *Earthdance.*
A little girl stars in a school play about the planets. In the story, her mom is away because
she is an astronaut.

Sweeney, Joan. *Me and My Place in Space.*
A child dressed like an astronaut describes outer space and the solar system.

Craft: For a simple craft project, kids can make star collage paintings. Give them dark blue
construction paper, adding star stickers to make the night sky.
Song: "Twinkle, Twinkle, Little Star."

AUSTRALIA

Czernecki, Stefan. *The Singing Snake.*
An Aboriginal folktale with stunning artwork. Snake captures Lark in his throat so he can
win a contest of who has the most beautiful voice.

Fox, Mem. *Possum Magic.*
To break a spell, grandma takes Hush around Australia trying different foods.

Fox, Mem. *Hattie and the Fox.*
Hattie the Hen is on the lookout for the fox, in this story with repetition and animal
noises.

Fox, Mem. *Shoes from Grandpa.*
In this cumulative tale, a little girl receives a variety of clothing for her birthday.

Fox, Mem. *Koala Lou.*
Koala Lou wishes her mother would pay her more attention so she tries to win the Bush
Olympics to get noticed.

Kent, Jack. *Joey.*
Joey the Kangaroo is outgrowing his mother's pouch.

Larranaga, Ana Martin. *Big Wide-Mouth Frog.*
In this version of the traditional tale, the frog meets a kangaroo, possum, koala, and emu
to find out what they eat.

Morpurgo, Michael. *Wombat Goes Walkabout.*
While searching for his mother, Wombat meets several other animals in this tale with
repeated phrases.

Murphy, Stuart J. *Jump Kangaroo Jump.*
Kangaroo and his friends divide into teams for the Field Day in this simple math
story.

Paterson, A.B. *Waltzing Matilda.*
A picture book version of the popular Australian song.

Ungerer, Tomi. *Adelaide.*
Adelaide the kangaroo has wings so she sets off to see the world.

Vaughan, Marcia. *Wombat Stew.*
A spoof of "Stone Soup," this energetic rhyming story stars a dingo who tries to get the other animals to help him make Wombat Stew.

Craft: Make paper boomerangs, or kangaroo paper bag puppets.
Song: "Waltzing Matilda."

BABY

Aliki. *Hush Little Baby.*
The traditional nursery song.

Blackstone, Stella. *Baby Rock, Baby Roll.*
Three babies run, sing, dance, and play in this rhythmic story. Also read *Baby High, Baby Low.*

Charlip, Remy. *Sleepytime Rhyme.*
Purple-hued illustrations and a brief rhyming text combine for a delightful bedtime story.

Cooke, Trish. *So Much.*
Told in a Jamaican cadence, a diverse family embraces the baby.

Gibson, Ginger F. *Tiptoe Joe.*
In this participation story, Joe encourages the other animals to follow him so he can show them a surprise.

Henkes, Kevin. *Julius, the Baby of the World.*
Lilly is annoyed at her baby brother, but defends him when cousin Garland teases him.

Hest, Amy. *The Babies Are Coming!*
One dozen babies prepare to come to lapsit storytime at the library.

Ho, Minfong. *Hush: A Thai Lullaby.*
Children will join in the repeated "Hush," and laugh at the animal noises in this charming book.

Hutchins, Pat. *Where's the Baby?*
The monster family looks for baby brother, following the muddy footprints.

Mahy, Margaret. *Boom, Baby, Boom, Boom!*
Baby drums on all kinds of things in the kitchen.

Meyers, Susan. *Everywhere Babies.*
A rhyming story showing a wide diversity of parents and babies.

Root, Phyllis. *What Baby Wants.*
Different family members try to make Baby stop crying.

Scott, Ann Herbert. *On Mother's Lap.*
Showing an Inuit mother and her toddler and baby, listeners will rock back and forth during this story of sibling rivalry.

Shields, Carol Diggory. *Baby's Got the Blues.*
The audience will repeat the title phrase in this joyous look at what a baby has to deal with
 on a day-to-day basis.

Craft: Distribute muslin squares for children to decorate with markers, as mini-quilts.
Song: "Hush, Little Baby."
App: *Hello, Baby Animals!* Shortstack.

BEACH

Bridwell, Norman. *The Missing Beach Ball.*
Clifford, Cleo, and T-Bone go to the beach, but their beach ball is washed away by a
 big wave.

Brown, Marc. *D. W. All Wet.*
D.W. is afraid of the water.

Cash, Megan M. *I Saw the Sea and the Sea Saw Me.*
A girl uses her five senses to experience the sea.

Coplans, Peta. *Cat and Dog.*
In this fun counting story, Dog and Cat picnic at the beach.

Cottle, Joan. *Miles Away From Home.*
Miles has a great vacation at the beach.

Daly, Niki. *The Boy on the Beach.*
One of the few beach stories with an African child, set in South Africa. A boy is lost at the
 beach but the lifeguard gets him an ice cream and finds his parents.

Ehrlich, H. M. *Louie's Goose.*
Louie's stuffed animal goose gets tattered after a day at the beach.

Enderle, Judith Ross. *Six Sandy Sheep.*
The six sheep surf, sail, scuba, search for seashells, and do other beach activities.

Hill, Eric. *Spot Goes to the Beach.*
Spot and his Dad go to the beach.

Hubbell, Patricia. *Sea, Sand, and Me!*
A young girl does a variety of activities at the seashore, including making sandcastles.

Karas, Brian. *Atlantic.*
Dramatic illustrations depict the Atlantic Ocean in this simple nonfiction book.

Levine, Evan. *Not the Piano, Mrs. Medley!*
Mrs. Medley is loaded down with items to take to the beach.

Mathers, Petra. *Lottie's New Beach Towel.*
Lottie, the chicken, thinks of several ingenious uses for her beach towel.

Rey, H. A. *Curious George Goes to the Beach.*
The mischievous monkey feeds the seagulls and rescues a picnic basket.

Ryan, Pam Munoz. *Hello, Ocean.*
A story about using your five senses to experience the ocean, featuring a rhyming text.

Yamashita, Haruo. *Mice at the Beach.*
Dad saves the day when one of his mice children is stuck out on a sandbar after the tide has come in.

Yektai, Niki. *Bears at the Beach: Counting 10 to 20.*
Not a story but a fun counting exercise.

Craft: A simple craft can be done with sand paintings. Buy colored sand from an art supply story, or color sand from a gardening shop. Drizzle white glue on thick paper, and then dust with the colored sand.

BEDTIME

Arnold, Tedd. *No Jumping on the Bed.*
Even though he has been warned not to, Walter jumps on his bed and falls through to the apartments below him. Was he dreaming?

Asch, Frank. *Milk and Cookies.*
Baby Bear dreams he fed milk and cookies to a dragon while at Grandfather's house.

Browne, Anthony. *Willy the Dreamer.*
Willy dreams he is a movie star, rock star, wrestler, explorer, and other careers.

Chapman, Jan. *I'm Not Sleepy!*
A little owl insists he is not sleepy, even though daytime has come which means it is time for him to go to bed.

Fox, Mem. *Time for Bed.*
Animal parents try to get their babies to go to sleep.

Fox, Mem. *A Bedtime Story.*
Polly needs help reading a bedtime story, so she has to convince her parents to stop reading their own books to read to her.

Ho, Minfong. *Hush: A Thai Lullaby.*
Animal sounds and repetition make this a great choice for toddler and preschool storytime.

Jewel. *Sweet Dreams.*
A star-scattered sky illustrates this lyrical lullaby.

Meadows, Michelle. *Piggies in Pajamas.*
A rhyming text and joyous cartoon illustrations show a passel of pigs who try to stay up later than their bedtime.

Wood, Audrey. *Sweet Dream Pie.*
The Brindles make Sweet Dream Pie from a secret recipe, which causes everyone in town who eats it to have fantastic dreams!

Ziefert, Harriet. *It's Time to Say Good Night.*
In this circular story, a boy greets each thing he sees at the start of his day, then says good
    night to each as it gets dark.

Craft: Make door hangers that say "Quiet, I'm Reading."
App: *Sandra Boynton Collection.* Loud Crow.

BEES

Carle, Eric. *The Honeybee and the Robber.*
A popup book with tabs and other moveable elements, about a bee defending the hive from
    a bear out to steal the honey.

Ernst, Lisa Campbell. *A Colorful Adventure of the Bee Who Left Home One Monday Morn-
    ing . . .*
A concept book about colors.

High, Linda Oatman. *Beekeepers.*
A girl helps her grandfather who is a beekeeper.

Huber, Raymond. *Flight of the Honeybee.*
In this informational picture book, honey bee Scout goes looking for food.

McDonald, Megan. *Ant and Honeybee—What a Pair!*
The two insects choose costumes for a party, with unfortunate results.

Lobel, Arnold. *The Rose in My Garden.*
A cumulative story about a bee, a snail, and other creatures on the rose in the garden.

Smallman, Steve. *The Very Greedy Bee.*
Lots of sound effects are included in this amusing story of a bee that eats too much nectar.

Wong, Janet S. *Buzz.*
A young boy hears a buzzing bee outside his window one morning, then hears all the other
    things that buzz like dad's shaver, the juicer, the garage door opener, etc.

Yorinks, Arthur. *Happy Bees.*
With great rhymes, we hear about the easy life of the bee.

Craft: Make a bumblebee paper plate craft by coloring a plate with yellow and black
    stripes, then adding eyes and wings made out of wax paper.
Song: "I'm Bringing Home a Baby Bumblebee."

BIRDS

Baker, Keith. *Little Green.*
A young boy paints a picture of the hummingbird outside his window.

Dunbar, Joyce. *Baby Bird.*
A bird learning to fly falls out of his nest, and meets several other animals.

Ehlert, Lois. *Feathers for Lunch.*
Will the cat catch the birds to have for his dinner?

Freschet, Berniece. *Owl in the Garden.*
Children will make the bird sounds depicted in this story about a blue jay.

Gray, Rita. *Have You Heard the Nesting Bird?*
Short rhyming verses depict the sounds made by birds in this factual tale.

Henkes, Kevin. *Birds.*
This story incorporates the concepts of color, shape, size, and numbers into the tale of a bird outside a child's window.

Hutchins, Pat. *Good Night, Owl!*
There are lots of bird sounds for the audience to chant in this funny story about an owl trying to sleep.

Kent, Jack. *Round Robin.*
Robin is so fat he has to hop south for the winter, instead of flying. A funny book on migration.

Massie, Diane. *The Baby Beebee Bird.*
A new bird at the zoo keeps everyone awake in this participation story.

Stockdale, Susan. *Bring on the Birds.*
In this informational picture book, various birds are described in a rhyming text.

Sturgis, Brenda Reeves. *The Lake Where Loon Lives.*
In this cumulative story, various animals that live in Maine's lakes are described.

Waddell, Martin. *Owl Babies.*
With repetition that will get the audience participating, this sweet story focuses on Sarah, Percy, and Bill, owl siblings who are waiting for their mother to return with food.

Craft: An easy "Owl" paper bag puppet can also teach kids about basic shapes. Cut out circles for eyes, a triangle for the beak, and rectangles for the wings, and glue to a paper lunch bag.

App: *Don't Let the Pigeon Run This App.* Disney.

BIRTHDAYS

Elya, Susan M. *F is for Fiesta.*
Rhyming verse describes various items used at a birthday party, using both English and Spanish words.

Flack, Marjorie. *Ask Mr. Bear.*
Danny asks several animals what they could give him as a present for his mother—the audience can participate by making the sounds of each animal.

Gorbachev, Valeri. *Nicky and the Fantastic Birthday Gifts.*
Nicky creates an imaginative picture for his mother's birthday.

Harper, Charise M. *The Best Birthday Ever! By Me (Lana Kittie).*
A little kitten demonstrates how to be a gracious host at one's birthday party in this very funny book with bright cartoon illustrations.

Hill, Eric. *Spot's Birthday Party.*
Toddlers will enjoy guessing who is under the various flaps, looking for the birthday party guests.

Hurd, Thacher. *Little Mouse's Birthday Cake.*
Thinking his friends have forgotten him, Little Mouse goes skiing by himself on his birthday.

Hutchins, Pat. *Happy Birthday, Sam!*
Sam solves several problems on his birthday.

Jocelyn, Marthe. *Hannah and the Seven Dresses.*
Hannah can't decide what to wear on her birthday.

Keats, Ezra Jack. *A Letter to Amy.*
Peter invites Amy to his birthday party.

Khan, Rukhsana. *Big Red Lollipop.*
Rubina can't convince her mother that her little sister should not come to a friend's birthday party.

Kulka, Joe. *Wolf's Coming!*
All the animals in the forest hide from the wolf, but not because they are afraid.

Machado, Ana Maria. *What a Party!*
Invited to bring guests and food, a birthday party becomes chaotic in this funny multicultural story.

Mora, Pat. *Uno, Dos, Tres = One, Two Three.*
A very brief rhyming text using a few Spanish words tells the story of two sisters looking for a gift for their mother.

Rockwell, Anne. *Hugo at the Window.*
A dog looks out his window at his friends at various shops on the street—what are they buying?

Watanabe, Shigeo. *It's My Birthday.*
A little bear celebrates his fourth birthday with his family in this very brief story.

Watt, Melanie. *Scaredy Squirrel Has a Birthday Party.*
Scaredy Squirrel plans his own birthday party.

Craft: Make simple party hats.
Song: "Happy Birthday."
App: *Together Time with Song and Rhyme for Parent and Preschooler.* Mulberry Media Interactive Inc.

BODY PARTS

Arnold, Tedd. *Parts.*
A boy is afraid he is falling apart when he loses a tooth.

Bauer, Marion Dane. *Thank You for Me!*
A celebration of what our body can do, from hands that clap to a body that twirls.

Carle, Eric. *From Head to Toe.*
Children will want to move along with the animals in this call and response story.

Cummings, Phil. *Goodness, Gracious!*
A child imagines situations with pirates, witches, and others to name the parts of the body.

Davick, Linda. *I Love You, Nose! I Love You, Toes!*
A toddler's body parts are celebrated in this rhyming story.

Fox, Mem. *Ten Little Fingers and Ten Little Toes.*
A rhyming book filled with multicultural babies.

Hindley, Judy. *Eyes, Nose, Fingers and Toes.*
Cartoon toddlers show the parts of the body.

Martin, Bill. *Here Are My Hands.*
A brief but lively rhyming story about the parts of the body.

Rotner, Shelley. *The Body Book.*
Photographs and a simple text describe the parts of the body.

Craft: Have kids trace their hands, or make paper plate masks of their own faces.
Song: "Head and Shoulders," and "The Hokey Pokey."

BUBBLES

Anderson, Peggy. *To the Tub.*
In this sequel to *Time for Bed, the Babysitter Said,* Froggie won't take his bath.

Birdseye. Tom. *Soap! Soap! Don't Forget the Soap!*
In this Appalachian folktale, a boy is sent to the store to buy soap but he is very forgetful.

Brown, Margaret Wise. *The Dirty Little Boy.*
A newly illustrated version of the story about a little boy who copies the bathing practices of different animals.

DePaola, Tomie. *Strega Nona Takes a Vacation.*
Strega Nona sends home candy and bubble bath while on vacation, and Big Anthony gets stuck with too many bubbles!

Inkpen, Mick. *Thing!*
Kipper finds a gadget that blows bubbles.

Kudrna, C. I. *To Bathe a Boa.*
It's a struggle to bathe any pet, especially a boa constrictor.

Sutherland, Harry. *Dad's Car Wash.*
Dad makes bath time fun when he pretends it is a carwash for kids.

Woodruff, Elvira. *Show and Tell.*
Andy brings magic bubbles for show and tell.

Woodruff, Elvira. *Tubtime.*
Two sisters share an unusual bubble bath full of animals.

Ziefert, Harriet. *No Bath Tonight!*
A little boy stalls at bath time by wondering if various animals are hiding in the tub.

Craft: Using watercolor paints mixed with some bubble solution, let the kids make bubble paintings.

BUILDING AND CONSTRUCTION

Ashburn, Boni. *The Fort That Jack Built.*
In this take-off on the cumulative tale "The House that Jack Built," a little boy builds a pillow fort in the living room.

Banks, Kate. *Night Worker.*
Alex says goodnight as his father goes off to work as a nighttime construction worker.

Barton, Byron. *Building a House.*
In a clear and simple way, Barton shows the various people needed to build a house, including a plumber, carpenter, electrician, roofer, mason, painter, and more!

Barton, Byron. *Machines at Work.*
A general construction machinery book.

Bean, Jonathan. *Building Our House.*
The details of how a house is built are described through the experience of one family.

Hale, Christy. *Dreaming Up: A Celebration of Building.*
Children's play emulates how buildings are designed in this poetic look at architecture.

Horvath, James. *Build, Dogs, Build: A Tall Tail.*
A construction crew made up of dogs must tear down an old building, then construct a new apartment building in this rhyming story.

Merriam, Eve. *Bam Bam Bam.*
Rhyming text with onomatopoeia describe the process of building a skyscraper.

Morris, Ann. *Tools.*
Color photos from around the world depict how various occupations use a variety of tools.

Rockwell, Anne. *The Toolbox.*
A story about Dad's tools on his workbench.

Shulman, Lisa. *Old MacDonald Had a Woodshop.*
A sheep builds a farm in this cumulative story.

Various. *The Three Little Pigs.*
Even toddlers know which house is built to last in this classic.

Craft: Put out Duplo blocks for a free building activity.

BUTTERFLIES

Brawley, Helen. *Percival the Plain Little Caterpillar.*
A book about colors that has a great story about how a caterpillar becomes a butterfly.

Carle, Eric. *The Very Hungry Caterpillar.*
Listeners will chant the days of the week, the food items, and the repeated "but he was still
hungry!" when reading this storytime classic.

Edwards, Pamela Duncan. *Clara Caterpillar.*
An unusual story about a cream-colored, plain butterfly, who finds out she is just as good
as the colorful butterflies.

Horacek, Petr. *Butterfly, Butterfly.*
Lucy's garden is full of various insects, including butterflies.

Jarrett, Clare. *Arabella Miller's Tiny Caterpillar.*
Arabella feeds a caterpillar and watches while it becomes a chrysalis and then a butterfly.

Kroll, Virginia. *Butterfly Boy.*
Set in Mexico, a boy and his grandfather look for butterflies.

Martin, Bill. *Ten Little Caterpillars.*
Various types of butterflies are featured in the rhythmic counting book.

Millbourne, Anna. *The Butterfly.*
Lovely soft watercolors illustrate this very simple look at a butterfly's life cycle.

Swope, Sam. *Gotta Go! Gotta Go!*
A little caterpillar knows she needs to get to Mexico, but doesn't know that she is going to
become a Monarch Butterfly.

Tarbett, Debbie. *Ten Wriggly, Wiggly Caterpillars.*
Pop-ups and 3-D elements highlight this counting book.

Craft: Make a butterfly from a coffee filter. Use watercolor paints to decorate the coffee
filter (the filter paper causes the paint to run and look beautiful). Then, use a pipe
cleaner to cinch the coffee filter in the middle to form the wings, and curl the ends of
the pipe cleaner to form antennae.
App: *Very Hungry Caterpillar and Friends: Play and Explore.* StoryToy.

CAMPING

Brown, Marc. *Arthur Goes to Camp.*
Arthur is afraid of many things at camp, including the mysterious things that start to occur.

Carlson, Nancy. *Arnie Goes to Camp.*
Arnie is hesitant about sleepaway camp, but it turns out to be a lot of fun!

Christelow, Eileen. *Jerome Camps Out.*
Jerome is looking forward to the school camping trip, even though the class bully is
coming, too.

Cousins, Lucy. *Maisy Goes Camping.*
Maisy the mouse and her friends take a camping trip.

Giff, Patricia. *Ronald Morgan Goes to Camp.*
Ronald is not very good at sports, but wants to earn a camp medal.

Henkes, Kevin. *Bailey Goes Camping.*
Bailey the bunny is too little to go camping, so he makes his own campout at home.

Marshall, James. *The Cut-Ups at Camp Custer.*
Spud and Joe are out to catch the practical joker at summer camp.

McPhail, David. *Pig Pig Goes to Camp.*
Pig Pig is not excited about going to summer camp, but has a great time once he gets there.

Parr, Todd. *Otto Goes to Camp.*
Everyone thinks Otto brings too many unnecessary things to camp, but one item turns out
    to be surprisingly useful.

Raffi. *Shake My Sillies Out.*
This Raffi song is set at a summer camp.

Seligson, Susan. *Amos Camps Out.*
Amos the dog brings his motorized couch to camp.

Longstreth, Galen Goodwin. *Yes, Let's.*
A rhyming text describes a family hike through the woods.

Watt, Melanie. *Scaredy Squirrel Goes Camping.*
Scaredy Squirrel doesn't like camping but learns to appreciate the outdoors when he goes
    hiking, looking for an electrical outlet for his television.

Wolff, Ashley. *Stella and Roy Go Camping.*
Siblings find evidence of a bear near their campsite.

Crafts: Make binoculars out of toilet tissue cardboard rolls. Tape the rolls together, and
    use a string or piece of yarn to hang the "binoculars" around your neck. Decorate
    with markers or colored paper.
Songs: "A-Camping We Will Go."

CANADA

Andrews, Jan. *Very Last First Time.*
A girl learns the traditional method of finding mussels under the ice when the tide goes out.

Arnosky, Jim. *Beaver Pond, Moose Pond.*
A realistic story of a beaver pond that is inhabited by other forest animals.

Carrier, Roch. *The Hockey Sweater.*
This longer picture book is better suited to school-age children. It tells the true story of a
    boy who receives a sweater celebrating the hockey team that is the rival of his favor-
    ites, and he is forced to wear it.

Numeroff, Laura. *If You Give a Moose a Muffin.*
Another of Numeroff's circular stories, this one stars a moose.

Perkins, Lynne Rae. *Pictures from Our Vacation.*
A little girl takes photos of the trip to the family farm in Canada.

Root, Phyllis. *Looking for a Moose.*
In a takeoff on "We're Going on a Bear Hunt," four children go looking for a moose.

Stafford, Liliana. *The Snow Bear.*
Beautifully illustrated story of a polar bear.

Trottier, Maxine. *Migrant.*
Anna and her family are migrant workers from Mexico, working in Canada to harvest fruits and vegetables.

Wood, Douglas. *Rabbit and the Moon.*
Adapted from a Cree legend, a crane flies a rabbit to the moon.

Craft: Make paper moose antlers attached to paper headbands.

CARIBBEAN

Adoff, Arnold. *Flamboyan.*
Set in Puerto Rico, this longer rhyming picture book features a girl who can fly.

Carlstrom, Nancy. *Baby-O.*
In this cumulative story, a family takes their wares to market. The storytime listeners will call out the repeated phrases.

Faustin, Charles. *A Caribbean Counting Book.*
Deeply saturated colors illustrate this collection of counting rhymes from several Caribbean countries.

Garne, T. S. *One While Sail.*
The numbers one through 10 are demonstrated with island items such as a sail, clouds, or boats, with folk art-style paintings and a rhyming text.

Gershator, Phillis. *Kallaloo!*
A West Indian version of "Stone Soup," in which a shell is used to start the pot of soup.

Gershator, Phillis. *Rata-Pata-Scata-Fata.*
Torn paper collages illustrate this tale of a boy in St. Thomas, who repeats the title phrase whenever his mother asks him to help with a chore.

Gershator, Phillis. *Sweet, Sweet Fig Banana.*
Set in Haiti, a young boy grows a banana tree.

Isadora, Rachel. *A Caribbean Dream.*
Watercolor paintings and a rhyming text show island children swimming, playing, and so forth.

Lessac, Frane. *My Little Island.*
Lessac shows his childhood on the island of Monserrat in this popular Reading Rainbow book.

Marley, Cedella. *Every Little Thing.*
Based on the Bob Marley song "Three Little Birds," a little boy stays positive with the encouragement of the birds.

Trice, Linda. *Kenya's Song.*
Kenya can't decide which is her favorite song that she has learned at the Caribbean Cultural Center.

Williams, Karen Lynn. *Circle of Hope.*
A boy plants a tree and hopes it will grow, in this story set in Haiti.

Craft: Make drums from coffee cans; decorate paper to glue on the sides.

CATS

Allenby, Victoria. *Nat the Cat Can Sleep Like That.*
Nat the cat likes to sleep all day and play all night.

Day, Nancy Raines. *A Cat's Year.*
The first year in a newborn cat's life helps children learn the months of the year.

Dean, James. *Pete the Cat: Wheels on the Bus.*
The traditional song is sung by Pete the Cat and his friends.

Fleming, Denise. *Mama Cat Has Three Kittens.*
Fluffy, Skinny, and Boris follow Mama Cat. Repetition will engage young listeners and the vibrant artwork can be seen from the back row!

Gag, Wanda. *Millions of Cats.*
Listeners will chant along with this classic storytime favorite.

Galdone, Paul. *Cat Goes Fiddle-I-Fee.*
Traditional folksong set on a farm. The repetition will get everyone to sing along!

Harper, Dan. *Telling Time with Big Mama Cat.*
Plastic moveable clock hands help kids learn to tell time as they hear about a cat's daily activities.

Henkes, Kevin. *Kitten's First Full Moon.*
This Caldecott winner concerns a cat who thinks the moon is a bowl of milk.

Keats, Ezra Jack. *Hi, Cat!*
Archie is followed by a stray cat which disrupts things but remains a friend.

Kraus, Robert. *Where Are You Going, Little Mouse?*
Ignored at home, Little Mouse runs away but the cat still can't catch him!

Martin, Bill. *Kitty Cat, Kitty Cat, Are You Going to School?*
In a rhyming question and answer format, this simple story shows a cat going to school.

Mockford, Caroline. *Cleo the Cat.*
The first of several books starring Cleo, an orange cat, featuring a rhyming text.

Ryder, Joanne. *Come Along, Kitten.*
A rhyming story of a dog that takes care of the family's new kitten.

Yolen, Jane. *How Do Dinosaurs Love Their Cats?*
Learn some basic cat care tips from these dinosaurs.

Craft: Make simple masks using paper plates and construction paper ears, whiskers, and other facial features.

Song: "Three Little Kittens Who Lost Their Mittens."

App: *Dr. Seuss Beginner Book Collection #1 and #2.* Oceanhouse Media.

CHEMISTRY

Barton, Chris. *The Day-Glo Brothers.*
In this Sibert Honor book, learn the true story of how Bob and Joe Switzer invented fluorescent paint.

Beech, Linda. *The Magic School Bus Gets Baked In a Cake: A Book about Kitchen Chemistry.*
Ms. Frizzle and her students learn about chemistry.

Katz, Alan. *Stalling.*
Dan stalls bedtime with various activities, including mixing up leftovers to make slime!

Plourde, Lynn. *Science Fair Day.*
Ima asks all the other students what they are doing before working on her own project.

Seuss, Dr. *Bartholomew and the OObleck.*
A green, slimy substance comes to earth—can Bartholomew save everyone from the disaster?

Sierra, Judy. *The Secret Science Project That Almost Ate the School.*
In this rhyming story, a girl sends away for super slime to use for her science project.

Wilson, Karma. *Whopper Cake.*
In this rhyming story, Grandpa makes Grandma an enormous birthday cake.

Craft: Check your science experiment books for instructions on how to clean pennies with vinegar, or how to make "slime" out of clear glue, liquid starch, and food coloring.

CHICKENS

Alborough, Jez. *Six Little Chicks.*
In this story that encourages audience participation, a mother hen looks after her five chicks and one egg.

Allen, Pamela. *Fancy That!*
A hen hatches her eggs to the sound of barnyard noises.

Barton, Byron. *The Little Red Hen.*
The classic repetitive story paired with toddler—friendly bold color illustrations.

Dunbar, Joyce. *Eggday.*
Dora the duck holds a contest to see who can lay the best egg.

Emberley, Rebecca. *Chicken Little.*
Brightly colored collage illustrations are paired with a cumulative text in this classic story
about "the sky is falling!"

Galdone, Paul. *Little Tuppen.*
A little chick needs a sip of water, so his mother keeps trading for different items so she
can bring him a cup of water.

Ginsberg, Mirra. *The Chick and the Duckling.*
Chick imitates everything the Duckling does, but gets into trouble when it is time to go
swimming.

Ginsberg, Mirra. *Good Morning, Chick.*
A little chick falls into a puddle when he tries to imitate a rooster.

Gorbachev, Valeri. *Chickens, Chickens.*
Two chickens visit the playground for the first time where a beaver teaches them how to
go down a slide.

Heller, Ruth. *Chickens Aren't the Only Ones.*
A rhyming science story explaining how snakes, turtles, and other animals lay eggs.

Hutchins, Pat. *Rosie's Walk.*
Rosie is unaware that a fox is following her as she walks around the farm.

Kasza, Keiko. *Wolf's Chicken Stew.*
A hungry wolf tries to trick mother hen into letting him eat the chicks.

Krilanovich, Nadia. *Chicken, Chicken, Duck.*
A group of farm animals play a noisy game.

Pomerantz, Charlotte. *Here Comes Henny.*
A humorous tongue twister where Henny carries a "sack" in which she has a "back pack
packed with snicky-snackies for her picky chickies."

Stoeke, Janet Morgan. *Minerva Louise.*
A hen has fun exploring a house.

Williams, Garth. *The Chicken Book.*
Five little chicks learn that it takes more than wishing to get what they want.

Wormell, Mary. *Hilda Hen's Search.*
A mother hen tries several places before she finds the perfect spot to hatch her eggs.

Craft: Make puffball chicks.
App: *Simms Taback Children's Book Collection.* CJ Educations.

CHINA

Demi. *The Empty Pot.*
Ping learns a lesson in honesty from the emperor in this tale. Have each child plant a seed
in a cup to take home from storytime.

Demi. *Liang and the Magic Paintbrush.*
When a poor boy paints a picture, it comes to life. A Reading Rainbow book.

Hong, Lily. *Two of Everything.*
A farmer and his wife find a magic pot—whatever you put into it doubles.

Thong, Roseanne. *Red Is a Dragon: A Book of Colors.*
A Chinese-American girl uses traditional Chinese items to describe the colors.

Thong, Roseanne. *Round Is a Mooncake: A Book of Shapes.*
A Chinese-American girl uses traditional Chinese items to describe shapes.

Tucker, Kathleen. *Seven Chinese Sisters.*
A dragon kidnaps the baby sister and her older siblings use their magical powers to get her back.

Yi, Hu Yong. *Good Morning China.*
Beautiful paintings show daily life in China, with a simple text describing what a child sees there.

Young, Ed. *Lon Po Po.*
In this variation on Little Red Riding Hood, three sisters outwit the granny wolf who is trying to eat them.

Craft: Make Chinese paper lanterns, as seen here: www.enchantedlearning.com/crafts/chinesenewyear/lantern/

CIRCUS

Bronson, Linda. *The Circus Alphabet.*
Dramatic three-dimensional illustrations depict a circus.

Ehlert, Lois. *Circus.*
Ehlert's signature cut paper collages illustrate this circus of flying zucchini and clowns.

Emberley, Rebecca. *My Mother's Secret Life.*
When mother yells at the messy house "This place looks like a three-ring circus!" it really turns into one!

Falconer, Ian. *Olivia Saves the Circus.*
At show and tell, Olivia describes how she substituted for all the circus performers who were out sick, by flying on a trapeze, and so forth.

Freeman, Don. *Bearymore.*
While hibernating, Bearymore dreams up a new circus act.

Harrison, Hannah. *Extraordinary Jane.*
A little dog with no discernible talent is part of a family of circus dogs.

Peek, Merle. *The Balancing Act: A Counting Song.*
Elephants balance on a tightrope in this subtraction song.

Priceman, Marjorie. *Emeline at the Circus.*
Emeline becomes the star of the circus, unbeknownst to her preoccupied teacher.

Sampson, Michael. *Star of the Circus.*
Sizes are depicted when each circus animal is pushed off the stage by a larger animal.

Schnachner, Judith Byron. *Skippyjon Jones Cirque de Ole.*
Skippyjon the cat wants to perform his high-wire act in the circus.

Slate, Joseph. *Miss Bindergarten Plans a Circus with Kindergarten.*
The popular kindergarten teacher and her 26 alphabetically named students put on a circus at school.

Van Dusen, Chris. *The Circus Ship.*
A rhyming text tells the story of circus animals adopted by islanders off the coast of Maine, after their ship has an accident.

Craft: Make a clown paper plate mask.

COLORS

Austin, Mike. *Monsters Love Colors.*
Playful monsters scribble with their crayons to mix colors.

Baker, Keith. *Little Green Peas: A Big Book of Colors.*
Bouncy rhymes introduce nine different colors.

Barry, Frances. *Duckie's Rainbow.*
With rainbow-shaped pages, this simple story shows readers the colors of the rainbow.

Beaumont, Karen. *I Ain't Gonna Paint No More*
Exploding with energy, a little girl paints every space in her house; told to the tune of "It Ain't Gonna Rain No More."

Cabrera, Jane. *Cat's Colors.*
A cat describes 10 colors and tells which is his favorite.

Crews, Donald. *Freight Train*
Very simple book about colors, using train cars as examples.

Ehlert, Lois. *Planting a Rainbow.*
Flowers demonstrate the colors.

Emberley, Ed. *Go Away, Big Green Monster.*
Die-cut pages help kids send away monsters and learn their colors.

Fontes, Justine. *Black Meets White.*
Die-cuts, flaps, and popups show the joys of the underrepresented colors of black, white, and gray.

Fox, Mem. *Where is the Green Sheep.*
In this joyful, brief story, the opposites and rhymes hold the attention of the youngest listeners.

Hubbard, Patricia. *My Crayons Talk.*
A very brief text and child-like crayon drawings make this perfect for toddler storytime.

Martin, Bill. *Brown Bear, Brown Bear, What Do You See?*
The classic repetition story that uses animals to teach colors.

Pinkwater, Manus Daniel. *Bear's Picture.*
Two "fine, proper gentlemen" tell a bear he cannot paint a picture, but the bear proves them wrong.

Reynolds, Peter. *The Dot.*
Vashti is certain she is no good at art, until a kind teacher encourages her.

Seeger, Laura Vaccaro. *Lemons Are Not Red.*
Older kids will predict what is in each picture, with colors that may surprise you.

Tullet, Herve. *Press Here.*
In this simple but dazzling interactive book, the reader will shake the colored dots to get them to move.

Waddell, Martin. *Alice the Artist.*
Alice paints a picture, but friends drop by and tell her to add things, until she decides to do it her own way.

Walsh, Ellen Stoll. *Mouse Paint.*
Three white mice find a yellow, red, and blue jar of paint and mix the colors; also available as a Big Book.

Wellington, Monica. *Colors for Zena.*
A young girl learns how various colors are made from the three primary colors.

Wilson, Karma. *Bear Sees Colors.*
Bear and mouse go walking and see various colors in this rhyming story.

Wolff, Ashley. *Baby Bear Sees Blue.*
Baby bear leaves his den and sees various colors in nature.

Craft: Since many of these stories have a theme of creativity, try something open-ended like watercolor paints, instead of a craft that has to look a certain way.

App: *Go Away, Big Green Monster!* Night & Day Studios.

COOKING

Brown, Marcia. *The Bun.*
In this classic cumulative tale with similarities to the "Gingerbread Man" folktale, a bun rolls out of the kitchen and is pursued by various people and animals.

Brunhoff, Laurent De. *Babar Learns to Cook.*
A famous TV chef comes to the palace to teach Babar how to cook.

Denise, Anika. *Baking Day at Grandma's.*
In this joyous book that will encourage participation, three bear cubs help grandma bake a cake.

Dragonwagon, Crescent. *This Is the Bread I Baked for Ned.*
Learn the steps in making bread in this cumulative tale.

Falwell, Cathryn. *Feast for Ten.*
A family makes a chicken dinner in this counting book.

Gelsanliter, Wendy. *Dancin' In the Kitchen.*
Inspired to dance by listening to the radio in Grandma's kitchen, everyone helps make dinner while dancing!

Goodman, Susan. *All in Just One Cookie.*
This brief informational book describes where the ingredients for cookies come from.

Lin, Grace. *Dim Sum for Everyone!*
A celebration of Chinese food!

Morris, Ann. *Bread, Bread, Bread.*
Color photos from around the world show the different types of bread in various cultures in this informational book.

Stevens, Janet. *Cook-A-Doodle-Doo!*
Big Brown Rooster gets his friends to help him make strawberry shortcake.

Sturges, Philomen. *Little Red Hen Makes a Pizza.*
Even though the other animals don't help, the Little Red Hen shares her pizza.

Woodson, Jacqueline. *We Had a Picnic This Sunday Past.*
A large African American family shares favorite foods at a picnic.

Craft: Make chef hats out of white tissue paper, taped to a paper headband.

CRICKETS

Carle, Eric. *The Very Quiet Cricket.*
A cricket meets other friendly insects during the day.

Caudill, Rebecca. *A Pocketful of Cricket.*
A 1964 Caldecott Honor book with illustrations by Evaline Ness, in which a boy finds a cricket.

DiTerlizzi, Angela. *Some Bugs.*
A rhyming text describes insects that are in many backyards.

Fleming, Denise. *Barnyard Banter.*
Filled with animal sounds, this short rhyming story talks about farm animals.

Harrington, Janice. *Busy-Busy Little Chick.*
Based on a Central African folktale, this story shows a chick helping to build a new nest for his mother and siblings.

Maxner, Joyce. *Nicholas Cricket.*
A bug jazz band plays at the late night forest dance.

Underwood, Deborah. *The Loud Book!*
A celebration of the sounds from morning until night includes the sound of crickets.

Wheeler, Lisa. *Old Cricket.*
Old Cricket is too tired and cranky to help his wife prepare for the winter.

Wood, Audrey. *Quick As a Cricket.*
A rhyming story about a boy who acts like various animals.

Craft: Make the crickets at www.storknet.com/cubbies/kidscrafts/sep05.htm which are made from combs.

CRIME FIGHTERS

Christelow, Eileen. *The Robbery at the Diamond Dog Diner.*
Two robbers kidnap Glenda Feathers, believing she can lay eggs containing diamonds.

Cottringer, Anne. *Eliot Jones, Midnight Superhero.*
An ordinary boy becomes a superhero at night.

Hinkes, Ed. *Police Cat.*
Noodles, the cat, polices the neighborhood in his uniform, and performs a heroic rescue!

Hurd, Thacher. *Mystery on the Docks.*
Ralph rescues the opera singer Eduardo from kidnappers.

Kitamura, Satoshi. *Sheep in Wolves' Clothing.*
Three sheep hire detective Elliott Baa to help them locate their stolen fleece.

Palatini, Margie. *The Web Files.*
In this spoof of TV's "Dragnet," two ducks investigate a robbery on a farm.

Pilkey, Dav. *Dog Breath: The Horrible Trouble of Hally Tosis.*
Hally the dog's terrible breath comes in handy when two burglars enter the Tosis house!

Rathmann, Peggy. *Officer Buckle and Gloria.*
Gloria the police dog is the star of school safety assemblies.

Rocco, John. *Super Hair-O and the Barber of Doom.*
A boy is worried that a haircut will make him lose his super powers.

Rosen, Michael. *Send for a Superhero!*
Dad reads a bedtime story about Extremely Boring Man who thwarts villains by putting them to sleep.

Sharmat, Marjorie Weinman. *Nate the Great.*
The first in a popular easy reader series that stars a boy detective. Nate helps Annie find a lost picture.

Craft: Go to the publisher's website that has lots of ideas relating to the *Nate the Great* series of easy readers: www.randomhouse.com/teachers/pdf/nateactivities.pdf

DAYS OF THE WEEK

Adams, Pam. *Mrs. Honey's Hat.*
With repetition to engage listeners, something different is removed from the hat each day.

Carle, Eric. *The Very Hungry Caterpillar.*
This storytime classic involves a little caterpillar that eats something different each day of the week.

Domanska, Janina. *Busy Monday Morning.*
A child describes his busy week on the farm.

Hanson, Warren. *It's Monday, Mrs. Jolly Bones!*
An engaging rhyming text describes the different silly chores done on different days of the week.

Himmelman, John. *Chickens to the Rescue.*
The audience will call out the repeated title phrase in this silly story about a new catastrophe on the farm on each day of the week.

Koller, Jackie French. *Seven Spunky Monkeys.*
A monkey goes missing each day of the week in this book that also involves counting.

Kraus, Robert. *Come Out and Play, Little Mouse.*
Repetition involves the audience in this amusing story of a mouse that outwits a cat.

Levine, Arthur. *Monday Is One Day.*
Each day is described by a working parent and child who are looking forward to the weekend in this brief rhyming book.

Lobel, Anita. *One Lighthouse, One Moon.*
The cat and people who live in a lighthouse describe the days, months, and counting concepts.

McQuinn, Anna. *Lola Loves Stories.*
Lola and Dad go to the library every Saturday, and she reenacts a different story on the different days of the week.

Tompert, Ann. *Harry's Hats.*
In this simple easy reader, Harry wears a different hat each day for a related activity.

Ward, Cindy. *Cookie's Week.*
Cookie the cat gets into a mischief each day.

Young, Ed. *Seven Blind Mice.*
Each day a different mouse describes the strange new thing near their pond, helping listeners learn colors as well as the days of the week.

Craft: Make a Very Hungry Caterpillar paper chain, with the name of the day of the week on each chain: www.first-school.ws/theme/printables/days-week.htm

DINOSAURS

Barton, Byron. *Dinosaurs, Dinosaurs.*
Even toddlers enjoy this clear and simple description of various types of dinosaurs.

Edwards, Pamela Duncan. *Dinorella.*
Dinosaurs stand in for people in this spoof of Cinderella. The main character resembles a diplodocus helped by her Fairydactyl.

Guiberson, Brenda Z. *The Greatest Dinosaur Ever.*
Dramatic, realistic paintings highlight this informational book about 12 different dinosaurs.

Houran, Lori Haskins. *Dig Those Dinosaurs.*
A paleontologist describes how dinosaur bones are uncovered.

Lund, Deb. *Dinosailors.*
Some seasick dinosaurs decide to bring their ship home.

Manning, Linda. *Dinosaur Days.*
Each day of the week some mischievous dinosaurs wreak havoc at a girl's house.

Schnetzler, Pattie. *Ten Little Dinosaurs.*
Learn the real names of dinosaurs in this counting book.

Yolen, Jane. *How Do Dinosaurs Say Goodnight?*
A very brief, amusing rhyme about dinosaurs going to bed. Also try *How Do Dinosaurs Get Well Soon?*

Craft: Make a dinosaur paper bag puppet.

DOGS

Bee, William. *Digger Dog.*
In this participation story, Digger Dog uses big machinery to dig up huge bones.

Feiffer, Jules. *Bark George.*
In this hilarious book, a dog visits the vet because he makes every animal sound except barking.

Frazee, Marla. *Boot and Shoe.*
In this circular tale, two sibling dogs run around and around searching for each other.

Graham, Bob. *Benny: An Adventure Story.*
Benny tires of being a magician's assistant and goes in search of a family.

Hurd, Thacher. *Art Dog.*
Racecar driving artist Art Dog helps to solve crimes in the big city.

Keats, Erza Jack. *Whistle for Willie.*
Willie's owner Peter tries to learn to whistle, so he can whistle for him to come.

Masurel, Claire. *Ten Dogs in the Window.*
In this rhyming story, similar to "Ten in Bed," dogs are purchased from the pet store window by people who resemble the dogs they choose.

Murray, Alison. *Hickory Dickory Dog.*
Rufus the dog follows Zach to school and joins in on the activities.

Pilkey, Dav. *Dog Breath.*
Hally Tosis, a dog with horrible green breath, helps catch two robbers.

Reiser, Lynn. *Hardworking Puppies.*
Ten puppies find 10 different jobs, including work pulling a dog sled, and saving swimmers.

Shannon, David. *Good Boy, Fergus!*
Fergus loves to chase cats and motorcycles, but hates baths!

Shaskan, Stephen. *A Dog Is a Dog.*
A rhyming text compares dogs to other animals.

Craft: Make a dachshund like *Whistle for Willie.* Photocopy an illustration of Willie, then
   make him a very wide dachshund by putting an accordion-folded strip of black paper
   in his middle.
Song: "How Much Is That Doggie in the Window," and "B-I-N-G-O."
App: *Wild about Books.* Random House Digital.

DRAGONS

DePaola, Tomie. *The Knight and the Dragon.*
A shy knight and an equally shy dragon meet up for their first battle.

Emberley, Ed. *Klippity Klop.*
Sound effects are the highlight of this brief story of a knight, who is looking for a dragon.

Falwell, Cathryn. *Dragon Tooth.*
Sara makes a cardboard box dragon to take her attention away from a sore loose tooth.
   Children can make a dragon just like the one Sara does in the story, with just egg
   cartons, boxes, paper, glue, and markers.

Hall, Bruce Edward. *Henry and the Kite Dragon.*
Good for older children, this story is set in New York's Chinatown in 1920.

Kent, Jack. *There's No Such Thing As a Dragon.*
No one believes Billy when he wakes up and finds a dragon at the foot of his bed, until the
   dragon grows so large it moves the house down the street.

Mayer, Mercer. *The Bravest Knight.*
A boy imagines what it would be like to live and fight dragons, like knights in
   stories do.

Nolan, Jerdine. *Raising Dragons.*
A small African American girl describes finding a large egg that hatches into a dragon, and
   how she cares for it. One of the few multicultural dragon stories.

Roberts, Bethany. *Gramps and the Fire Dragon.*
Gramps and Jesse imagine a dragon story while starring into the fireplace.

Robertson, M. P. *The Egg.*
George finds a giant egg that hatches a dragon.

Stock, Catherine. *Emma's Dragon Hunt.*
Grandfather Wong teaches Emma the many good things about dragons.

Thong, Roseanne. *Red Is a Dragon.*
Great for toddlers and preschoolers, this simple concept book of colors uses things in the
   Chinese-American community as examples.

Tucker, Kathy. *The Seven Chinese Sisters.*
Each sister has a special power, like excelling at karate, talking to dogs, or cooking, that
    helps them defeat a dragon who has taken the youngest sister.

Craft: Make a dragon paper bag puppet. Find the instructions at www.enchantedlearning
    .com/crafts/chinesenewyear/lion/

EARTH DAY

Base, Graeme. *The Water Hole.*
In this counting book, various animals drink from a shrinking water hole. Base's dramatic
    paintings depict animals from around the world, and kids can pick out "hidden" ani-
    mals in each picture.

Brown, Marc. *Arthur Turns Green.*
Arthur works on his school project, which D.W. confuses for a machine that turns everyone green.

Burton, Virginia Lee. *The Little House.*
Originally published in 1942, this timeless Caldecott winner depicts urban overgrowth and
    how it can damage our environment.

Cole, Henry. *On Meadowview Street.*
In this picture book, Caroline convinces her new suburban neighborhood to include an
    actual meadow.

Fleming, Denise. *Where Once There Was a Wood.*
Fleming's handmade paper collages dramatically illustrate a simple story of a forest
    replaced by houses and the animals that lost their home.

Glaser, Linda. *Our Big Home: An Earth Poem.*
Celebrating water, the sun, and wind, this rhythmic story relates how humans share the
    planet with animals.

Ross, Anna. *Grover's Ten Terrific Ways to Help Our Wonderful World.*
Grover and his friends on Sesame Street show how we can all do little things that will add
    up to a cleaner planet.

Wheeler, Eliza. *Miss Maple's Seeds.*
A woman who lives in a tree cares for seeds until it is time for them to be planted in spring.

Wright, Maureen. *Earth Day, Birthday!*
A monkey says today is his birthday, but the other animals say it is Earth Day.

Craft: Make leaf rubbings or rock mosaics.
App: *Parker Penguin.* Nosy Crow.

EGGS

Aston, Dianna Hutts. *An Egg Is Quiet.*
Beautiful illustrations highlight this brief informational book on eggs.

Bunting, Eve. *Hurry! Hurry!*
The animals on the farm hurry to the barn to see an egg hatch.

Cutbill, Andy. *The Cow That Laid an Egg.*
A cow finds and egg and cares for it like her very own.

Dunbar, Joyce. *Egg Day.*
Dora the duck gets the farm animals to participate in a contest to find out who lays the
   best egg.

Dunrea, Olivier. *Ollie.*
Ollie is a stubborn egg that won't hatch until Gossie and Gertie use reverse psychology
   on it!

Ernst, Lisa Campbell. *Zinnea and Dot.*
Two chickens fight over who is the mother of an egg, until they decide to co-parent the
   chick that hatches.

Heller, Ruth. *Chickens Aren't the Only Ones.*
Beautiful color illustrations highlight this look at the various animals that lay eggs.

Imai, Miko. *Little Lumpty.*
Inspired by Humpty Dumpty, Lumpty climbs the town wall but cannot get down.

Meddaugh, Susan. *Harry on the Rocks.*
Harry strands his boat on an island and he sees an egg hatch—it is a strange lizard with
   wings!

Polacco, Patricia. *Rechenka's Eggs.*
An injured goose lays 13 fancy decorated eggs for the Easter Festival.

Simmons, Jane. *Daisy and the Egg.*
Daisy waits for a new brother or sister to hatch.

Ward, Jennifer. *What Will Hatch?*
Die-cut holes reveal different types of animals that hatch from eggs.

Craft: Children can glue small bits of colored tissue paper to an outline of an egg to make
   a decorated egg picture.
App: *Parker Penguin.* Nosy Crow.

FATHER'S DAY

Blumle, Elizabeth. *My Father the Dog.*
A girl suspects her dad may really be a dog in disguise because he is so good at playing
   catch, fetching the paper, etc.

Carle, Eric. *Mister Seahorse.*
Great for Father's Day, Mister Seahorse greets other ocean fathers who care for their
   young.

Dorros Arthur. *Papa and Me.*
A bilingual boy spends a day with his dad, who only speaks Spanish.

Germein, Katrina. *My Dad Thinks He's Funny.*
A boy finds his dad's jokes on the corny side in this hilarious story.

Hines, Anna Grossnickle. *Daddy Makes the Best Spaghetti.*
Dad can do lots of cool things like cook, make bath time fun, and so on.

Kroll, Steven. *Happy Father's Day.*
Mom and each of the children have a special surprise for Dad.

London, Jonathan. *Froggy's Day with Dad.*
Froggy's plans go awry (as always) when he takes his Dad miniature golfing on Father's Day.

Martin, David. *Piggy and Daddy Go Fishing.*
Piggy is excited about going fishing but feels sorry for the worms and the fish.

Paradis, Susan. *My Daddy.*
A boy is amazed at what his dad can do—cross the street without help, stay up past midnight, etc.

Pringle, Laurence. *Octopus Hug.*
Dad invents lots of games to play while mom is out. Features an African American dad.

Walker, Anna. *I Love My Dad.*
Ollie, a young zebra, describes the things he likes to do with his dad.

Craft: Make Father's Day cards. Be sure to offer options for Grandfathers, Uncles, or other male family members.
App: *Together Time with Song and Rhyme for Parent and Preschooler.* Mulberry Media Interactive Inc.

FIREFIGHTERS

Bond, Felicia. *Poinsettia and the Firefighters.*
A little pig calls the fire department when some power lines start a fire outside her window.

Fox, Christyan. *Fire Fighter Piggy Wiggy.*
A pig daydreams what it would be like to be a firefighter.

Hamilton, K. R. *Firefighters to the Rescue!*
A day in the life of a firefighter, from cooking at the station to rescuing a pet.

Hubbell, Patricia. *Firefighters! Speeding! Spraying! Saving!*
In this dynamic book, lots of sound words describe what is happening during a fire.

MacLean, Christine. *Even Firefighters Hug Their Moms.*
A boy imagines several careers he could aspire to, including firefighting.

Rey, H. A. *Curious George and the Firefighters.*
While on a class field trip to the firehouse, Curious George ends up going on an emergency call!

Sis, Peter. *Fire Truck.*
A little boy imagines he is a fire truck.

Teague, Mark. *Firehouse!*
Edward and Judy visit the firehouse.

Craft: See if your local fire station can bring a truck to show the children and talk to them briefly about fire safety. Or, make firefighter hats out of red construction paper.

FIVE SENSES

Aliki. *My Five Senses.*
Available as a Big Book, this simple nonfiction look at the five senses features Aliki's signature cartoon illustrations and a very easy to understand, brief text.

Brocket, Jane. *Cold, Crunchy, Colorful: Using Our Senses.*
Large color photos are captioned with a sentence that explains how the pictured object is explored with one of the five senses.

Cash, Megan M. *I Saw the Sea and the Sea Saw Me.*
A girl pleasantly demonstrates the five senses while at the seashore, until a jellyfish appears.

McMillan, Bruce. *Sense Suspense: A Guessing Game for the Five Senses.*
In Spanish and English, this guessing game uses clear color photos to encourage children to name which sense is being used in the picture. Many of the photos were taken at a beach.

Raschka, Chris. *Five for a Little One.*
A rabbit explores the five senses in this nonlinear book with a rhythmic, brief text and expressive watercolor illustrations.

Reiser, Lynn. *My Cat Tuna.*
A cat uses his five senses to experience a summer day. With flaps to lift, and a very simple text.

Rotner, Shelley. *Senses at the Seashore.*
Bright color photos show children frolicking at the beach, with brief captions highlighting the senses: "hear the lifeguard's whistle, taste the sweet juicy watermelon."

Ryan, Pamela Munoz. *Hello, Ocean!*
A rhyming text told from the point of view of a little girl and her encounter with the ocean.

Stojic, Manya. *Rain.*
Several animals hear, feel, smell, see, and taste the rain that is coming to their dry savannah home.

Zarin, Cynthia. *What Do You See When You Shut Your Eyes?*
Children experience the five senses while walking around the neighborhood, and even when they are dreaming.

Craft: Play a five senses game: Blindfold the children and have them sniff a lemon, or touch a stuffed animal, or listen to a shell to see if they can "hear" the ocean.

FLEAS

Downey, Lynn. *Flea's Sneeze.*
Animal noises, repeated sneezing, and a rhyming text make for a humorous barnyard story.

Edwards, Pamela Duncan. *Ed & Fred Flea.*
Brothers Ed and Fred are fleas that live on a dog.

Emberley, Ed. *The Wing on a Flea.*
A book about shapes.

Kralovansky, Susan Holt. *There Was a Tall Texan Who Swallowed a Flea.*
In this cumulative rhyming story, a cowboy swallows various critters to rid himself of a flea.

Lillegard, Dee. *Sitting In My Box.*
A box soon crowds with various animals, until a flea joins them.

Lionni, Leo. *I Want to Stay Here! I Want to Go There! A Flea Story.*
Like "The Country Mouse and the City Mouse," two fleas part ways because one likes to travel, and one likes to stay home.

Lish, Ted. *Three Little Puppies and the Big Bad Flea.*
In this spoof of "Three Pigs," three puppies build their houses out of flimsy materials, so soon they are invaded by fleas.

Ward, Jennifer. *There Was a Coyote Who Swallowed a Flea.*
A twist on the cumulative tale, "I Know an Old Lady Who Swallowed a Fly," this is set in the Southwest.

Wood, Audrey. *The Napping House.*
A cumulative story about the various family members who pile onto a bed. Also available as a Big Book and flannelboard.

Craft: Make a dog paper bag puppet with a little puffball flea.
Song: "Boom, Boom, Ain't It Great to be Crazy."

FLIES

Arnold, Tedd. *Hi, Fly Guy!*
Buzz captures a fly so he can enter the pet show. This is the first in a series of easy readers, and all are brief enough to read at a storytime.

Aylesworth, Jim. *Old Black Fly.*
This rhyming ABC book is hilarious, with riotous watercolor paintings by Stephen Gammell. Available in a Big Book edition.

Faulkner, Keith. *The Wide Mouth Frog.*
In this pop-up book, a frog asks various animals what they eat, volunteering that he eats flies.

Howitt, Mary. *The Spider and the Fly.*
Droll illustrations depict the Victorian-era poem in this Caldecott Honor book best suited
    to older preschoolers and school-age children.

Jorgensen, Gail. *Gotcha!*
A fly interrupts a bear's birthday party, causing the bear to chase the fly.

Kennedy, Kim. *Frankenfrog.*
After creating an enormous fly, the scientist needs to create an equally large frog to catch it!

Oppenheim, Joanne. *You Can't Catch Me!*
A fly challenges several animals to catch him; the storytime crowd will chant the repeated
    phrases.

Rosen, Michael. *Tiny Little Fly.*
Fly is shooed away by three different animals as he swoops and zooms, looking for a place
    to land.

Taback, Simms. *There Was an Old Lady Who Swallowed a Fly.*
The traditional song done with brightly colored, die-cut illustrations.

Trapani, Iza. *Shoo Fly.*
Everyone will be singing "Shoo fly, don't bother me!" when you read this book version of
    the folksong.

Craft: Make a fly mask, made with egg cartons for the fly's big eyes. Or, try the cute
    frog catching a fly with its tongue at www.thebestkidsbooksite.com/craftdetails3
    .cfm?CraftID = 840
Song: "Five Green and Speckled Frogs."

FOURTH OF JULY

Bertrand, Diane G. *Uncle Chente's Picnic.*
Bilingual Spanish/English. A rainstorm and power failure can't stop the special picnic in
    honor of Uncle Chente.

Chall, Marsha. *Happy Birthday, America.*
Kay and her extended family celebrate.

Guthrie, Woody. *This Land Is Your Land.*
Enjoy one of the picture book versions of Guthrie's moving song.

Joosse, Barbara. *Fourth of July.*
At first, Ross is too little to participate in the July 4th celebration, but when he can
    walk the length of the parade carrying a banner, he proves he is old enough for
    sparklers.

Keller, Holly. *Henry's Fourth of July.*
Henry describes his family's trip to the annual holiday picnic.

Osborne, Mary Pope. *Happy Birthday, America!*
A family celebrates with a parade, carnival, picnic, and fireworks.

Pomeranc, Marion. *American Wei.*
Wei loses his tooth at his family's American citizenship ceremony, and the diverse group
of new citizens helps him find it.

Roberts, Bethany. *Fourth of July Mice.*
Four mice celebrate the holiday in this sweet rhyming story.

Seymour, Tres. *Jake Johnson—The Story of a Mule.*
Farmer Puckett's stubborn mule won't take the fireworks to the fair on the 4th of July.

Wardlaw, Lee. *Red, White, and Boom!*
A rhyming celebration of Independence Day.

Wong, Janet S. *Apple Pie Fourth of July.*
Her family runs a Chinese restaurant so a girl has to work during the Fourth of July
parade.

Ziefert, Harriet. *Hats Off to the Fourth of July.*
Rhyming story of a customary small town celebration.

Craft: Flags made from craft sticks or paper.
Song: "Yankee Doodle."

FOXES

Aylesworth, Jim. *Gingerbread Man.*
The classic story of the cookie who thought he could out-fox a fox; kids will chant along
with the famous phrase.

Bloom, Suzanne. *Fox Forgets.*
Bear worries when Fox forgets to give a message to Goose.

Church, Caroline. *One Smart Goose.*
A smart goose bathes in the mud so the fox cannot see his white feathers in the
moonlight.

Edwards, Pamela Duncan. *Four Famished Foxes and Fosdyke.*
Combining a great lesson on the letter "F" with a funny story, this is a new take on the "fox
in the hen house" story.

Ehlert, Lois. *Moon Rope.*
With text in Spanish and English, this Peruvian folktale involves a mole and a fox trying to
climb a rope up to the moon.

Fox, Mem. *Hattie and the Fox.*
Kids will repeat the exclamations made by each animal in this cumulative story. Available
in a Big Book edition.

Galdone, Paul. *What's In Fox's Sack?*
The same folktale as *Going to Squintim's*, aimed at slightly younger readers.

Hindley, Judy. *Do Like a Duck Does.*
Mother duck tricks the fox into imitating a duck.

Hogrogian, Nonny. *One Fine Day.*
Based on an Armenian folktale, this cumulative story shows a fox trading for various items, so he can reclaim his tail.

Hutchins, Pat. *Rosie's Walk.*
A very short text involves Rosie the chicken being followed by a fox.

Janovitz, Marilyn. *Little Fox.*
Little Fox breaks the family's favorite chair, the one where Mom reads stories to him.

Kasza, Keiko. *My Lucky Day!*
A fox thinks it is his lucky day when a pig visits, until the pig tricks him into making him a meal, giving him a massage, and so forth.

Ward, Helen. *Rooster and the Fox.*
Adapted from "The Canterbury Tales," a proud rooster is tricked by a sly fox.

Waring, Richard. *Hungry Hen.*
A hungry fox patiently waits for a hen to plump up, until the hen is bigger than the fox!

Westwood, Jennifer. *Going to Squintim's: A Foxy Folk Tale.*
Based on the English folktale, this repetitive, humorous story involves a fox "trading" up from a bee to a boy that the fox hopes to eat.

Willems, Mo. *That Is Not a Good Idea!*
Resembling a silent film with title cards, this hilarious story concerns a fox and some very smart chickens.

Williams, Sue. *Dinnertime!*
One by one, six little rabbits escape a fox.

Crafts: If you're looking for a unique craft, make fox tails. Cut out tagboard tails and punch a hole in the upper end. Let the kids color. Then thread yarn through the hole and tie the tails on the kids. Use this with *One Fine Day.*
Songs: "A Hunting We Will Go" and "Fox Went Out on a Chilly Night."

FROGS

Anderson, Peggy. *Time for Bed, the Babysitter Said.*
Joe won't go to bed in this short rhyming story.

Arnold, Tedd. *Green Wilma.*
Wilma looks for flies to eat and disrupts school.

Faulkner Keith. *The Wide Mouthed Frog.*
Pop-ups highlight this short, funny story.

French, Vivian. *Growing Frogs.*
Blending information on tadpole development with a story, this picture book describes a little girl's efforts to watch a tadpole turn into a frog.

Kalan, Robert. *Jump, Frog, Jump!*
In this cumulative tale, a frog must jump to escape capture.

Lionni, Leo. *It's Mine!*
Three frogs argue over who owns the pond, until a storm shows them the value of sharing.

London, Jonathan. *Froggy Gets Dressed.*
The kids will scream with laughter when Froggy forgets to put on his underwear!

Mack, Jeff. *Ah Ha!*
Using just the exclamation in the title, this lively book describes the challenges faced by a frog.

Manushkin, Fran. *Peeping and Sleeping.*
Barry and his dad walk by a pond and try to figure out who or what is making that sound!

Craft: Make a frog paper bag puppet.
Song: "Five Green and Speckled Frogs."
App: *Franklin Frog.* Nosy Crow.

GARDENING

Aston, Dianna Hutts. *A Seed Is Sleepy.*
Lovely illustrations and a very brief text describe how seeds grow in this informational book.

Cole, Henry. *Jack's Garden.*
In this cumulative tale, the listener will see what Jack plants and how it grows.

DeRobertis, Barbara. *Count On Pablo.*
Pablo helps his Abuela sell vegetables at the market in this counting story.

Ehlert, Lois. *Planting a Rainbow.*
Covering both the concept of colors and the "how to" of planting flowers, this brightly illustrated book is perfect for a wide age range.

Florian, Douglas. *Vegetable Garden.*
A rhyming, brief story about a family planting and tending their vegetable garden.

French, Vivian. *Oliver's Vegetables.*
Grandpa lets Oliver choose the vegetable to have for dinner each night, from Grandpa's backyard garden.

Hall, Zoe. *The Surprise Garden.*
Planting unmarked seeds results in wonderful surprises in the vegetable garden.

Lin, Grace. *The Ugly Vegetables.*
A little girl thinks her mother's Chinese vegetables are ugly until she tastes the wonderful soup they make.

Park, Linda Sue. *What Does Bunny See?*
The rhyming text will help the audience call out the color of each flower in this interactive story.

Rockwell, Lizzy. *Plants Feed Me.*
A very simple nonfiction science book that describes the parts of a plant.

Root, Phyllis. *Soup for Supper.*
A giant and a small woman vie for the best veggies for their soup.

Westcott, Nadine B. *The Giant Vegetable Garden.*
The townsfolk let their vegetables overgrow, in order to win prizes at the Fair.

Wilner, Isabel. *A Garden Alphabet.*
A rhyming alphabet full of all things related to gardening.

Craft: Have the children plant seeds in paper cups. Hopefully, many of them can re-plant these in their backyards or in patio pots, but even kids with no "planting" space can grow herbs (like rosemary) on their kitchen windowsills.
App: *Endless Alphabet.* Originator, Inc.

HABITATS

Berkes, Marianne Collins. *Over in the Ocean in a Coral Reef.*
The many animals of the coral reef are celebrated in this variation of the song "Over in the Meadow."

Berkes, Marianne Collins. *Over in a River: Flowing Out to the Sea.*
North American river animals and their habitats are the focus of this counting book, using the rhyme of the folksong "Over in the Meadow."

Cole, Henry. *On the Way to the Beach.*
Many kids will relate to this brief story about walking on the beach; gatefold pages open to show various animals in that habitat.

Cousins, Lucy. *Maisy's World of Animals.*
In this clever pop-up look at habitats, Maisy goes to the Arctic, mountains, desert, savanna, ocean, jungle, and Antarctic.

Cowcher, Helen. *Rain Forest.*
A simple description of the Rain Forest of South America, with distinctive color illustrations.

Fleming, Denise.
In the Small, Small Pond.
In the Tall, Tall Grass.
Where Once There Was a Wood.
Fleming's handmade colorful paper collages illustrate these rhyming descriptions of the animals found in various habitats. Fun even for toddler time.

Mazer, Anne. *The Salamander Room.*
A boy imagines changing his room into a habitat for salamanders.

Mora, Pat. *Listen to the Desert/Oye Al Desierto.*
A simple, melodic description of the desert, told in English and Spanish.

Craft: Make stick puppets of the animals in your featured book.
App: *Parker Penguin.* Nosy Crow.

HALLOWEEN

Bennett, Kelly. *Vampire Baby.*
Tootie's big brother thinks she might be a vampire when her teeth grow in and she bites.

Crow, Kristin. *Bedtime at the Swamp.*
With a repeated phrase that will appeal to listeners, a boy and his cousins try to outrun whatever is making those sounds in the swamp—until mom tells them to come inside for bath time.

Emberley, Ed. *Go Away Big Green Monster!*
A great book for empowering toddlers to not be afraid. As each page is turned, another part of the monster disappears. A hand puppet with removable parts which is based on this book can be purchased from Lakeshore Learning.

Hayes, Sarah. *This Is the Bear and the Scary Night.*
Told in the same rhythm as "The House That Jack Built," a teddy bear is left in the park and goes through several adventures before he is returned to his owner.

Howard, Arthur. *Hoodwinked.*
A little witch wants a pet that is scary, but not too scary.

Paquette, Ammi-Joan. *Ghost in the House.*
A little ghost and some other creatures explore a haunted house, in this amusing story with engaging repetition.

Pearson, Susan. *We're Going on a Ghost Hunt.*
The audience can help act out this ghostly take on the "We're Going on Bear Hunt" chant.

Reiner, Carl. *Tell Me a Scary Story . . . But Not Too Scary!*
Grandpa tells a little boy about the neighbor and a marble that looks like an eyeball.

Rueda, Claudia. *Let's Play In the Forest While the Wolf Is Not Around.*
Based on a traditional song from Europe, a group of children play while a wolf gets dressed.

Savage, Stephen. *Ten Orange Pumpkins.*
This rhyming counting book features various people taking away pumpkins.

Stevenson, Harvey. *Big, Scary Wolf.*
Dad convinces Rose, who can't sleep because of the shadows in her room, that the shadows can't be a wolf.

Willem, Mo. *Leonardo the Terrible Monster.*
Leonardo is terrible at being a monster—he is not the least bit scary!

Craft: Make simple Jack-o-Lantern masks from orange paper.
Song: "Five Little Pumpkins Sitting on a Gate."
App: *Go Away, Big Green Monster!* Night & Day Studios.

HAMSTERS AND GERBILS

Baker, Alan. *Benjamin's Portrait.*
A hamster tries his paw at portrait painting.

Brown, Marc. *Arthur and the School Pet.*
D.W. volunteers to take care of the class gerbil during Christmas vacation.

Inkpen, Mick. *Kipper and Roly.*
Kipper buys Roly the hamster as a gift for Pig, but soon decides he can't part with him!

Kirk, Daniel. *Bus Stop, Bus Go.*
A hamster gets loose on the school bus.

Lord, Cynthia. *Happy Birthday, Hamster.*
Hamster and Dog prepare for Hamster's surprise birthday party.

Rathmann, Peggy. *10 Minutes till Bedtime.*
The countdown begins as a child gets ready for bed, by reading to pet hamsters, taking a bath, dressing in pajamas, and so forth.

Scillian, Devin. *Memoirs of a Hamster.*
The cat convinces the hamster to leave his cage, but the big world is much more frightening than he expected.

Suen, Anastasia. *Hamster Chase.*
Using the characters created by Ezra Jack Keats, this easy reader describes the class pet getting loose.

Craft: Go to www.hamstertours.com for Peggy Rathmann's great site relating to *10 Minutes till Bedtime.* You can print out a "Hamster Scope" craft or learn to make a Hamster RV.

HATS

Berenstain, Stan and Jan. *Old Hat, New Hat.*
A very simple story of opposites.

Blos, Joan. *Martin's Hats.*
Martin changes hats frequently as he encounters each new adventure.

Katz, Karen. *Twelve Hats for Lena.*
Lena makes a new hat for each month of the year; this should inspire lots of great hat craft projects!

Morris, Ann. *Hats, Hats, Hats.*
Another of Morris's amazing simple nonfiction books, this focuses on hats around the world.

Slobodkina, Esphyr. *Caps for Sale.*
The classic story; this is available as a Big Book, or as story apron figures.

Smith, William. *Ho for a Hat.*
A simple lesson on hats through history, told by a boy and his dog.

Spinelli, Eileen. *Do You Have a Hat?*
A rhyming text describes hats worn by famous people throughout history.

VanLaan, Nancy. *This Is the Hat.*
This rhyming, cumulative story of a hat used as a home for various animals will invite participation from the storytime audience.

Ward, Jennifer. *The Sunhat.*
In this cumulative story, several animals try to squeeze into Rosa's hat.

Won, Brian. *Hooray for Hat!*
The audience will shout out the repeated title phrase in this delightful look at how a hat can cheer up the grumpiest person (or animal)!

Crafts: Newspaper hats: www.uggabugga.com/Arts%20&%20Crafts/Origami/Origami %20-%20Hat%20Instructions.htm.
App: *Dr. Seuss Beginner Book Collection #1 and #2.* Oceanhouse Media.

HAWAII

Fellows, Rebecca. *A Lei for Tutu.*
Nahoa looks forward to Lei Day, until Tutu gets sick.

George, Jean Craighead. *Dear Katie, the Volcano is a Girl.*
Science and folklore mix in this story of Katie and her grandmother.

Gillespie, Jane. *S Went Surfing in Hawaii.*
Each letter of the alphabet does different activities while on vacation in Hawaii.

Guback, Georgia. *Luka's Quilt.*
When Tutu (grandmother) makes a Hawaiian-style quilt, Luka wishes for a more colorful one.

London, Jonathan. *Froggy Goes to Hawaii.*
Froggy is so excited to be on vacation in Hawaii that he doesn't pay attention to his parents.

Martin, Rafe. *Shark God.*
A brother and sister are imprisoned by a king, but because they freed a shark caught in a net, the Shark God comes to their rescue.

Mohan, Beverly. *Punia and the King of the Sharks.*
To get lobsters, Punia must outwit the sharks guarding their cave.

Rattigan, Jama Kim. *Dumpling Soup.*
A family eats foods reflecting their Hawaiian, Korean, and Japanese cultures.

Rumford, James. *Island Below the Star.*
Five brothers, each with a special skill, sail to Hawaii.

Samuels, Barbara. *Aloha, Dolores.*
Dolores and her cat Duncan enter a contest to win a trip to Hawaii.

Takayama, Sandi. *Sumorella: A Hawaii Cinderella Story.*
Mango Boy is teased for being skinny, so he dreams of becoming a Sumo wrestler.

Tune, Suelyn C. *How Maui Slowed the Sun.*
A pourquoi story about the long days in Hawaii.

Williams, Laura. *Torch Fishing With the Sun.*
Makoa worries about his aging grandfather.

Craft: The easiest paper lei is made with simple photocopied flowers strung on a shoelace or piece of yarn, with one-inch pieces of plastic drinking straws used to separate the flowers.

HEALTHY EATING

Barrett, Judi. *Cloudy with a Chance of Meatballs.*
It rains food in this popular picture book that was adapted into a hit feature film.

Berenstain, Jan and Stan. *The Berenstain Bears and Too Much Junk Food.*
Mama sets out to convince the family that they are eating too much junk food.

Brown, Marcia. *Stone Soup.*
Soldiers gently motivate a town to contribute vegetables to their soup in this classic folktale
    on cooperation.

Carlson, Nancy. *Get Up and Go.*
A kid-friendly look at exercise.

Child, Lauren. *I Will Never Not Ever Eat a Tomato.*
Lola's brother tricks her into eating vegetables.

DePaola, Tomie. *Strega Nona's Harvest.*
Strega Nona tries to teach Anthony how to plant and nurture a vegetable garden.

Ehlert, Lois. *Eating the Alphabet.*
An alphabetical tour of fruits and vegetables.

Ehlert, Lois. *Growing Vegetable Soup.*
Complete with a soup recipe, this simple story with vivid color illustrations shows how to
    plant vegetables.

Falwell, Cathryn. *Feast for 10.*
The entire family helps prepare dinner.

French, Vivian. *Oliver's Vegetables.*
Grandpa makes a deal with Oliver—Oliver can pick the vegetables from the garden, but he
    must eat them for dinner.

Leedy, Loreen. *The Edible Pyramid: Good Eating Every Day.*
The animals at a fancy restaurant show which foods fit into the food pyramid.

Rubel, Nicole. *Ralph Feels Rotten.*
In this easy reader, Ralph gets sick after eating out of the trash can.

Gregory, Rex Barron. *Showdown at the Food Pyramid.*
Healthy foods battle snack foods who have taken over the food pyramid.

Hoban, Russell. *Bread and Jam for Frances.*
In this classic picture book, Frances only eats bread and jam until her mom makes
    spaghetti.

Hoberman, Mary Ann. *The Seven Silly Eaters.*
A rhyming story where each family member wants something different to eat.

Rockwell, Lizzy. *Good Enough to Eat.*
A simple look at healthy foods.

Rosenthal, Amy K. *Little Pea.*
Little Pea hates the candy he is asked to eat for dinner.

Sayre, April Pulley. *Rah, Rah, Radishes! A Vegetable Chant.*
In this clear informational book, a rhyming text and color photos depict various vegetables.

Schnitzlein, Danny. *The Monster Who Ate My Peas.*
A young boy tries to bribe a monster into eating his peas.

Sharmat, Mitchell. *Gregory the Terrible Eater.*
Gregory the goat likes fruits and vegetables, not tin cans, in this popular Reading Rainbow book.

Spinelli, Eileen. *Miss Fox's Class Shapes Up.*
The popular teacher motivates the class to eat healthy and exercise.

Yaccarino, Dan. *The Lima Bean Monster.*
After Sammy and his friends dump their vegetables in a vacant lot, the lot turns into the Lima Bean Monster.

Craft: Distribute tomato plants to each child (see if you can get a local garden store to donate them), or, make potato stamps: www.firstpalette.com/Craft_themes/Colors/Potato_Stamps/Potato_Stamps.html
Song: "Apples and Bananas."

HELPING

Barton, Byron. *The Little Red Hen.*
In this classic story that invites audience participation, the Little Red Hen asks for help but doesn't receive it.

Bracken, Beth. *Henry Helps with the Baby.*
Big brother Henry helps his parents by taking care of his baby sister. Also see *Henry Helps with the Dog* and other books in the series.

Brown, Marc. *Arthur Helps Out.*
Arthur helps around the house before going out to play.

Cadena, Beth. *Supersister.*
A little girl helps around the house in anticipation of the birth of her baby sister.

Clement, Andrew. *The Handiest Things in the World.*
Photos and a brief text show the various things that hands can do.

Costello, David. *I Can Help.*
A monkey helps a lost duck, who in turn helps another animal, and so on in a chain reaction of helpfulness.

Hughes, Shirley. *Alfie Gives a Hand.*
Alfie wants to help out at a friend's birthday party but must first learn to do without his blanket.

Mayer, Mercer. *I am Helping.*
In this board book, Little Critter helps around the house, sometimes with disastrous results.

Morris, Ann. *Teamwork.*
With striking color photos and a very brief text, Morris demonstrates the idea of teamwork and helping each other, in countries around the world.

Muth, Jon. *Zen Ties.*
A panda encourages others to help their neighbors.

Panzieri, Lucia. *The Kindhearted Crocodile.*
Wanting to be a pet, a crocodile demonstrates how helpful he can be to a family.

Paradore, Coleen. *26 Big Things Small Hands Can Do.*
From A to Z, this book demonstrates things young children can do to be helpful.

Wells, Rosemary. *Hands Off Harry.*
Part of the "Kindergator" series, Harry needs to learn about others' personal space.

Craft: Instead of the usual arts and crafts program, hold a canned food drive or other charitable event where the kids can contribute. For example, they can make greeting cards for hospital patients.

App: *Together Time with Song and Rhyme for Parent and Preschooler.* Mulberry Media Interactive Inc.

HIBERNATION

Arnosky, Jim. *Every Autumn Comes the Bear.*
Dramatic full color illustrations add details to this brief story of a bear that shows up at a farm, before finding his way to a den to hibernate.

Brian, Janeen. *Too Tight, Benito!*
Because Benito Bear has grown over the summer, he has trouble finding a comfortable place to hibernate.

Carnesi, Monica. *Sleepover with Beatrice and Bear.*
Beatrice the rabbit wants to accompany Bear when he goes to hibernate.

Cooper, Elisha. *Bear Dreams.*
A bear persuades his friends to play instead of hibernating.

Dabcovich, Lydia. *Sleepy Bear.*
Sleepy Bear wakes up in spring.

Fleming, Denise. *Time to Sleep.*
Bear notices that winter is coming, so he tells the snail, who tells another animal, who tells another, until the warning comes back to bear.

Fox, Mem. *Sleepy Bears.*
In this rhyming counting book, mama bear sings each cub to sleep.

Grindley, Sally. *What Will We Do Without You?*
The other animals miss Jefferson Bear while he is hibernating.

Helquist, Brett. *Bedtime for Bear.*
Even though it is time for Bear to hibernate, his animal friends encourage him to play with them.

Henkes, Kevin. *Old Bear.*
Old Bear dreams he is a cub enjoying the four seasons.

Krensky, Stephen. *Chaucer's First Winter.*
Instead of sleeping in winter, Chaucer stays up, afraid he will miss some fun.

London, Jonathan. *Froggy Gets Dressed.*
Froggy wants to play in the snow, but eventually goes back to bed since he should be
    hibernating!

Meadows, Michelle. *Hibernation Station.*
A rhyming text introduces children to a variety of animals that hibernate.

Murray, Marjorie Dennis. *Don't Wake the Bear!*
Several animals snuggle up to a hibernating bear to keep warm.

Rosen, Michael. *I'm Going On a Bear Hunt.*
Technically not a hibernation story, this is a great interactive chant, which involves finding
    a bear in a cave.

Ward, Andrew. *Baby Bear and the Long Sleep.*
Baby Bear can't settle down for his long winter's nap.

Yolen, Jane. *Sleep, Black Bear, Sleep.*
Told in a rhyming text, this describes different animals that settle down for winter.

Craft: Make bear paper bag puppets.
App: *Alphabet Animals: A Slide-and-Peek Adventure.* Auryn.

HORSES

Asch, Frank. *Goodnight Horsey.*
A request for a bedtime glass of water results in a fantastic horsey ride with a surprise
    ending.

Bemelmans, Ludwig. *Madeline in London.*
Madeline and her schoolmates give Pepito a horse for his birthday.

Brett, Jan. *Fritz and the Beautiful Horses.*
Fritz the pony saves the local children when the bridge is damaged.

Chandra, Deborah. *A is for Amos.*
A little girl rides her horse Amos in this imaginative alphabet story.

Doherty, Berlie. *Snowy.*
Rachel wants to bring Snowy to school for pet day, but the horse has to pull the canal barge
    as part of the family's business.

Greenfield, Eloise. *On My Horse.*
A young African American boy describes riding on a horse in this very simple rhyming story.

Hubbell, Patricia. *Horses: Trotting! Prancing! Racing!*
Lively rhyming couplets describe facts about horses, including the many jobs they do.

Jeffers, Susan. *All the Pretty Horses.*
The bedtime lullaby is depicted in this very short but memorable picture book.

Jeffers, Susan. *My Pony.*
A little girl imagines having her own horse, a pony named Silver.

Lester, Alison. *Noni the Pony.*
Noni the pony enjoys farm life with a cat and dog in this rhyming story.

London, Jonathan. *If I Had a Horse.*
A girl imagines riding a horse in the jungle and through her town. A few Spanish words are included in the text.

London, Jonathan. *Mustang Canyon.*
Little Pinto, a colt, runs with the other wild mustangs in Monument Valley.

Mullin, Patricia. *One Horse Waiting for Me.*
In this rhyming counting story, different types of horses are depicted, including rocking horses and a merry go round.

Rash, Andy. *Are You a Horse?*
After receiving a saddle for his birthday, Roy goes around asking various animals and things if they are horses in this comic story reminiscent of *Are You My Mother?*

Smee, Nicola. *Clip-Clop.*
Cat, Dog, Pig, and Duck implore Horse for a raucous ride in this hilarious participation story.

Smee, Nicola. *Splish-Splash.*
In this follow up to *Clip-Clop,* Horse takes his smaller farm friends on a boat ride.

Stein, David Ezra. *Cowboy Ned & Andy.*
Horse Andy searches the desert for a birthday cake for Ned.

Wilson, Karma. *Horseplay!*
The farmer tries to get his rowdy horses to settle down and go to sleep in this rhyming story.

Yolen, Jane. *Hush, Little Horsie.*
A rhyming celebration where the mama horse assures her foal that she will watch over him.

Craft: Make simple cowboy kerchiefs out of muslin squares. The children can decorate them with rubber stamps or markers.

HOUSES AND HOMES

Ackerman, Karen. *I Know a Place.*
Kids will repeat the title phrase, since it occurs several times in this comforting story.

Barrett, Judith and Ron. *Old MacDonald Had an Apartment House.*
Old MacDonald plants vegetables in his apartment, which grow into his neighbors rooms and creates chaos!

Barton, Byron. *Building a House.*
A brief description of what is involved in building a house, including plumbing and
electricity.

Burton, Virginia Lee. *The Little House.*
The classic story about a house in the country which is soon surrounded by new buildings,
which eventually becomes a town.

Desimini, Lisa. *My House.*
Imaginative photo collages illustrate this celebration of home.

Emmett, Jonathan. *No Place Like Home.*
Mole is looking for a new home, and gets help from Hedgehog, Squirrel, and Rabbit.

Enderle, Judith Ross. *Upstairs.*
Elbie looked forward to new neighbors in his apartment house, but the new tenants start a
farm in their apartment!

Grifalconi, Ann. *Village of Round and Square Houses.*
In this tale from Cameroon, grandmother explains why men and women live in different
shaped houses.

Hoberman, Mary Ann. *A House Is a House for Me.*
A rhyming story that describes different kinds of dwellings.

LeSieg, Theodore (Dr. Seuss). *In a People House.*
A mouse gives a guided tour to a bird, of the various things in a "people house."

Morris, Ann. *Houses and Homes.*
Color photos and a very brief text describe houses around the world.

Rockwell, Anne and Harlow. *Nice and Clean.*
A simple explanation of how to clean the house, where all family members join in
the task.

Various. *The House That Jack Built.*
There are several versions of this Mother Goose cumulative story.

Craft: Each child can make a house that looks like his or her own home, whether it is an
apartment, mobile home, etc. Use a milk carton or shoe box for the base, and the kids
can add paper windows, doors, and other elements.
App: *Jack and the Beanstalk.* Nosy Crow.

INDIA

Arnold, Marsha. *Heart of a Tiger.*
A cat wants to be called Tiger, so he must show the other animals he is brave and deserving
of such a name.

Brown, Marcia. *Once a Mouse.*
A wise man changes a mouse into a cat so he will not be eaten, and continues changing the
animal until he gets too big to control.

Demi. *One Grain of Rice.*
As a reward, a girl receives one grain of rice, doubled each day until the reward can feed the whole village.

Galdone, Paul. *The Monkey and the Crocodile.*
Who will win the game of wits between the monkey and the crocodile?

Kostecki-Shaw, Jenny Sue. *Same, Same but Different.*
Pen pals Kailash in India and Elliot in the United States notice that they have very similar interests.

Rumford, James. *Nine Animals and the Well.*
Each animal wants to bring the best present to the king in this tale about the origin of numerals one to nine.

Smith, Jeremy. *Lily's Garden of India.*
Mother's garden has sections reflecting the culture of different countries, and India may be Lily's favorite.

Young, Ed. *Seven Blind Mice.*
Which mouse can guess the giant thing in front of them? This simple tale helps children learn colors and days of the week.

Zia, F. *Hot, Hot Roti for Dada-ji.*
Aneel shares stories and cooking with his grandfather.

Craft: Make an elephant paper bag puppet.

JAPAN

Gollub, Matthew. *Ten Oni Drummers.*
In this counting story, 10 Oni (ogres) appear on the beach and make noise, eventually sending nightmares away.

Johnston, Tony. *Badger and the Magic Fan.*
A badger steals a magic fan that can make a person's nose grow, and uses it on a rich man's daughter.

Morimoto, Junko. *Two Bullies.*
Two wrestler-sized bullies each proclaim superiority over the other but they are too cowardly to fight.

Say, Allen. *Bicycle Man.*
Two American soldiers walk by a playground, and join in the fun by doing bike tricks. A Reading Rainbow book.

Sierra, Judy. *Tasty Baby Bellybuttons.*
Oni, a type of giant ogre, goes after the treat of baby bellybuttons. But one baby fools them!

Uchida, Yoshiko. *Two Foolish Cats.*
Two cats find rice cakes—who should have them? They ask a monkey to decide how to divide the treat evenly.

Wells, Rosemary. *Yoko Finds Her Way.*
Yoko and her mother are going to Japan, but Yoko gets lost at the airport.

Yashima, Taro. *Umbrella.*
Momo receives boots and an umbrella for her birthday, and watches for rain every day so she can try out her gifts.

Yashima, Taro. *Crow Boy.*
A shy country boy must leave home at dawn to walk miles to the village school.

Craft: Make paper fish: www.enchantedlearning.com/crafts/japan/koi/, using tissue paper, and hang them up like windsocks.

KNIGHTS

Aitken, Amy. *Ruby the Red Knight.*
A young girl named Ruby imagines that she is a member of the Knights of the Round Table.

Bently, Peter. *King Jack and the Dragon.*
Three young children play at fighting dragons before it is time to go home to bed.

Davey, Own. *Night Knight.*
A boy imagines he is a great knight, while he gets ready for bed.

Emberley, Ed. *Klippity Klop.*
Similar to "Going on a Bear Hunt," this story encourages audience participation.

Hazen, Barbara Shook. *The Knight Who Was Afraid of the Dark.*
Sir Fred is afraid of the dark, a fact the castle bully tries to exploit to get even with Sir Fred.

Kraegel, Kenneth. *King Arthur's Very Great Grandson.*
Henry longs to be a hero like this great grandfather, but potential opponents just want to be friends.

O'Connor, Jane. *Sir Small and the Dragonfly.*
In this easy reader, Sir Small must rescue Princess Teena from the Dragonfly.

Thomas, Shelley Moore. *Good Night, Good Knight.*
The Good Knight comes to the rescue of three little dragons who can't go to sleep without drinks of water, bedtime stories, and goodnight kisses.

Wojtowycz, David. *Elephant Joe, Brave Knight!*
Elephant Joe and Zebra Pete set out to save a damsel in distress.

Ziefert, Harriet. *Night, Knight.*
Homonyms are the theme of this very easy reader book.

Crafts: Use black construction paper and tissue paper to make simple "stained glass" decorations.
App: *Jack and the Beanstalk.* Nosy Crow.

LADYBUGS

Brown, Ruth. *Ladybug, Ladybug.*
A ladybug runs into various animals while she is rushing home to see her children.

Carle, Eric. *The Grouchy Ladybug.*
This ladybug picks a fight with each animal she sees, including a whale. There is also a lesson on telling time in the story.

Conklin, Gladys. *Lucky Ladybugs.*
In this factual story with watercolor illustrations, the reader can learn about ladybugs.

Dahl, Michael. *Lots of Ladybugs: Counting by Fives.*
As the title indicates, this book helps children learn to count by fives, but it also has a story about ladybugs.

Donaldson, Julia. *What the Ladybug Heard.*
The quiet ladybug helps the other animals foil the robbers' plan to steal the prize-winning cow.

Gerth, Melanie. *Ten Little Ladybugs.*
Listeners will get practice in counting backward in this book with tactile ladybugs.

Finn, Isobel. *The Very Lazy Ladybug.*
A ladybug rides on a dog and other animals, but doesn't learn to fly until she is forced to do so.

Fox, Mem. *Yoo-Hoo, Ladybug!*
Children will look for the ladybug in this illustrated puzzle story.

O'Malley, Kevin. *Little Buggy Runs Away.*
Told in dialogue balloons and deeply saturated full color paintings, a little ladybug runs away from home but is afraid when night comes.

Thomas, Jan. *Can You Make a Scary Face?*
The ladybug encourages the audience to act out various commands in this engaging story that invites active participation.

Tickle, Jack. *Look Out, Ladybug!*
Ladybug has some difficulties as she learns to fly.

Craft: Check out www.daniellesplace.com/html/ladybugcrafts.html for several craft ideas, including ladybug hats, pencil toppers, and rock creatures.

App: *Endless Alphabet.* Originator, Inc.

LEAVES AND TREES

Ehlert, Lois. *Red Leaf, Yellow Leaf.*
Watch a maple tree grow from seed to sapling and watch the leaves change color.

Gove, Doris. *My Mother Talks to Trees.*
A girl joins her mother on a walk where she learns not to be embarrassed when her mother talks to trees.

Hall, Zoe. *Fall Leaves Fall.*
Clear illustrations that carry to a large crowd make this story of two brothers playing in the
     leaves perfect for toddler storytime.

Houghton, Eric. *The Crooked Apple Tree.*
A favorite tree will be missed when the family moves.

Lionni, Leo. *A Busy Year.*
Mouse watches his friend the tree grow and lose its leaves throughout the year.

Maestro, Betsy. *Why Do Leaves Change Color?*
This easy nonfiction book describes how and why leaves change color.

Matheson, Christie. *Tap the Magic Tree.*
In this interactive story, children will want to touch the pages to make the leaves fall or
     change color.

Stein, David. *Leaves.*
A curious bear wonders why the leaves are changing colors.

Udry, Janice. *A Tree is Nice.*
In this Caldecott winner, there are many reasons to appreciate trees.

Wells, Rosemary. *Ruby's Falling Leaves.*
Max helps his big sister Ruby collect leaves for a school project.

Craft: Make leaf rubbings: gather a variety of leaves, and then have plenty of paper and
     crayons with the paper peeled off. The child puts a piece of paper on top of the leaf
     and rubs it with the side of the crayon.

LIZARDS

Carle, Eric. *The Mixed Up Chameleon.*
In this classic picture book, a chameleon learns to change his shape and size as well as his
     color.

Carlson, Nancy. *Henry's Show and Tell.*
Henry brings his pet lizard for show and tell, but it escapes!

Chisato, Tashiro. *Chameleon's Colors.*
Chameleon is tired of changing colors, but the other animals wish they could so he helps
     them by painting them in exciting patterns.

Cowley, Joy. *Chameleon, Chameleon.*
Dramatic color photos are the highlight of this very simple nonfiction book on
     chameleons.

Craig, Lindsey. *Dancing Feet!*
Six different animals, including a lizard, get up and dance in this rhyming guessing game
     that will inspire interaction with the audience.

Gravett, Emily. *Blue Chameleon.*
Chameleon wants to make a friend but has a difficult time.

Hadithi, Mwenye. *Crafty Chameleon.*
In this African pourquoi tale, a chameleon tries to escape from a leopard and a crocodile.

Koontz, Robin. *Lizzie Little, the Sky is Falling!*
Lizzie the lizard gets the other desert animals to help her when she believes the sky is falling.

Lionni, Leo. *A Color of His Own.*
A chameleon wishes to stay one color, but learns to be himself.

Na, Il Sung. *Hide & Seek.*
Elephant counts to 10 and plays hide and seek with the other animals, who are all easy to pick out of the illustrations except the chameleon.

Perlman, Janet. *The Delicious Bug.*
Two chameleons catch a bug on their tongues at the same time and fight over who gets to eat it.

Shannon, George. *Lizard's Song.*
Bear tries to learn the words to Lizard's song; the audience will chant along to this humorous tale.

Craft: Make simple lizards out of Play-doh or other crafting clay.
App: *Simms Taback Children's Book Collection.* CJ Educations.

MAGICIANS

Agee, Jon. *Milo's Hat Trick.*
Milo the Magnificent has difficulty with his magic tricks.

Cate, Annette. *The Magic Rabbit.*
Ray the magician is separated from his bunny in the big city.

Christelow, Eileen. *Olive and the Magic Hat.*
Olive and Otis play with their father's top hat. Father thinks the hat is magic when he can hear it "talk."

DePaola, Tomie. *Strega Nona's Magic Lessons.*
Big Anthony thinks only women can be stregas (witches), so he dresses up as a girl to learn some of Strega Nona's magic.

Grossman, Bill. *My Little Sister Ate One Hare.*
Dressed as a magician, a little girl enjoys eating snakes and other critters, until she "urps" when she has to eat peas! A fun counting story.

Lester, Helen. *The Wizard, the Fairy, and the Magic Chicken.*
Three boastful magicians try to outdo each other, but they need to work together to undo the trouble they have caused.

Meddaugh, Susan. *Cinderella's Rat.*
One of the rats that were turned into a coachman for Cinderella tells his side of the story.

Paul, Ruth. *Hedgehog's Magic Tricks.*
Friends help out hedgehog when his magic show isn't very magical.

Sperring, Mark. *Max and the Won't Go to Bed Show.*
Max puts on a wild variety show, including magic, so he won't have to go to bed.

Turkle, Brinton. *Do Not Open.*
A woman finds a magic bottle on the beach—should she open it?

Crafts: Make a Wizard's pointed hat out of paper.
App: *Jack and the Beanstalk.* Nosy Crow.

MAIL CARRIERS

Ahlberg, Jane and Allan. *The Jolly Postman.*
Packed with letters and foldouts, fairy tale characters correspond with one another.

Carter, Don. *Send It!*
Cut paper collages show a mailman on his route.

Keats, Ezra Jack. *A Letter to Amy.*
The boy from *Peter's Chair* and *The Snowy Day* sends a birthday party invitation to his
    friend Amy.

Kent, Jack. *Joey Runs Away.*
The postman delivers Joey back to his mom after he runs away.

Kightley, Rosalinda. *The Postman.*
Rhyming tale of a mail carrier going around the city.

Poydar, Nancy. *Mailbox Magic.*
A boy sends away for a special cereal bowl.

Rylant, Cynthia. *Mr. Grigg's Work.*
Neighbors fill in for the postmaster when he is sick with the flu.

Scott, Ann Herbert. *Hi!*
A small child says "Hi!" to everyone in line at the post office.

Vries, Anke de. *Raf.*
Ben loses his stuffed animal giraffe Raf, but soon receives postcards from him.

Wells, Rosemary. *Bunny Mail.*
Max sends Santa a request for a bike, while sister Ruby plans a July 4th parade. Grandma
    receives letters from each of them.

Craft: Obtain donated postcards from staff and volunteers. Children (with a parent's help)
    can write a postcard to their grandparent or other relative. Have the library mail the
    cards and cover postage.

MATH

Appelt, Kathi. *Bats on Parade.*
A bat marching band lines up in different formations to teach basic multiplication in this
    humorous rhyming story.

Cuyler, Margery. *Guinea Pigs Add Up.*
A bouncy rhyme describes an ever-increasing guinea pig family at a school.

Dodds, Dayle Ann. *Minnie's Diner.*
A funny rhyming story about doubling, where Minnie serves a group of brothers, each twice as large as his younger sibling.

Franco, Betsy. *Double Play: Monkeying Around with Addition.*
Chimps learn about doubling when they are on the playground in this rhyming story.

Fromental, Jean-Luc. *365 Penguins.*
A family receives a penguin each day in the mail, which soon turns into a disaster.

Horton, Joan. *Math Attack!*
Under the stress of math homework, numbers start to fly out of the brain of a young girl.

Jenkins, Emily. *Lemonade in Winter.*
Siblings set up a lemonade stand to earn money.

Maloney, Peter. *One Foot Two Feet.*
Die-cut pages help children see in a new way in this unusual counting story.

Markel, Michelle. *Tyrannosaurus Math.*
Fifteen math concepts are introduced by a charming T Rex.

McElligott, Matthew. *Bean Thirteen.*
Two bugs try to divide 13 beans evenly.

McElligott, Matthew. *Lion's Share.*
At the lion's party, each guest takes half of the cake, until it is Ant's turn and only a crumb is left.

Oxley, Jennifer. *The Chicken Problem.*
When 100 chickens escape their coop, Peg and Cat use math to gather them up.

Reynolds, Aaron. *Superhero School.*
Instead of learning to fly, kids at Superhero school are stuck in math class, but that comes in handy when they are attacked.

Rosenthal, Amy K. *This Plus That: Life's Little Equations.*
This fanciful book shows how addition can help make good things happen.

Craft: Make a Lotto-style matching game: www.simplydaycare.com/lotto-games.html
App: *Drive About: Number Neighborhood.* Artgig Studios.

MEXICO

Aardema, Verna. *Borreguita and the Coyote.*
In this folktale from Mexico, a sheep outwits a coyote. The children can make the repeated animal sounds found throughout the story.

Brown, Monica. *Chavela and the Magic Bubble.*
Chavela blows a large bubble and floats to Mexico, where her great-grandfather once worked harvesting gum tree sap.

Elya, Susan M. *Eight Animals on the Town.*
Spanish words are woven into this story about animals that go shopping.

Guy, Ginger. *Fiesta!*
A very simple story, with a few Spanish words, about a birthday party.

Mora, Pat. *Uno, Dos, Tres = One, Two, Three.*
Two sisters count in English and Spanish, trying to find a birthday present for Mother.

Ryan, Pam Munoz. *Mice and Beans.*
While a grandmother prepares for a birthday party, mice have plans of their own.

Winter, Jeanette. *Josefina.*
A counting book about the real-life artist Josefina Aguilar, who makes painted clay figures.

Craft: Tissue paper flowers are a traditional craft from Mexico that a preschooler can make with the help of an adult. For the instructions, see http://spoonful.com/crafts/tissue-paper-flowers

MIGRATION

Berne, Jennifer. *Calvin Can't Fly.*
A starling reads books instead of flying south with his cousins.

Hills, Tad. *How Rocket Learned to Read.*
A little bird teaches a dog how to read, then flies away for the winter.

Harris, Sue. *The Little Seal.*
A harp seal migrates south with his mother, but misses his friends back home.

Johnson, Amy Crane. *Lewis Cardinal's First Winter.*
Lewis is reluctant to migrate until Solomon Raven explains why he must.

Kent, Jack. *Round Robin.*
Round Robin is too plump to fly south so he must walk in this cartoon-like picture book.

Meddaugh, Susan. *Tree of Birds.*
Harry finds an injured bird named Sally. The other birds won't fly south without Sally, so Harry must find a way to make sure they don't freeze in the winter.

O Flatharta, Antoine. *Hurry and the Monarch.*
Hurry, the tortoise, befriends a monarch butterfly who stops in Texas on its way from Canada to Mexico.

Sockabasin, Allen. *Thanks to the Animals.*
Set in Maine and reflecting Passamaquoddy culture, a baby falls off the bobsled heading south for the winter, but his father walks back to find him.

Wild, Margaret. *Lucy Goosey.*
Lucy is having so much fun she doesn't want to leave when it is time to migrate with the other geese.

Wolff, Ashley. *A Year of Birds.*
Children learn about the months of the year and various types of birds.

Craft: Along with hibernation, bird migration is a topic preschoolers learn in autumn. For an activity, make bird feeders out of pinecones: http://web4.audubon.org/educate/educators/bird_feeders.html

App: *Don't Let the Pigeon Run This App.* Disney.

MONSTERS

Arnold, Tedd. *Five Ugly Monsters.*
A variation on "Five Little Monkeys Jumping on the Bed."

Austin, Mike. *Monsters Love School.*
Nervous about the first day of school, the monsters learn how to succeed in this new environment.

Emberley, Ed. *Go Away, Big Green Monster!*
Kids will shout out the "Go away" to each part of the monster's face—a fun, interactive storytime favorite, also available as a puppet.

Hutchins, Pat. *The Very Worst Monster.*
Hazel Monster, sister to baby Billy Monster, describes how she can be more monstrous than the new baby.

Lester, Helen. *The Loch Mess Monster.*
A very messy monster learns to pick up after himself.

Mayer, Mercer. *There's a Monster in My Closet.*
Another storytime classic, about a boy who has to console the frightened monster. The boy has a toy gun which some parents may want to avoid.

Miranda, Anne. *Monster Math.*
A brief, rhyming story to help us count the monsters. No numerals are shown, just the word for the number and the monsters to be counted.

O'Keefe, Susan. *One Hungry Monster.*
A funny, rhyming counting story that ends in a food fight worthy of the Three Stooges.

Rubin, Adam. *Big Bad Bubble.*
Four monsters face their greatest fear—bubbles!

Sendak, Maurice. *Where the Wild Things Are.*
The classic tale, available in Spanish and Chinese, stars Max who tames the Wild Things.

Willis, Jeanne. *The Monster Bed.*
Dennis the monster is afraid to go to bed; maybe there are humans under the bed! Look closely for the stuffed animal that resembles one of Sendak's *Wild Things*, at the foot of Dennis's bed.

Winthrop, Elizabeth. *Maggie and the Monster.*
One of the few picture books that show a monster who is a girl.

Yolen, Jane. *Creepy Monsters, Sleepy Monsters: A Lullaby.*
Two siblings enjoy familiar activities until it is time to go to bed.

Craft: Make a paper bag puppet based on *Go Away, Big Green Monster.*
App: *Go Away, Big Green Monster!* Night & Day Studios.

MOTHER GOOSE

Ahlberg, Janet and Allan. *Each Peach Pear Plum.*
This serves as a guessing game if you have a small enough group to spot the Mother Goose characters hidden in each illustration.

Baker, Keith. *Hickory Dickory Dock.*
A variety of animals react to the clock striking the time in this variation of the popular rhyme.

Conway, David. *The Great Nursery Rhyme Disaster.*
Miss Muffet explores the other characters in her nursery rhyme book.

Galdone, Paul. *Three Little Kittens.*
This picture book story of the popular rhyme will have kids singing along.

Hennessy, B.G. *The Missing Tarts.*
With delightful illustrations by Tracey Campbell Pearson, this book serves as a rhyming guessing game. See if the children can identify the Mother Goose character in each rhyme before you get to the end of a verse.

Imai, Miko. *Little Lumpty.*
Lumpty knows the story of Humpty Dumpty, yet he still ventures onto a wall. He's stuck there until his resourceful mother thinks of a solution to the problem.

Marshall, James. *Old Mother Hubbard and Her Dog.*
A longer Mother Goose rhyme that introduces some new vocabulary to kids, and Marshall's cartoon illustrations modernize the story.

Opie, Iona and Wells, Rosemary. *My Very First Mother Goose* and *Here Comes Mother Goose.*
Children are familiar with Wells' characters, so these two books are a great way to introduce certain characters like Humpty Dumpty, which we will see in some of the other books.

Pearson, Tracey Campbell. *Sing a Song of Sixpence.*
One rhyme illustrated as a picture book; this is fun paired with *The Missing Tarts.*

Craft: Glue cotton balls to a cut-out of a lamb, to accompany "Mary Had a Little Lamb."
Song: "Mary Had a Little Lamb."
App: *Together Time with Song and Rhyme for Parent and Preschooler.* Mulberry Media Interactive Inc.

MOTHER'S DAY

Bauer, Marion Dane. *My Mother Is Mine.*
Animal mothers are shown taking care of their children, as a human child makes a Mother's Day card.

Christelow, Eileen. *Five Little Monkeys Jumping on the Bed.*
Wait for the surprise ending, where Mother is jumping on the bed!

Flack, Marjorie. *Ask Mr. Bear.*
In this classic, a young boy asks several animals their advice as to what he should give his
   mother as a birthday gift.

French, Vivian. *A Present for Mom.*
Stanley can't decide what to give his mother for Mother's Day.

Guardino, Debbie. *Is Your Mama a Llama?*
A rhyming, humorous text invites audience participation in this story of animal mothers.

Mora, Pat. *Uno, Dos, Tres = One, Two, Three.*
A very brief rhyming story, using Spanish and English, about finding a birthday present
   for Mama.

Murphy, Jill. *Five Minutes Peace.*
Mother elephant wants just "five minutes peace" from her three rambunctious offspring.

O'Connor, Jane. *Fancy Nancy's Marvelous Mother's Day Brunch.*
Lift the flaps to see what Nancy is making for brunch!

Simpson, Martha. *What Not to Give Your Mom on Mother's Day.*
A boy tries to figure out what would be an appropriate gift for his mother.

Smalls-Victor, Irene. *Jonathan and His Mommy.*
Get everyone on their feet to follow along with the characters as they walk, jump,
   and dance down the street, in this story depicting an African American mother
   and son.

Craft: Make a Mother's Day card, or make paper flower daffodils using a cupcake paper
   and a pipe cleaner, with leaves cut from construction paper.
App: *Together Time with Song and Rhyme for Parent and Preschooler.* Mulberry Media
   Interactive Inc.

MOVEMENT

Carle, Eric. *From Head to Toe.*
Get the audience up to mimic the movements in this story, about animals that move various
   parts of the body.

Chapman, Lynne. *Baby Can . . . Bounce!*
Baby animals demonstrate various movements the audience can replicate.

Craig, Lindsey. *Dancing Feet!*
A catching rhyming book that will have the audience on their feet.

Cronin, Doreen. *Bounce.*
A dog demonstrates the various ways you can bounce.

Cronin, Doreen. *Wiggle.*
This rhyming text describes the various ways you can wiggle.

Frazee, Marla. *Walk On!*
A baby learns to walk in this hilarious story.

London, Jonathan. *Wiggle Waggle.*
A story about how various animals walk and move; have the listeners copy the movements.

Newcome, Zita. *Toddlerobics.*
Toddlers stretch and do other exercises in this amusing book. Also try *Toddlerobics: Animal Fun.*

Rosen, Michael. *We're Going On a Bear Hunt.*
The popular campfire call and response story, where the audience can re-enact the movements done in the story.

Reid, Rob. *Wave Goodbye.*
Many of us use the rhyme in this story as a closing song at storytime—wave your hands, feet, lips, and other body parts!

Walton, Rick. *My Two Hands/My Two Feet.*
Two back-to-back rhyming stories about the hands and feet.

Wood, Audrey. *Quick as a Cricket.*
A boy copies the motions of various animals. Also available in a Big Book edition.

Craft: Paper windsocks: cutout a few shapes (like stars) within a piece of paper, and then form the paper into a tube. Tape tissue paper streamers along the bottom of the tube, then hang up like a windsock!
Songs: "Shake Your Sillies Out" by Raffi, "The Hokey Pokey."
App: *Sandra Boynton Collection.* Loud Crow.

MUSIC

Ajmera, Maya, Elise Hofer Derstine, and Cynthia Pon. *Music Everywhere!*
Color photos and a very brief text show children from around the world playing musical instruments.

Busse, Sarah Martin. *Banjo Granny.*
Owen's grandma travels across the country to play his favorite bluegrass music.

Cox, Judy. *My Family Plays Music.*
The whole family plays musical instruments.

James, Simon. *Baby Brains Superstar.*
A precocious baby becomes a rock star due to his uncanny ability to play electric guitar.

Kraus, Robert. *Musical Max.*
Practice makes perfect! Max's rehearsals annoy his neighbors, until he stops playing and the silence bothers them even more.

Krosoczka, Jarrett. *Punk Farm.*
Old MacDonald is shocked to see that his animals have formed a punk rock band.

Lyon, George Ella. *Five Live Bongos.*
Five siblings use anything around the house to make music, from banging on pots and pans to drumming on things they find at the junkyard.

Marsalis, Wynton. *Squeak, Rumble, Whomp! Whomp! Whomp!*
Onomatopoetic text describes music in a young boy's neighborhood.

Pinkney, Brian. *Max Found Two Sticks.*
A boy drums on buckets and other found objects instead of speaking, but his family knows what his music communicates.

Wissinger, Tamera Will. *This Old Band.*
In this humorous counting story based on the song "This Old Man," cowboys start their own band.

Yaccarino, Dan. *Oswald Makes Music.*
Inspired by a band they hear in the park, Oswald and his dog try to make music, but they don't have instruments.

Ziefert, Harriet. *Animal Music.*
A picture book containing two stories: one is about an animal marching band, the other is about a farm animal dance band.

Craft: Make tambourines by stapling two paper plates together that are filled with uncooked rice, beans, or popcorn. Of course, the kids can decorate the plates with brightly colored markers or streamers.

App: *Together Time with Song and Rhyme for Parent and Preschooler.* Mulberry Media Interactive Inc.

NAMES

Daly, Niki. *The Boy on the Beach.*
The lifeguard helps a lost boy find his parents, when the boy spells out his name in the sand.

Dylan, Bob. *Man Gave Names to All the Animals.*
The lyrics of the song are illustrated with colorful cartoons.

Engel, Diana. *Josephina Hates Her Name.*
Wishing she had a short name like friends Amy and Sarah, her mother explains how she is named after a long-lost aunt.

Fox, Mem. *Wilfred Gordon McDonald Partridge.*
Wilfrid befriends several residents at the senior home, including Miss Nancy.

Henkes, Kevin. *Chrysanthemum.*
She always loved her name until the kids at school make fun of it.

Lester, Helen. *A Porcupine Named Fluffy.*
Fluffy doesn't live up to his name, but realizes it could be worse when he befriends a rhino named Hippo!

Mosel, Arlene. *Tikki Tikki Tembo.*
A longtime storytime favorite that is available in a Big Book edition. Eldest son's long name is so difficult to say it can be hazardous when he falls in a well.

Peek, Merle. *Mary Wore Her Red Dress.*
A picture book based on the popular folksong; adapt it to the names of kids at your storyhour.

Slate, Joseph. *Miss Bindergarten Gets Ready for Kindergarten.*
A great alphabet book that incorporates the names of 26 students, and works as a story about the first day of school.

Craft: Make nameplates out of paper for the child's bedroom door.
Song: "John Jacob Jingleheimer Schmidt," "The Name Game (Banana-Fana Fo Fana)," and "Aikendrum."
App: *How Rocket Learned to Read.* Random House Digital.

NOISES

Blake, Quentin. *All Join In.*
Short verse celebrating a variety of noises.

Brown, Margaret Wise. *The Noisy Book.*
One of several books by Brown, featuring a little dog and noises he hears in various locations.

Coy, John. *Vroomaloom Zoom.*
Carmella and her dad drive through the woods hearing all types of noises.

Dodd, Emma. *Dog's Noisy Day.*
In this sequel to *Dog's Colorful Day*, the little white dog encounters several sounds as he takes his morning walk.

Edwards, Michelle and Phyllis Root. *What's That Noise?*
Brothers Alex and Ben are kept awake by a scary noise.

Edwards, Pamela. *Slop Goes the Soup: A Noisy Warthog Word Book.*
A very brief but funny story full of sound words like crash, clatter, and whoosh.

Feiffer, Jules. *Bark, George.*
A mother dog takes her puppy to the vet to find out why he isn't barking.

Fleming, Candace. *Muncha! Muncha! Muncha!*
Rabbits take over a farmer's garden.

Fuge, Charles. *Yip! Snap! Yap!*
Dogs make different types of barking and growling sounds, and the audience is encouraged to make the same noises.

Kuskin, Karla. *All Sizes of Noises.*
Full of onomatopoeia, we watch John wake up and go throughout his day making various sounds.

Kuskin, Karla. *Roar and More.*
Animal noises are featured in this book, similar to *All Sizes of Noises.*

Martin, Bill. *Polar Bear, Polar Bear, What Do You Hear?*
A participation story similar to *Brown Bear, Brown Bear, What Do You See?*

Massie, Diane. *The Baby Beebee Bird.*
A little bird keeps the entire zoo awake by chirping all night.

Maynard, Bill. *Quiet, Wyatt!*
Wyatt, the smallest kid on the block, is constantly told to be quiet. When he does so, people miss what he can tell them.

Most, Bernard. *The Cow That Went Oink.*
A cow and a pig teach each other their languages.

Pearson, Tracey Campbell. *Bob.*
Bob, the rooster, asks several animals for help in learning how to crow.

Showers, Paul. *The Listening Walk.*
A girl and her father take a walk, and identify the various sounds they hear along the way.

Spence, Robert. *Clickety Clack.*
A train gets increasingly noisier as quacking ducks and other creatures get on board.

Underwood, Deborah. *The Loud Book!*
A brief but lively text describes various sounds throughout the day.

Wells, Rosemary. *Noisy Nora.*
Nora, the middle child, makes noise to get attention from her busy parents.

Zolotow, Charlotte. *The Quiet Mother and the Noisy Little Boy.*
Mother thinks her son Sandy is noisy, until they meet the boisterous boy next door.

Crafts: Try making these noisemakers: www.marthastewart.com/portal/site/mslo/menuitem.3a0656639de62ad593598e10d373a0a0/?vgnextoid=33598670de42f010VgnVCM1000003d370a0aRCRD&rsc=also_try
Songs: "Old MacDonald."
App: *Dr. Seuss Beginner Book Collection #1 and #2.* Oceanhouse Media.

OCEAN LIFE

Adams, Georgie. *Fish Fish Fish.*
Colorful collage illustrations depict various fish in the ocean.

Carle, Eric. *Mister Seahorse.*
Great for Father's Day, Mister Seahorse greets other ocean fathers who care for their young.

Cousins, Lucy. *Hooray for Fish.*
Author of the "Maisy" series presents this large, brightly colored story of a fish who knows many ocean creatures.

Clements, Andrew. *Big Al.*
Big Al, the blowfish, is teased for being ugly, but when he helps the other fish who are caught in a net, they see beyond his appearance to become friends.

Farrell, Darren. *Thank You, Octopus.*
Octopus helps his buddy get ready for bed.

Galloway, Ruth. *Fidgety Fish.*
Brightly colored cartoon illustrations help tell the story of Tidler, who is swallowed by a bigger fish.

Kranking, Kathleen. *The Ocean Is.*
Color photos and rhyming verse describe what is in the ocean.

Kraus, Robert. *Herman the Helper.*
Herman the octopus is a great help to the other ocean creatures.

Lionni, Leo. *Swimmy.*
A little black fish has the solution to the problem of being prey for bigger fish.

Metzger, Steve. *Five Little Sharks Swimming in the Sea.*
A counting book patterned after the fingerplay "Five Little Monkeys Jumping on the Bed."

Oppel, Kenneth. *Peg and the Whale.*
Peg is raised on a ship, and is a great fisherman. She sets her sights on catching a whale.

Pallota, Jerry. *Dory Story.*
The ocean's food chain is explained in this simple story of a boy's imagination.

Rose, Deborah Lee. *Into the A, B, Sea: An Ocean Alphabet.*
Twenty-six ocean animals are featured in this entertaining alphabet book.

Ryan, Pamela Munoz. *Hello, Ocean!*
Using her five senses, a girl describes how she experiences the wonders of the ocean.

Sherry, Kevin. *I'm the Biggest Thing in the Ocean.*
A giant squid brags about being large until he meets someone bigger.

Stockdale, Susan. *Fabulous Fishes.*
A simple rhyming text describes various fish in this informational picture book.

Ward, Helen. *Old Shell, New Shell: A Coral Reef Tale.*
A hermit crab looks for a new, bigger shell. He encounters a variety of ocean life while on
    his search.

Ward, Jennifer. *Somewhere In the Ocean.*
A counting book in rhyme, showing ocean creatures and their young.

Wood, Audrey. *Ten Little Fish.*
Brightly colored computer-generated illustrations complement this simple counting story.

Craft: Paper plate octopus: the plate is the octopus's body; have the kids color and put on
    eyes, mouth, and so forth. Then they attach eight paper streamers to the plate for legs;
    this is a great counting activity.
App: *Ten Little Fish.* CJ Educations.

OUTER SPACE

Asch, Frank. *Moon Bear.*
Bear is worried that the moon is shrinking, so he decides to take action.

Best, Cari. *Shrinking Violet.*
Shy Violet stars in the school play about the Solar System.

Branley, Franklyn M. *The Planets of the Solar System.*
A great nonfiction book, useful for introducing facts on the Solar System. There are instruc-
    tions for a craft mobile at the back of the book.

Brewster, Patience. *Ellsworth and the Cats from Mars.*
A cat dreams about green furry cats visiting from Mars. The small pictures and longer text make this better for older children.

Malone, Peter. *Star Shapes.*
A rhyming text describes some of the animal constellations.

Mayo, Margaret. *Zoom, Rocket, Zoom!*
A rhythmic text describes astronauts working in outer space.

McNamara, Margaret. *The Three Little Aliens and the Big Bad Robot.*
In this spoof of "Three Little Pigs," three aliens set off to find a new planet.

McNaughton, Colin. *Here Come the Aliens.*
Kids will laugh out loud at this silly story about space aliens.

Puttock, Simon. *Earth to Stella.*
This colorful picture book stars a girl named Stella, who imagines she is an astronaut exploring outer space.

Reidy, Jean. *Light Up the Night.*
In this cumulative rhyming story, a boy takes a nighttime ride when his blanket becomes a rocket ship.

Sadler, Marilyn. *Alistair from Outer Space.*
While on the way to the library to return his books, Alistair is kidnapped by aliens.

Saltzberg, Barney. *The Soccer Mom from Outer Space.*
Sometimes parents act like they are from outer space!

Shields, Carol D. *Martian Rock.*
A rhyming story that describes the planets in the Solar System; with a surprise ending!

Viva, Frank. *A Long Way Away.*
A picture book that reads front to back, then back to front, about a journey from the deep sea to outer space.

Willis, Jeanne. *Earthlets, As Explained by Professor Xargle.*
A class of alien children learn about humans before visiting our planet.

Yaccarino, Dan. *Zoom! Zoom! Zoom! I'm Off to the Moon!*
A boy flies his spaceship to the moon.

Yorinks, Al. *Company's Coming!*
Moe and Shirley invite some visitors from outer space to stay for dinner.

Craft: Make the mobile of the solar system found at: www.craftsforkids.com/projects /real_solar_system.htm
Song: "Twinkle, Twinkle, Little Star."

PENGUINS

Apperley, Dawn. *Flip and Flop.*
Little brother Flop wants to play with his big brother, but Flip only wants to play with his friends.

Bickford, Tessa. *Go, Jojo, Go! A Little Penguin on a Big Swim.*
Color photos show penguins as they learn to swim.

Boynton, Sandra. *Your Personal Penguin.*
This board book features a rhyme about a penguin, along with Boynton's signature cartoon
 illustrations.

Buzzeo, Toni. *One Cool Friend.*
Elliot befriends a penguin at the aquarium.

Chester, Jonathan. *Splash! A Penguin Counting Book.*
Photos of Adele penguins highlight this counting book.

Gravois, Jeanne. *Quickly, Quigley.*
Children will call out the title, which is repeated several times throughout this story about
 a little penguin.

Guion, Melissa. *Baby Penguins Love Their Mama!*
Mama penguin teaches the babies how to slide, waddle, and do other tasks.

Lester, Helen. *Tacky the Penguin.*
Tacky is much different than the other penguins, which comes in handy when hunters come
 to their ice flow.

Metzger, Steve. *Five Little Penguins Slipping on the Ice.*
A lively counting song about penguins.

Yoon, Salina. *Penguin on Vacation.*
Penguin is tired of the snow and cold so he goes on vacation to the beach.

Craft: Visit www.first-school.wtheme/animals/birds/penguin.htm
App: *Parker Penguin.* Nosy Crow.

PETS

Baek, Matthew J. *Be Gentle with Dog, Dear!*
Baby Elissa needs to learn to be kind to dog Tag.

Biedrzycki, David. *Me and My Dragon.*
A boy describes how he cares for his pet dragon.

Boelts, Maribeth. *Before You Were Mine.*
A little dog is adopted from a shelter.

Brown, Peter. *Children Make Terrible Pets.*
A bear asks her mother if she can keep the child she found in the woods as her pet.

Capucilli, Alyssa. *Biscuit Wins a Prize.*
In this very easy reader, Biscuit is entered in his first dog show.

Cooper, Melrose. *Pets!*
A rhyming celebration of pets includes "Sleek pets, slick pets, do-amazing-tricks pets."

Gwynne, Fred. *Easy To See Why.*
The audience will chant "easy to see why," which is repeated throughout this story concerning dogs that resemble their owners.

Graham, Margaret. *Benji and His Friend Fifi.*
Fifi, the poodles, runs off while getting groomed for the pet show, but neighbor mutt Benji runs after her.

Keats, Ezra Jack. *Pet Show!*
Kids from the neighborhood all win a prize, from the brightest goldfish, to the busiest ants, to Archie's germ in a glass jar. Libraries may want to model their pet shows after this one since everyone walks away a winner!

LaRochelle, David. *The Best Pet of All.*
A young boy's mother won't let him have a dog, so he brings home a dragon as a pet.

London, Jonathan. *Froggy and the Doggy.*
Froggy and his sister get a new pet.

Plourde, Lynn. *Dino Pets.*
A boy brings home various dinosaurs from the pet store to figure out which would make the best pet.

Craft: Make a paper bag puppet of your favorite pet animal.
App: *How Rocket Learned to Read.* Random House Digital.

PHOTOSYNTHESIS

Bang, Molly. *Living Sunlight: How Plants Bring the Earth to Life.*
The sun describes photosynthesis using a rhyming text in this thoughtful book. Also available on DVD.

Carle, Eric. *The Tiny Seed.*
Carle's signature collages illustrate this tale of a seed that sprouts, showing the plant's life cycle through the seasons.

Cole, Henry. *Jack's Garden.*
In this cumulative story, Jack plants a beautiful garden.

Ehlert, Lois. *Planting a Rainbow.*
Along with the concept of colors, this shows how flowers grow from bulbs, seeds, or seedlings.

Ehlert, Lois. *Red Leaf, Yellow Leaf.*
A maple leaf shows how plants grow from seed to sapling in this beautifully illustrated story.

Fogliano, Julie. *And Then It's Spring.*
A boy waits anxiously for the seeds he planted to sprout.

Ghigna, Charles. *Little Seeds.*
A simple rhyming text describes a child who has planted flower seeds in the garden.

Heller, Ruth. *The Reason for a Flower.*
Lavish illustrations depict the life cycle of a flower.

Hood, Susan. *Rooting for You: A Moving Up Story.*
A seed is hesitant to stick his head out of the dirt and sprout, but gets some encouragement.

Kraus, Ruth. *The Carrot Seed.*
In this classic tale, a small boy plants a seed and waits for it to come up.

Worth, Bonnie. *Oh Say Can You Seed?*
The Cat in the Hat examines various parts of a flower and explains photosynthesis.

Craft: For an activity, take-home plants are great. You can also make tissue paper flowers, seed mosaics, or other flower activities.

PIRATES

Fox, Mem. *Tough Boris.*
Boris is not so tough when his parrot dies.

Greene, Rhonda Gowler. *No Pirates Allowed! Said Library Lou.*
Big Pirate Pete thinks there is treasure in the library, but Library Lou must convince him the treasure is in the books.

Horowitz, Dave. *Twenty-Six Pirates: An Alphabet Book.*
A pirate for each letter of the alphabet populates this humorous tale.

Leuck, Laura. *I Love My Pirate Papa.*
A little boy describes all the things he appreciates about his father, who is a pirate.

Long, Melinda. *How I Became a Pirate.*
A boy describes how he learned about pirate behavior. Also try the sequel, *Pirates Don't Change Diapers.*

McFarland, Lyn Rossiter. *Pirate's Parrot.*
A teddy bear replaces the pirate's parrot, and he proves to be up to the job.

McPhail, David. *Edward and the Pirates.*
When Edward learns to read, he can enter the world of imaginary characters, including pirates!

Sobel, June. *A Pirate ABC.*
A band of pirates plan to capture the entire alphabet.

Crafts: Make spyglasses out of toilet paper or paper towel tubes.

PIZZA

Auch, Mary Jane. *The Princess and the Pizza.*
To win the prince, a practical princess must pass a series of tests, which include cooking a pizza.

Barbour: Karen. *Little Nino's Pizzeria.*
Tony helps out at this family's restaurant.

Dobson, Christina. *Pizza Counting.*
Using pizzas, readers learn about counting and fractions.

Herman, Gail. *Pizza Cats.*
Three stray cats takeover a pizza parlor.

Maccarone, Grace. *Pizza Party.*
In this simple easy reader, a group of kids make a pizza.

Rubin, Adam. *Secret Pizza Party.*
Raccoon loves pizza so he crashes the party next door.

Smith, Maggie. *Pigs in Pajamas.*
In this story celebrating the letter P, pizza is one of the foods delivered to the pig's sleepover
    party.

Steig, William. *Pete's a Pizza.*
Pete and his dad have a great game where dad pretends to make Pete into a pizza.

Stoodt, Jeffrey. *Pizza Pokey.*
A pizza-themed version of "The Hokey Pokey" song.

Sturges, Philemon. *The Little Red Hen Makes a Pizza.*
Unlike the original story, this little red hen shares her pizza with the pals who refused to
    help make it.

Walters, Virginia. *Hi Pizza Man!*
Kids will call out the repeated phrases in this simple but entertaining book.

Wellington, Monica. *Pizza at Sally's.*
Using vegetables from her garden, Sally makes pizza for her customers.

Craft: A simple pizza craft takes one paper plate. Then, the children cut out red circles
    (pepperoni), yellow triangles (cheese), and green rectangles (bell pepper), and glue
    them on the plate to make a pizza. This craft helps reinforce the concept of the easier
    shapes.

POTATOES

Black, Michael Ian. *I'm Bored.*
A little girl tries to prove to a potato that children are not tedious.

Bloom, Amy. *Little Sweet Potato.*
Little Sweet Potato searches for a home where he will be accepted, even though he is
    lumpy and bumpy.

Cazet, Denys. *Minnie and Moo and the Potato from Planet X.*
Minnie and Moo, those two wacky cows, help an alien who has landed on their farm.

Coy, John. *Two Old Potatoes and Me.*
A father and daughter grow potatoes in the backyard, from two old, eye-growing potatoes
    that they cut into chunks.

DeFelice, Cynthia. *One Potato, Two Potato.*
Based on a folktale, this story describes an old, poor couple who find a magic pot of
    potatoes.

Denise, Anika. *Pigs Love Potatoes.*
A counting book featuring pigs helping mama cook potatoes.

Doodler, Todd H. *One Potato, Two Potato.*
How many potatoes will fit into Mr. Potato Head's birthday party?

Farish, Terry. *The Cat Who Liked Potato Soup.*
An old man leaves his cat to go fishing, and the cat is afraid he won't return.

French, Vivian. *Oliver's Vegetables.*
Oliver will only eat French Fries until Grandpa shows him the other veggies growing in
    the backyard.

Katz, Michael. *Ten Potatoes in a Pot.*
A collection of counting rhymes. Just read one or two rhymes between each picture
    book.

Leedy, Loreen. *The Potato Party and Other Troll Tales.*
Seven short illustrated stories; the title one is perfect for this theme.

Lied, Kate. *Potato: A Tale from the Great Depression.*
Expressive cartoon illustrations by Lisa Campbell Ernst help tell this true story of a family
    who finds work picking potatoes.

Pomeroy, Diana. *One Potato: A Counting Book of Potato Prints.*
This counting book is illustrated with potato prints—it can inspire your art project.

Rockwell, Anne. *Sweet Potato Pie.*
The farm is a busy place, but everyone stops work when it is time for Grandma's sweet
    potato pie.

Selsam, Millicent. *More Potatoes!*
In this easy reader science book, a girl learns how potatoes are grown from the corner
    grocer and a local farmer.

Speed, Toby. *Brave Potatoes.*
At the County Fair, the potatoes stage a breakout and ride the Ferris Wheel to escape a
    mad chef.

Craft: Make potato prints: before the storytime, cut the potatoes into shapes. Kids just dip
    them in paint and "stamp" art paper. For instructions, check out www.kinderplanet
    .com/vegprint.htm

PRINCE AND PRINCESS

Andersen, Hans Christian. *The Princess and the Pea.*
One of Andersen's briefer stories, this is appropriate for preschoolers.

Harper, Charise Mericle. *Princess Patty Meets Her Match.*
Patty sets off to find her Prince Charming.

Kastner, Jill. *Princess Dinosaur.*
Princess Dinosaur plays with all the toys.

Katz, Karen. *Princess Baby.*
Princess does not like being called nicknames.

Kemp, Anna. *The Worst Princess.*
Princess Sue is grateful to be rescued by a prince, but she realizes she would prefer a less
    traditional partner.

Lester, Helen. *Princess Penelope's Parrot.*
The spoiled princess cannot get her parrot to talk.

Lobel, Arnold. *Prince Bertram the Bad.*
Prince Bertram goes too far when he throws a stone at a witch.

Munsch, Robert. *The Paper Bag Princess.*
This princess does not need help defeating a fire-breathing dragon.

Oppenheim, Joanne. *The Prince's Bedtime.*
The prince refuses to go to bed, until an old woman offers the best method to get him to
    go to sleep.

Priceman, Marjorie. *Princess Picky.*
Princess Perfect refuses to eat her vegetables, so she is called Princess Picky.

Todd, Mack. *Princess Penelope.*
Penelope is sure she must be a princess, even if she doesn't live with a "royal" family.

Craft: One of the easiest crafts is to make are crowns made out of construction paper, then
    decorated with glitter.
App: *Jack and the Beanstalk.* Nosy Crow.

QUEENS AND KINGS

Aardema, Verna. *The Riddle of the Drum.*
In this folktale from Mexico, suitors must demonstrate some special skills before they can
    marry the Princess.

DeRegniers, Beatrice Schenk. *May I Bring a Friend?*
When the King and Queen invite him to tea, a boy asks if he can bring various animals.

Funke, Cornelia. *Princess Knight.*
Princess Violetta is appalled that her father plans to give away her hand in marriage to
    whoever wins a jousting tournament, so she decides to participate!

Lester, Helen. *Princess Penelope's Parrot.*
The greedy princess tries to teach her new parrot how to speak with unexpected results.

Miller, M. L. *Dizzy From Fools.*
The Princess learns how to be a jester despite her father's objections.

Lobel, Arnold. *Giant John.*
A giant is hired to perform odd jobs around the castle.

Miura, Taro. *The Tiny King.*
The tiny king is lonely in his large castle until he meets a big princess.

Singleton, Debbie. *The King Who Wouldn't Sleep.*
A clever farmer helps the king fall asleep by using a counting activity.

Wood, Audrey and Don. *King Bidgood's in the Bathtub.*
This popular repetitive story will have your audience chanting along.

Crafts: Make a crown or jester's hat. Crowns can be made of cardstock paper, fitted like a headband, and decorated with glitter. Jester hats can be made from a paper bag: Cut out the bottom and roll like a cuff to make the headband, then cut the other end into points and curl down, rolling on a crayon.
App: *Jack and the Beanstalk.* Nosy Crow.

RAIN

Aardema, Verna. *Bringing the Rain to Kapiti Plain.*
Written in the same pattern as "The House That Jack Built," this African folktale describes a drought.

Ashman, Linda. *Rain!*
In this joyous story with a very brief text, a boy enjoys the rain.

Barrett, Judi. *Cloudy With a Chance of Meatballs.*
A very funny story about what would happen if it rained giant food items.

Bluemle, Elizabeth. *Tap Tap Boom Boom.*
A rainstorm in the big city sends folks to the subway.

Freeman, Don. *A Rainbow of My Own.*
A small boy imagines that he owns the rainbow.

Gibson, Amy. *Split! Splat!*
A girl enjoys being out in the rain, where she can sing her own rain song.

Hesse, Karen. *Come On, Rain!*
One of the few books about rain in the city, with African American characters celebrating the end of the drought.

Hillenbrand, Will. *Kite Day: A Bear and Mole Story.*
Bear and Mole fly their kite on a windy day, until it begins to rain.

Keats, Ezra Jack. *A Letter to Amy.*
Peter loses the invitation he wants to send Amy, while walking to the mailbox in the rain.

Parker, Mary Jessie. *The Deep, Deep Puddle.*
After a rainstorm, various animals fall into a puddle in this counting book filled with onomatopoeia.

Shaw, Charles. *It Looked Like Spilt Milk.*
The classic picture book, where different white blobs resemble an ice cream cone, a rabbit, and so forth.

Craft: Try an art project based on Charles Shaw's *It Looked Like Spilt Milk*: cut out a white "cloud" and glue to blue (sky) paper.

SHADOWS

Asch, Frank. *Bear Shadow.*
Bear tries to get rid of his shadow.

Bartolos, Michael. *Shadowville.*
At nighttime, shadows go into their own private world.

Berge, Claire. *Whose Shadow Is This? A Look at Animal Shapes.*
Guess the animal that gives off the shadow in the illustration.

Charlip, Remy. *Mother, Mother, I Feel Sick.*
Shadow pictures illustrate this popular jump rope rhyme.

Freeman, Don. *Gregory's Shadow.*
Gregory the groundhog is separated from his shadow; can he find it in time for
    Groundhog Day?

Leathers, Philippa. *The Black Rabbit.*
A large black rabbit is following little rabbit, until he discovers it is his shadow.

Lee, Suzy. *Shadow.*
An overhead light in her room allows a little girl to create an animal adventure.

Long, Greg. *Yeti, Turn Out the Light!*
Yeti can't sleep because he is afraid of the shadows on the wall.

MacKay, Elly. *Shadow Chasers.*
A rhythmic text details the concept of shadows in the summer sky.

Narahashi, Keiko. *I Have a Friend.*
A child describes her imaginary friend, who turns out to be her shadow.

Pallota, Jerry. *Who Will See Their Shadow This Year?*
In this Groundhog Day story, the animals are tired of winter, so they try to see their shad-
    ows to encourage the coming spring.

Swinburne, Stephen. *Guess Whose Shadow?*
Photos illustrate this guessing game about shadows.

Crafts: Make a stick puppet of a person on which the child could color in clothes, face or
    glue on a pair of pants and a shirt—using very simple pieces. They could add some
    yarn for hair. Then have them attach the same outline on another stick, but this time
    cut the outline in black construction paper to serve as the shadow.

SHAPES

Blackstone, Stella. *Ship Shapes.*
Search for various shapes in the illustrations of this story about a sea voyage and
    treasure hunt.

Boldt, Mike. *Colors Versus Shapes.*
The teams of Colors and of Shapes compete in a talent show.

Carle, Eric. *The Secret Birthday Message.*
Die cut pages feature shapes that lead the reader to a surprise in this clever story.

Chernesky, Felicia S. *Pick a Circle, Gather Squares: A Fall Harvest of Shapes.*
There are many examples of shapes at Pumpkin Farm.

Emberley, Ed. *The Wing on a Flea.*
Using a rhyming verse and bright paper cutouts on black backgrounds, this charming book shows the basic shapes and where they may occur.

Greene, Rhonda. *When a Line Bends . . . A Shape Begins.*
More details on what makes a shape are featured in this rhyming tale. The engaging illustrations include many of the shapes that kids can look for.

Henkes, Kevin. *Circle Dogs.*
Blocks of color take on characteristics of different common items in this imaginative story.

Micklethwait, Lucy. *I Spy Shapes in Art.*
Works of modern art are used to demonstrate various shapes.

Rikys, Bodel. *Red Bear's Fun with Shapes.*
Even toddlers will grasp the concept of shapes in this sweet story of a bear who finds shapes in the house and outside in nature.

Serfozo, Mary. *There's a Square.*
Another simple but charming rhyming story about shapes, this shows shapes as stick figure people.

Thong, Roseanne. *Round Is a Tortilla.*
Items from Mexican culture are used to demonstrate shapes in this rhyming story.

Zelinsky, Paul O. *Circle, Square, Moose.*
Moose invades a book of shapes, but Zebra comes to help him out and restore order.

Craft: Make Owl paper bag puppets using a triangle for the beak, circles for eyes, and rectangles for wings, or make a train engine out of shapes using a rectangle for the main portion, an upside down triangle for the spout, a square for the window, etc.

SNAKES

Ata, Te. *Baby Rattlesnake.*
In this Chickasaw Indian legend, a baby rattlesnake insists on getting a rattle even though he isn't old enough to take care of it.

Baker, Keith. *Hide and Snake.*
Listeners will look for the snake hidden in each picture.

Carle, Eric. *The Greedy Python.*
A python swallows 10 animals whole, but suffers from a stomach ache as a result.

Jonell, Lynne. *I Need a Snake.*
A boy wants a pet snake; illustrated with cartoon, child-like artwork.

Kellogg, Steven. *The Day Jimmy's Boa Ate the Wash.*
Jimmy brings his snake along on a field trip to a farm.

McNulty, Faith. *A Snake in the House.*
A pet snake is loose in the house!

Nygaard, Elizabeth. *Snake Alley Band.*
Sound effects are the highlight of this funny book about snakes making music.

Provencher, Rose-Marie. *Slithery Jake.*
In this rhyming story, a pet snake escapes from his cage.

Siegel, Randy. *My Snake Blake.*
A boy receives a long green snake as a pet, and it turns out to be a life saver!

Ungerer, Tomi. *Crictor.*
A boa constrictor is the pet of a kind old lady in France. He proves to be a hero when a
    burglar breaks into their apartment.

Walsh, Ellen Stoll. *Mouse Count.*
A snake puts sleeping field mice in a jar, one by one, in this counting story.

Yoon, Salina. *Opposnakes: A Lift-the-Flap Book about Opposites.*
Open the flaps to discover snakes in different colors, sizes, and shapes.

Craft: Make a spiral snake, like those found at www.dltk-kids.com/animals/mspiralsnake
    .htm

SNOW

Bauer, Caroline Feller. *Midnight Snowman.*
In a town where it rarely snows, neighbors take the opportunity to make a snowman after
    a storm.

Bean, Jonathan. *Big Snow.*
A boy waits and watches for snow all day, hoping to play with his sled.

Burton, Virginia. *Katy and the Big Snow.*
Katy is a snow removal machine who must dig out the city after a snowstorm.

Cuyler, Margery. *The Biggest, Best Snowman.*
Nell is told she is too small to help build the snowman, but she shows she is up to the job.

Ehlert, Lois. *Snowballs.*
A snow family is constructed—the artwork will inspire very creative snowman pictures.

Enderle, Judith. *Six Snowy Sheep.*
A fun rhyming story about counting sheep playing in the snow.

Goffstein, M. B. *Our Snowman.*
Big brother teaches little brother how to build a snowman.

Keats, Ezra Jack. *The Snowy Day.*
The Caldecott classic about a snowstorm in the city, and how Peter plays in the snow.

Kirk, Daniel. *The Snow Family.*
A boy makes a snow family just like his real one!

London, Jonathan. *Froggy Gets Dressed.*
Froggy usually hibernates all winter, but he wakes up to find that it has snowed!

Mack, Gail. *Yesterday's Snowman.*
A girl describes how she, her brother, and mother build a snowman, which melts before
   father gets home from work.

Norman, Kim. *If It's Snowy and You Know It, Clap Your Paws!*
A rollicking snow-filled take off of the song "If You're Happy and You Know It."

Pittman, Helena Clare. *The Snowman's Path.*
Nathan befriends a magical snowman.

Poydar, Nancy. *Snip, Snip, Snow!*
This simple story about a girl wanting to play outside includes instructions for making
   paper snowflakes.

Posner, Andrea. *Frosty Day.*
A special holiday just for snowmen!

Schertle, Alice. *All You Need Is a Snowman.*
A list of all the items you can use to make a snowman.

Waber, Bernard. *Bearsie Bear and the Surprise Sleepover Party.*
In this hilarious cumulative tale, Bearsie allows other forest animals into his bed during a
   blizzard, until Porcupine knocks on the door.

Ziefert, Harriet. *Snow Magic.*
The snow people have a party on the first day of winter.

Craft: Make snow pictures by gluing packing peanuts or cotton balls to construction paper.

SOLVE IT

Alarcon, Karen. *Louella Mae, She's Run Away!*
The whole family is looking for Louella Mae; can you guess who she is?

Baker, Keith. *Who Is the Beast?*
Just parts of an animal can be seen in the lush illustrations of the jungle; can you guess
   what beast it is?

Barnett, Mac. *Guess Again!*
Rhyming questions have surprising answers in this fun look at misguided riddles.

Davis, Katie. *Who Hops?*
Three animals that can hop are pictured with an animal that doesn't; guess which one.

Falconer, Ian. *Olivia and the Missing Toy.*
Olivia the Pig is determined to find out who stole her missing toy!

Guarino, Deborah. *Is Your Mama a Llama?*
A lilting rhyme describes various animals that help a llama find his mother.

Hill, Eric. *Spot the Dog.*
The popular "lift the flap" series of books are great for toddlers to solve simple picture riddles.

Inkpen, Mick. *In Wibbly's Garden.*
Wibbly the Pig is looking for his missing toy; lift the flaps to help him find it.

Kellogg, Steven. *The Missing Mitten Mystery.*
Annie looks for her missing mitten and imagines several unusual places it might be.

Miller, Margaret. *Whose Hat?*
Whose Shoe?
Who Uses This?
Just three of Miller's photo-guessing game books; even toddlers can solve these riddles!

Shea, Susan. *Do You Know Which One Will Grow?*
A rhyming text and flaps will encourage the audience to call out the answers in this factual look at living things.

Young, Ed. *Seven Blind Mice.*
The seven blind mice of the title each encounter a large object and try to guess what it is. The days of the week, colors, and numbers are all covered in this clever reworking of the classic folktale from India.

Craft: Print out some simple "dot to dot" activity sheets.
App: *Alphabet Animals: A Slide-and-Peek Adventure.* Auryn.

SOUTH AMERICA

Ehlert, Lois. *Moon Rope.*
A bilingual folktale from Peru, where a Fox persuades Mole to climb a rope to the moon.

Flora. *Feathers Like a Rainbow.*
Set in the Amazon rainforest, hummingbird shows how he gets his color by kissing the flowers.

Gerson, Mary Joan. *How Night Came From the Sea.*
A Brazilian folktale of how the daughter of the sea goddess married a mortal.

Knutson, Barbara. *Love and Roast Chicken.*
A funny story from the Andes, with a few Spanish words.

MacDonald, Margaret Read. *The Farmyard Jamboree.*
Inspired by a folktale from Chile, this has repetition and a song-like text.

McDermott, Gerald. *Jabuti the Tortoise.*
A folktale from the Amazon about why a tortoise has cracks in his shell.

Stanton, Karen. *Papi's Gift.*
Graciela can't wait for her birthday present, which is being mailed from Papi in the United States where he is working.

Torres, Leyla. *Saturday Sancocho.*
Set in Colombia, Grandmother and her granddaughter trade at the market until they have
   ingredients for their special Saturday meal.

VanLaan, Nancy. *So Say the Little Monkeys.*
Lots of sound effects will have the listeners chanting along to this Brazilian folktale.

Craft: Make Quetzal birds seen at www.dltk-kids.com/animals/mquetzal.html

STRAWBERRIES

Bruchac, Joseph. *The First Strawberries: A Cherokee Story.*
A Native American folktale about being kind to your family members.

Charles, N.N. *What Am I? Looking Through Shapes with Apples and Grapes.*
Rhyming guessing game about fruits, colors, and shapes.

Degan, Bruce. *Jamberry.*
In this rhythmic story, there are all types of berries to be found.

Formento, Alison. *These Bees Count!*
In this counting book, bees fly over strawberries and other plants as part of the honey-making
   process.

Litwin, Eric. *Pete the Cat: I Love My White Shoes.*
Pete's new sneakers turn various colors when he steps on strawberries, blueberries, and
   other messes.

Molk, Laurel. *Good Job, Oliver!*
Oliver Bunny tries to win the annual Strawberry Contest.

Naylor, Phyllis Reynolds. *Sweet Strawberries.*
A wife and her grumpy husband go to the market.

Stevens, Janet. *Cook-A-Doodle-Doo!*
Big Brown Rooster manages to bake a strawberry shortcake which would have pleased his
   great-grandmother, the Little Red Hen.

Wolff, Ashley. *Baby Bear Sees Blue.*
Baby Bear discovers many things out in nature, including red strawberries.

Wood, Audrey and Don. *The Little Mouse, the Red Ripe Strawberry, and the Big Hungry Bear.*
Little mouse is worried the bear will steal his strawberry (look for mouse wearing Groucho
   glasses).

Craft: Make strawberries out of red paper plates: children use yellow paint or yellow dot
   stickers to add the "seeds" and green construction paper stem tops.

SUN AND MOON

Asch, Frank. *Moon Bear.*
The bear is worried that the moon is shrinking and may disappear entirely.

Chall, Marsha Wilson. *Rupa Raises the Sun.*
When Rupa wants to sleep in, the townsfolk are concerned that the sun will not come up without Rupa's customary walk around the cookfire.

Gerstein, Mordicai. *The Sun's Day.*
Beginning at 6 A.M., we see what happens during the sun's day.

Ginsburg, Mirra. *Where Does the Sun Go at Night?*
A very brief story about the sun, who sleeps under a cloud blanket.

Henkes, Kevin. *Kitten's First Full Moon.*
A kitten thinks the moon is a distant bowl of milk.

Hol, Coby. *The Birth of the Moon.*
A pourquoi story about the phases of the moon; the sun gives the moonlight to animals so they may see at night.

Marino, Gianna. *Meet Me at the Moon.*
Mama elephant leaves her little one to climb the highest mountain to ask for rain.

Rinker, Sherri Duskey. *Goodnight, Goodnight, Construction Site.*
In this rhyming story, the construction vehicles say goodnight at sunset.

Tafuri, Nancy. *What the Sun Sees, What the Moon Sees.*
Flip over this dual story of what each heavenly body sees during a 24-hour day.

Craft: Make crowns that resemble the rays of the sun.

TEETH

Bate, Lucy. *Little Rabbit's Loose Tooth.*
When little rabbit finally loses his first tooth, he isn't sure if the tooth fairy will come.

Berger, Joe. *My Special One and Only.*
Bridget goes to the store with money from the tooth fairy, but she loses her stuffed animal on the way.

Birdseye, Tom. *Airmail to the Moon.*
Ora Mae is sure someone stole her tooth, which she was saving to put under her pillow for the tooth fairy.

Brown, Marc. *Arthur's Tooth.*
Arthur is teased at school because he is the only one who hasn't lost a tooth yet.

Colato, Laìnez Renè. *The Tooth Fairy Meets El Raton Perez.*
When Miguel loses a tooth, both the U.S. Tooth Fairy and El Ratòn Pèrez from Mexico come to claim it.

Davis, Katie. *Mabel the Tooth Fairy and How She Got Her Job.*
Because Mabel the Fairy did not brush or floss, she is turned into the Tooth Fairy.

Gomi, Taro. *The Crocodile and the Dentist.*
Both the crocodile and the dentist are afraid of each other in this participation story.

Graham, Bob. *April and Esme, Tooth Fairies.*
Two new tooth fairy sisters set off on their first mission.

Johnston, Teresa. *My Tooth Is Loose, Dr. Moose.*
Three friends visit the dentist because they are losing their baby teeth.

Karlin, Nurit. *Tooth Witch.*
A little witch turns into the Tooth Fairy.

MacDonald, Amy. *Cousin Ruth's Tooth.*
The Fister family helps Ruth find her lost tooth.

Wilson, Karma. *Bear's Loose Tooth.*
Bear's friends reassure him that his baby tooth needs to fall out.

Wing, Natasha. *The Night before the Tooth Fairy.*
Told in the rhyme pattern of "The Night before Christmas," this story describes a boy losing a tooth.

Craft: Make a special holder for any lost teeth. You can make it as simple as an envelope decorated with glitter.
App: *Go Away, Big Green Monster!* Night & Day Studios.

TELEPHONES

Allen, Jeffrey. *Mary Alice, Operator Number 9.*
When the phone operator is sick, none of her substitutes can do the job. There is also a sequel, *Mary Alice Returns.*

Barnett, Mac. *Telephone.*
Birds resting on the telephone cables pass along a message from a mother bird to her little bird Peter in this humorous take on the "Telephone" game.

Bemelmans, Ludwig. *Madeline.*
The doctor phones for an ambulance when Madeline has appendicitis.

Cordell, Matthew. *Hello! Hello!*
Everyone is on their electronic devices, so a little girl encourages her family to turn them off.

Gambrell, Jamey. *Telephone.*
Animals call to tell about their problems.

Kurtz, Jane. *I'm Calling Molly.*
Christopher has just learned Molly's phone number, so he calls her daily to see if she can play.

Raschka, Chris. *Ring! Yo?*
We see just one side of a phone conversation between two friends.

Sadler, Marilyn. *Pass It On!*
Cow is stuck in a fence, so several animals pass along the message until help can come.

Wells, Rosemary. *Good Night, Fred.*
Fred breaks the phone while jumping on the couch; he is concerned since he thinks grandma lives in the phone.

Wells, Rosemary. *Shy Charles.*
When his babysitter falls down the stairs, Charles must call the emergency service.

Craft: Try the printouts at the following website, to help children practice their phone numbers: www.first-school.ws/activities/firststeps/telephone911.htm

THANKSGIVING

Anderson, Derek. *Over the River: A Turkey's Tale.*
Based on the traditional song, this tells the story of a boy hunting for his dinner.

Arnosky, Jim. *I'm a Turkey!*
Filled with facts, this rhyming story describes a turkey and his large flock.

Dean, Kim. *Pete the Cat: The First Thanksgiving.*
Pete the Cat celebrates Thanksgiving in this lift-the-flap book.

Falwell, Catherine. *Feast for 10.*
An African American family prepares dinner in this memorable counting book.

Goode, Diane. *Thanksgiving Is Here!*
Everyone gathers at grandmother's house for Thanksgiving.

Jackson, Alison. *I Know an Old Lady Who Swallowed a Pie.*
A spoof of the song "I Know an Old Lady Who Swallowed a Fly," where the title character swallows various elements of Thanksgiving dinner.

Johnston, Tony. *10 Fat Turkeys.*
In this rhyming counting book that invites participation, turkeys sit on a fence, but fall off one by one.

Pilkey, Dav. *Twas the Night before Thanksgiving.*
A class visit to a turkey farm inspires the kids to save the turkeys and have a vegetarian Thanksgiving.

Spinelli, Eileen. *The Perfect Thanksgiving.*
Two families celebrate Thanksgiving in their own way.

Craft: Make turkeys to decorate the table by gluing feathers into pinecones, and adding a red pipe cleaner as the head.

TREEHOUSES

Berenstain, Stan and Jan. *Berenstain Bear* series.
Read one of the many books in the Berenstain Bears series; after all, they live in a tree house!

London, Jonathan. *Froggy Builds a Tree House.*
Should Froggy allow girls as well as boys into his tree house?

Marshall, James. *Three Up a Tree.*
Sam, Spider, and Lolly trade stories in their tree house.

Mathis, Melissa Bay. *Animal House.*
Different animals offer advice on how to make a human child's tree house more fun.

McConnachie, Brian. *Lily of the Forest.*
A little girl is bored and she wanders off into the forest, where animals help her find her way.

Numeroff, Laura. *If You Give a Pig a Pancake.*
Among the many things the pig requests is a tree house in this circular story.

Rylant, Cynthia. *Henry and Mudge and the Tall Tree House.*
Uncle Jake builds Henry a tree house, but how can the big dog Mudge get up there?

Skorpen, Liesel M. *We Were Tired of Living in a House.*
Four siblings and their cat and dog try out different abodes, including a tree house and the beach.

Verburg, Bonnie. *The Tree House That Jack Built.*
In this rhyming cumulative story, a little boy builds a fantastic tree house.

Craft: Make trees out of paper towel rolls by adding cut out leaves.

TURTLES AND TORTOISES

Aesop. *Tortoise and the Hare.*
There are several versions of this fable; it also makes a great puppet show.

Buckley, Richard. *The Foolish Tortoise.*
With distinctive illustrations by Eric Carle, a tortoise learns he needs his shell to survive.

Castillo, Lauren. *Melvin and the Boy.*
A boy finds a turtle at the park, and takes him home.

Falwell, Cathryn. *Turtle Splash! Countdown at the Pond.*
In this counting rhyme, similar in pattern to "Over in the Meadow," the endnote spells out facts about pond ecology.

Gorbachev, Valeri. *Whose Hat Is It?*
When the wind blows a hat off its owner, turtle asks all the animals if it belongs to one of them.

Hadithi, Mwenye. *Tricky Tortoise.*
In this African folktale, a tortoise tricks an elephant.

Javernick, Ellen. *The Birthday Pet.*
Danny receives a pet turtle for his birthday.

Lowell, Susan. *The Tortoise and the Jackrabbit.*
A Southwestern version of Aesop's "The Tortoise and the Hare," this is available in a bilingual Spanish/English edition.

Maris, Ron. *I Wish I Could Fly!*
At first, turtle wishes he could fly, climb, or move like other animals, until he realizes he can do things they cannot do.

Michalak, Jamie. *Joe and Sparky Go to School.*
A giraffe and a turtle escape from the zoo on a yellow school bus.

Waddell, Martin. *Hi, Harry!*
A tortoise wants to play but everyone is too fast; who would be a good, slow playmate for Harry?

Craft: Make paper plate turtles by coloring the plates green, and adding cutouts of the head and four feet.
Song: "I Had a Little Turtle and He Lived in a Box"

UNITED KINGDOM

Galdone, Paul. *The Tree Sillies.*
Also available in a version with illustrations by Steven Kellogg. A suitor travels across England looking for three people sillier than his intended and her parents.

Hughes, Shirley. *An Evening at Alfie's.*
One of the delightful books about a little English boy and his family.

Jacobs, Joseph. *Johnny-Cake.*
Similar to "The Gingerbread Boy," with a cake that rolls away.

Kimmel, Eric. *The Old Woman and Her Pig.*
Less violent than other versions, this cumulative tale concerns an old woman trying to get her pig over the turnstile in the fence.

MacDonald, Margaret Read. *Slop!*
A Welsh tale with repetition that invites participation, this concerns an old couple who find out they are dumping slop on a Wee Man. A good tale for Earth Day, too.

Potter, Beatrix. *The Tale of Peter Rabbit.*
The popular tale of a rabbit warned not to steal from the farmer.

Richardson, Justin. *Christian, the Hugging Lion.*
Based on a true story, this concerns a lion cub purchased at Harrods department store and raised in a London apartment.

Various. *Jack and the Beanstalk.*
The classic folktale of a boy who finds magic beans that grow into a beanstalk to the sky.

Various. *Teeny Tiny Woman.*
A woman wants to make soup from a bone she found, until she hears the bone "talking" in the night.

Craft: Try some of these activities celebrating Beatrix Potter's *The Tale of Peter Rabbit*: www.peterrabbit.com/en/fun_and_games
App: *Jack and the Beanstalk.* Nosy Crow.

VALENTINE'S DAY

Bond, Felicia. *The Day It Rained Hearts.*
Originally published as *Four Valentines in a Rainstorm,* Cordelia is walking home when it begins to rain hearts.

Capucilli, Alyssa. *Biscuit's Valentine's Day.*
A puppy and little girl deliver valentine's greetings.

Carr, Jan. *Sweet Hearts.*
A panda family cuts out valentine hearts and decorates the house. The paper collage illustrations will inspire preschoolers to make homemade valentine cards.

Choldenko, Gennifer. *A Giant Crush.*
Jackson is too shy to approach the girl he likes, so he hides little gifts for her for Valentine's Day.

Demas, Corinne. *Valentine Surprise.*
A little girl makes a valentine heart for her mother.

Dodd, Emma. *Foxy in Love.*
Foxy helps Emily make a Valentine's Day card.

Hayes, Geoffrey. *A Very Special Valentine.*
In this simple board book with a pop-up valentine, Tyler makes his mother a card.

Henkes, Kevin. *Lilly's Chocolate Heart.*
Lilly saves her candy heart but tries to find a perfect place to hide it.

Petersen, David. *Snowy Valentine.*
Jasper Bunny searches for the perfect gift for Lilly.

Poydar, Nancy. *Rhyme Time Valentine.*
The wind blows away the valentines Ruby made for her class, so she figures out another way to spread her friendship greetings.

Rylant, Cynthia. *If You'll Be My Valentine.*
A brief rhyming tale of a boy making valentines for his family.

Schaefer, Lola. *Guess Who? A Foldout Valentine's Adventure.*
Simple rhyming clues will help the audience guess which animal is hidden in each picture.

Scotton, Rob. *Love, Splat.*
Splat the Cat has a special valentine for someone in his class.

Craft: Make friendship bracelets: www.finecraftguild.com/valentine-friendship-bracelet-cuff-kids-upcycling/

WEATHER

Aardema, Verna. *Bringing the Rain to Kapiti Plain.*
In this cumulative tale set in Africa, a boy tries to make it rain so his animals will have water.

Barrett, Judi and Ron. *Cloudy With a Chance of Meatballs.*
In this imaginative story, it starts to rain giant food items on the town of Chewandswallow.

Blackstone, Stella. *Bear In Sunshine.*
Bear likes to play in all types of weather.

Cobb, Vicki. *I Face the Wind.*
A simple nonfiction book on the winds. This contains some great activity ideas, too.

Ets, Marie Hall. *Gilberto and the Wind.*
This classic picture book is about a boy who is frightened of the wind until he realizes what good the breeze can do.

Harper, Jamie. *Miss Mingo Weathers the Storm.*
Flamingo teacher Miss Mingo takes her class on a field trip to a weather station.

Howell, Will. *I Call It Sky.*
A great story on how the weather changes with the seasons.

Lotz, Karen. *Can't Sit Still.*
Weather and the seasons are shown in the city. Get the audience on their feet and participate in the movements described in the story!

McKee, David. *Elmer's Weather.*
The patchwork elephant Elmer experiences different types of weather.

Rogers, Paul. *What Will the Weather Be Like Today?*
Rhyming verse describes the day's weather.

Singleton, Linda Joy. *Snow Dog, Sand Dog.*
During the different types of weather, a little girl makes a dog out of natural materials because she is allergic to dogs.

Weigelt, Udo. *All-Weather Friends.*
Moss, the frog, cannot predict the weather accurately, even when the other animals expect him to.

Craft: Check out some of these weather activities for children: www.dltk-kids.com/crafts /weather/index.htm
Song: "You Are My Sunshine" and "Ain't Gonna Rain No More."

WEDDINGS

Bottner, Barbara. *Flower Girl.*
Illustrated with color photos, this is a simple informational book on weddings.

Brannen, Sarah. *Uncle Bobby's Wedding.*
Chloe worries that when her favorite uncle Bobby marries his boyfriend Jamie, he won't have time for her.

Brown, Marc. *D. W. Thinks Big.*
Arthur gets to be the ring bearer in their aunt's wedding, but D.W. is too small to be a flower girl.

Cox, Judy. *Now We Can Have a Wedding!*
When two people from the same apartment building have a wedding, all the neighbors bring food from their cultures in this celebration of diversity.

Henkes, Kevin. *Lilly's Big Day.*
Lilly expects to be the flower girl at her favorite teacher's wedding, but he finds a different role for her to play.

Holabird, Katharine. *Angelina and the Royal Wedding.*
Angelina is picked to be a bridesmaid at the wedding of the princess.

Johnson, Angela. *The Wedding.*
Daisy is the flower girl at her sister's wedding; featuring an African American family.

Look, Lenore. *Uncle Peter's Amazing Chinese Wedding.*
Jenny is afraid her uncle won't have time for her after he is married, but learns differently at his wedding. Several references to Chinese wedding customs make this unique.

Mbuthia, Waithira. *My Sister's Wedding: A Story of Kenya.*
Wambui's family prepares for the special event with food, songs, dances, and gifts.

Morris, Ann. *Weddings.*
A very brief text is matched to color photos from weddings around the world.

Munsch, Robert. *Ribbon Rescue.*
A Native American girl is wearing a traditional ribbon dress, which comes in handy when several people at a wedding are missing things like shoelaces, etc.

Soto, Gary. *Snapshots from the Wedding.*
Sculpy clay figures illustrate this tale of a Mexican-American wedding.

Wells, Rosemary. *Max & Ruby at the Warthogs Wedding.*
Max loses the wedding ring in this hilarious story.

Zalben, Jane B. *Beni's First Wedding.*
Beni, the bear, attends his uncle's traditional Jewish wedding.

Craft: Make bouquets out of tissue paper flowers.

WIND

Asch, Frank. *Like a Windy Day.*
A little girl imagines how she would play if she were the wind in this participation story.

Bluemle, Elizabeth. *Tap Tap Boom Boom*
In this jazzy rhyming story, two city kids try to get out of the wind and rain.

Cobb, Vicki. *I Face the Wind.*
A simple nonfiction book on the winds. This contains some great activity ideas, too.

Ets, Marie Hall. *Gilberto and the Wind.*
This classic picture book is about a boy who is frightened of the wind until he realizes what good the breeze can do.

Hutchins, Pat. *The Wind Blew.*
A rhyming story of a playful wind.

Jackson, Alison. *When the Wind Blew.*
Fairytale characters are impacted by the wind, blowing Rock a Bye Baby to the Old Woman in the Shoe.

Judge, Rita. *Flight School.*
A penguin tries to master the wind to learn to fly.

Manceau, Edouard. *Windblown.*
Small pieces of paper are blown by the wind, and make up various animals in this charming collage tale.

Wright, Maureen. *Sneeze, Big Bear, Sneeze!*
A bear believes his sneezes are causing the leaves to fall and other things in nature, but the Wind clues him in that it is not Bear, it is the Wind doing all these things.

Craft: Make these fun pinwheels: www.momto2poshlildivas.com/2012/04/spring-craft-easy-kids-pinwheel.html

ZOOS

Caple, Kathy. *A Night at the Zoo.*
A boy and his grandfather fall asleep at the zoo.

Heder, Thyra. *Fraidyzoo.*
Little T's family makes zoo animals out of boxes and other recycled materials so she won't be scared on her next visit.

Hillenbrand, Will. *Down By the Station.*
In this well-known song, baby animals ride the train to the zoo.

Lobel, Arnold. *A Zoo for Mr. Muster.*
Mr. Muster enjoys visiting the zoo so much he brings the animals back to his apartment.

Massie, Diane Redfield. *The Baby Beebee Bird.*
In this participation story, the crowd will chant the repeated phrases the baby bird makes, which keep all the zoo animals awake.

O'Hora, Zachariah. *Stop Snoring, Bernard!*
Bernard's loud snoring disturbs the other animals at the zoo.

Park, Linda Sue. *Xander's Panda Party.*
Xander is not sure which zoo animals he should invite to his panda party.

Rathmann, Peggy. *Good Night, Gorilla.*
A zookeeper and his wife put the animals to bed.

Rice, Eve. *Sam Who Never Forgets.*
Sam the zookeeper goes about feeding the animals, but has he forgotten the elephant?

Sadler, Marilyn. *Alistair's Elephant.*
Alistair is followed home from the zoo by an elephant.

Sierra, July. *Wild about Books.*
A librarian sets up a library at the zoo! Told in the rhyming style of Dr. Seuss.

Craft: Make a simple paper plate mask of your favorite animal, or paper bag puppet.
App: *Wild About Books.* Random House Digital.

BIBLIOGRAPHY

SUGGESTED READINGS

Banks, Carrie Scott. *Including Families of Children with Special Needs*. Chicago, IL: Neal-Schuman, 2014.

Barr, Catherine and John T. Gillespie. *Best Books for Children: Preschool through Grade 6, 9th edition*. Westport, CT: Libraries Unlimited, 2010.

Bauer, Caroline Feller. *Leading Kids to Books through Crafts*. Chicago, IL: American Library Association, 2000.

Bauer, Caroline Feller. *Leading Kids to Books through Puppets*. Chicago, IL: American Library Association, 1997.

Bauer, Caroline Feller. *New Handbook for Storytellers*. Chicago, IL: American Library Association, 1995.

Bauman, Stephanie G., editor. *Storytimes for Children*. Santa Barbara, CA: Libraries Unlimited, 2010.

Bos, Bev. *Don't Move the Muffin Tin: A Hands-off Guide to Art for the Young Child*. Roseville, CA: Turn the Page Press, 1978.

Champlin, Connie. *Storytelling with Puppets: 2nd edition*. Chicago, IL: American Library Association, 1997.

Cobb, Jane. *I'm a Little Teapot!* Vancouver, BC: Black Sheep Press, 2001.

Cobb, Jane. *What'll I Do with the Baby-o?* Vancouver, BC: Black Sheep Press, 2007.

Crepeau, Ingrid M. and Ann M. Richards. *A Show of Hands: Using Puppets with Young Children*. St. Paul, MN: Redleaf Press, 2003.

Dailey, Susan M. *Sing a Song of Storytime*. New York: Neal Schuman, 2007.

Del Negro, Janice M. *Folktales Aloud: Practical Advice for Playful Storytelling*. Chicago, IL: American Library Association, 2014.

Diamant-Cohen, Betsy. *Mother Goose on the Loose*. New York: Neal-Schuman, 2006.

Driggers, Preston and Eileen Dumas. *Managing Library Volunteers: ALA Guides for the Busy Librarian—2nd edition*. Chicago, IL: American Library Association, 2011.

Ernst, Linda L. *Essential Lapsit Guide: A Multimedia How-To-Do-It Manual and Programming Guide for Stimulating Literacy Development from 12 to 24 Months*. Chicago, IL: American Library Association, 2014.

Fox, Mem. *Reading Magic: Why Reading Aloud to Our Children Will Change Their Lives Forever—2nd edition*. New York: Mariner, 2008.

Ghoting, Saroj. *Storytimes for Everyone! Developing Young Children's Language and Literacy*. Chicago, IL: American Library Association, 2013.

Ghoting, Saroj and Kathy Klatt. *STEP into Storytime: Using Storytime Effective Practice to Strengthen the Development of Newborns to Five-Year-Olds*. Chicago, IL: American Library Association, 2014.

Ghoting, Saroj Nadkarni and Pamela Martin-Diaz. *Early Literacy Storytimes @ Your Library*. Chicago, IL: American Library Association, 2006.

Gillespie, Kellie M. *Teen Volunteer Services in Libraries: A VOYA Guide from Voice of Youth Advocates*. Lanham, MD: VOYA Books, 2004.

Haven, Kendall and MaryGay Ducey. *Crash Course in Storytelling*. Westport, CT: Libraries Unlimited, 2006.

Hopkins, Carol Garnett. *Artsy Toddler Storytimes: A Year's Worth of Ready-to-Go Programming.* Chicago, IL: Neal-Schuman, 2013.

Isbell, Rebecca and Shirley C. Raines. *Tell It Again! 2: Easy to Tell Stories with Activities for Young Children.* Beltsville, MD: Gryphon House, 2000.

Jeffery, Debby Ann. *Literate Beginnings: Programs for Babies and Toddlers.* Chicago, IL: American Library Association, 1995.

MacDonald, Margaret Read. *Look Back and See: Twenty Lively Tales for Gentle Tellers.* New York: H.W. Wilson, 1991.

MacDonald, Margaret Read. *The Storyteller's Start-Up Book: Finding, Learning, Performing, and Using Folktales.* Little Rock, AR: August House, 2006.

MacMillan, Kathy. *Try Your Hand at This: Easy Ways to Incorporate Sign Language into Your Programs.* Lanham, MD: Scarecrow Press, 2005.

MacMillan, Kathy and Christine Kirker. *Baby Storytime Magic: Active Early Literacy through Bounces, Rhymes, Tickles, and More.* Chicago, IL: American Library Association, 2014.

Marino, Jane. *Babies in the Library!* Lanham, MD: Scarecrow Press, 2003.

McNeil, Heather. *Read, Rhyme and Romp: Early Literacy Skills and Activities for Librarians, Teachers, and Parents.* Santa Barbara, CA: Libraries Unlimited, 2012.

Minkel, Walter. *How to Do "The Three Bears" with Two Hands: Performing with Puppets.* Chicago, IL: American Library Association, 2000.

Nichols, Judy. *Storytimes for Two-Year-Olds: 3rd edition.* Chicago, IL: American Library Association, 2007.

Pavon, Ana-Elba and Diana Borrego. *25 Latino Craft Projects.* Chicago, IL: American Library Association, 2003.

Peck, Penny. *Crash Course in Children's Services: Revised edition.* Santa Barbara, CA: Libraries Unlimited, 2014.

Pica, Rae. *Jump Into Literacy: Active Learning for Preschool Children.* Beltsville, MD: Gryphon House, 2007.

Reid, Rob. *Family Storytime: Twenty-Four Creative Programs for All Ages.* Chicago, IL: American Library Association, 1999.

Reid, Rob. *Welcome to Storytime!: The Art of Story Program Planning.* Madison, WI: Upstart Books, 2012.

Scott, Barbara A. *1,000 Fingerplays and Action Rhymes.* New York: Neal-Schuman, 2010.

Schimmel, Nancy. *Just Enough to Make a Story: A Sourcebook for Storytelling.* Berkeley, CA: Sisters' Choice, 1992.

Sierra, Judy. *Mother Goose's Playhouse: Toddler Tales and Nursery Rhymes, with Patterns for Puppets and Feltboards.* Ashland, OR: Bob Kaminsky Media Arts, 1994.

Silberg, Jackie. *Reading Games for Young Children.* Beltsville, MD: Gryphon House, 2005.

Straub, Susan and K.J. Dell'Antonia. *Reading with Babies, Toddlers, and Twos: A Guide to Laughing, Learning, and Growing Together through Books.* Naperville, IL: Sourcebooks, Inc., 2013.

Stetson, Emily and Vicky Congdon. *Little Hands Fingerplays and Action Songs: Seasonal Activities and Creative Play for 2- to 6-Year-Olds.* Charlotte, VT: Williamson Publishing, 2001.

Thomas, Rebecca L. *A to Zoo: Subject Access to Children's Picture Books: 9th edition.* Santa Barbara, CA: Libraries Unlimited, 2014.

Trelease, Jim. *The Read-Aloud Handbook: 7th edition.* New York: Penguin, 2013.

Warner, Penny. *Baby's Favorite Rhymes to Sign: Sing and Sign the Classics with Your Baby . . . Before Your Baby Can Talk!* New York: Three Rivers Press, 2010.

RECOMMENDED WEBSITES

General Websites

PUBYAC Listserv

www.pubyac.org

The listserv PUBYAC offers great programming ideas; it also has a website with an archive where you can find ideas that were posted previously.

West Bloomfield Township Public Library

www.growupreading.org/

This site is a great place to start, to learn why we need to have storytimes, advice for parents, booklists, information on child development, phonemic and print awareness, and other factors important for emergent readers.

ALA Notable Children's Books

www.ala.org/alsc/awardsgrants/notalists/ncb

What are the newest and best books for youth? Check out the ALA/ALSC Notable Children's Books list, a great way to find must-purchase books for your library. Check this list for new recommended picture books to use at storytime.

Bibliotherapy Booklists

www.carnegielibrary.org/kids/books/bibtherapy.cfm

Complied by the staff of the Carnegie Library of Pittsburgh, this contains a wealth of lists of children's books that deal with issues such as bullies, death, homelessness, self-esteem, and other challenges. I don't use these at storytime, but they can be offered to parents who seek out books to help with a family issue.

Great Kid Books Blog

http://greatkidbooks.blogspot.com

School librarian Mary Ann Scheuer has a blog that talks about several subjects relating to children and librarians. She reviews apps, eBooks, and discusses the Common Core; check her recommendations for apps to use at storytime

Tiny Tips for Library Fun

http://tinytipsforlibraryfun.blogspot.com/

Wisconsin librarian Marge Loch-Wouters offers plenty of practical tips for children's librarians, including programming and storytime ideas.

Baby Storytimes

Kate McDowell's Website

http://katemcdowell.com/laptime/

McDowell started this website as the result of her practicum for her MLIS, and includes ideas for themes, tips on baby storytime, ideas for working with parents, and other practical advice.

Perry Public Library

www.perrypubliclibrary.org/rfb
This Ohio library's website has a great list of baby rhymes, with all the words.

Mel's Desk

http://melissa.depperfamily.net/blog/?page_id=3835
Melissa Depper offers outlines for nearly 50 baby storytimes, including song lyrics, literacy tips, and suggested books.

Toddler Storytimes

Mother Goose on the Loose

www.mgol.org/
The Mother Goose on the Loose program is a library-based storytime for young children and their parents, that encourages lots of singing and rhymes. The website explains why repetition is important for this age group, in getting them ready to learn to read.

Preschool Express Toddler Station

www.preschoolexpress.com/toddler_station.shtml
A wealth of activities you can demonstrate for the toddler and parent to repeat at home, from making toys to games and songs.

Little eLit: Early Literacy in the Digital Age

http://littleelit.com
A popular blog on using apps and other Web 2.0 media with younger children; blogger Cen Campbell often discusses how to use apps at storytime.

Very Best App for Young Children

www.alsc.ala.org/blog/2014/03/the-very-best-app-for-young-children/?utm_source=feedburner&
utm_medium=email&utm_campaign=Feed%3A+AlscBlog+%28ALSC+Blog%29
The Association of Library Service to Children lists apps appropriate for storytime planning.

TumbleBooks

www.tumblebooks.com/library/asp/customer_login.asp
An increasing number of libraries are offering online picture books to their patrons. TumbleBooks is one of the companies that libraries pay so their users can access the books in the online library. You can also offer a picture book from TumbleBooks at a storytime, to demonstrate the proper use for parents.

BookFlix

http://teacher.scholastic.com/products/bookflixfreetrial/
Similar to TumbleBooks, BookFlix offers a collection of online children's books, many paired with video content, to libraries that pay for the service.

Storyline Online

www.storylineonline.net

Storyline Online is a free website that offers something similar to TumbleBooks and BookFlix. Sponsored by the Screen Actors Guild, this site shows famous actors reading popular picture books, similar to how picture books are read on the PBS series "Reading Rainbow."

Once Upon an App

www.coloradolibrariesjournal.org/articles/once-upon-app-process-creating-digital-storytimes-pre schoolers

Two librarians explain how to incorporate digital content into storytimes to support early literacy skills and practices.

Preschool and Family Storytimes

Bay Views/BayNews

www.bayviews.org

From the Association of Children's Librarians of Northern California. A monthly newsletter that also contains a column on storytime, with a new theme every month.

Everything Preschool

www.everythingpreschool.com

Also arranged by themes, these lesson plans include books! In fact, the book jackets are shown so you can see which picture books you might have and which may carry well to a group. Under each theme there are also songs, coloring pages, art ideas, recipes, games, and science ideas.

Preschool Express

www.preschoolexpress.com/theme_station.shtml

Thousands of ideas to enliven your storytime, but no books listed. Go to the Theme Station for crafts and activities by theme, the Story Station for rhymes and stories to tell, the Toddler Station for active movement ideas, the Pattern Station for craft printables, and more.

Step by Step Theme Pages

http://stepbystepcc.com/themes2.html

Run by a daycare provider named Jana, this is very similar to how most libraries compile their storytime themes. Under each theme, she lists picture books first, then songs and fingerplays, then craft ideas. It appears that she regularly updates this site.

Mid-Hudson Library System Story Hour Page

http://midhudson.org/program/ideas/Story_Hour.htm

Links to sites on flannelboards, music, crafts, and a wealth of other information relating to story-times is designed for library staff.

Lee & Low Books

http://blog.leeandlow.com/2014/03/21/where-can-i-find-great-diverse-childrens-books/

The publisher Lee & Low Books has a great resource page listing several other publishers as well as lists of multicultural books for children.

Poway School District Kindergarten Readiness

http://powayusd.sdcoe.k12.ca.us/news/ebulletin/december03/kindergarten-readiness.htm

From the Poway School District in California, this website lists 26 topics, one of each letter of the alphabet, on kindergarten readiness.

Family Education Kindergarten Readiness Resources

http://school.familyeducation.com/kindergarten/kindergarten-readiness/72117.html

This useful list of articles by various children's education specialists discusses kindergarten readiness and other related issues.

Songs and Fingerplays

Reading Is Fundamental

www.rif.org/kids/leadingtoreading/en/babies-toddlers/finger-plays.htm

The Reading Is Fundamental's site contains short videos of a person performing fingerplays for toddlers and babies.

Kididdles

www.kididdles.com/lyrics/allsongs.html

A great resource for song lyrics to popular preschool schools; some of the lyric pages let you hear the music, too.

BusSongs

http://bussongs.com/songs/well-all-join-in-the-circle.php

This site is run by volunteers who wanted to preserve and promote traditional songs used at storytimes and at summer camps. Each entry has lyrics, facts about the song, and some have videos.

Songs for Teaching

www.songsforteaching.com/fingerplays/index.htm

www.songsforteaching.com/movement.htm

The Fingerplays area has a great list of commonly used fingerplays; many come with an audio clip so you can learn the melody. There are also photos of a person doing the fingerplay, so you can copy the movement. There is an area for action songs; many of these also include an audio clip.

Born to Read Songs and Fingerplays

www.ala.org/alsc/issuesadv/borntoread/toddlerrhymesgames

Provided by the American Library Association's Born to Read initiative, this site lists several tickle and bouncing rhymes that are perfect for a baby storytime.

CanTeach

www.canteach.ca/elementary/songspoems.html

Poems and songs are listed here by theme. This is intended for teachers but also lists links for school librarians that can be helpful.

Fred Rogers Center for Early Learning and Children's Media

www.fredrogerscenter.org/resources/play-and-learn/
The Fred Rogers Center, named after the renowned television teacher for preschoolers, offers recommendations for apps to use for storytime, many of them featuring music.

Grow a Reader

https://itunes.apple.com/us/app/grow-a-reader/id594398910?mt=8
The Calgary Public Library offers a free app that encourages parents to sing with their children.

King County Library System's Rhymes and Songs

http://wiki.kcls.org/index.php/Category:Rhymes_&_Songs
From the King County Library system in Washington, this site contains hundreds of storytime songs and rhymes, demonstrated with videos featuring staff members performing the songs.

Bilingual Storytimes

Bibliotecas Para La Gente

www.bibliotecasparalagente.org
This website has a wealth of great ideas for doing storytimes in Spanish, or in English and Spanish, and is sponsored by the Northern California Chapter of REFORMA.

El Dia de los Ninos—Texas State Library

www.tsl.state.tx.us/ld/projects/ninos/songsrhymes.html
Traditional Spanish children's songs and rhymes are listed here, with the words in both English and Spanish, and with sound files.

Lectorum/Scholastic

www.lectorum.com/
Lectorum is the Spanish books division of Scholastic publishers.

Pan Asian Books

www.panap.com/
Located in the San Francisco Bay Area, this book distributor has a website you can use to order children's books in a variety of Asian languages.

Shen's Books

www.shens.com/
Specializing in multicultural children's books, Shen's also has some bilingual books. This website allows for easy ordering.

Children's Book Press

www.childrensbookpress.org/
This unique publisher started as a nonprofit organization, and publishes children's books celebrating world cultures. Now part of Lee & Low Books, many of their picture books feature English and another language.

Washington County Library—Spanish Fingerplays

www.wccls.org/rimas

Videos of popular Spanish fingerplays performed by library staff will help you quickly learn some songs for your storytime.

StoryBlocks—Spanish Songs for Children

www.storyblocks.org/videos/language/espanol/

Provided by Colorado Libraries for Early Literacy, this site contains videos of library staff demonstrating popular children's Spanish songs and fingerplays.

Arts and Crafts Websites

Enchanted Learning

www.enchantedlearning.com

You don't have to be a member to use this site, which contains lots of homework areas, helpful pages, and great craft ideas for storytimes and programs.

The Activity Idea Place: An Early Childhood Educator's Resource

www.123child.com/

Hundreds of themes, with ideas for crafts, games, recipes, songs, and fingerplays (but not books), this is a great secondary source for storytime ideas.

Multicultural Preschool Ideas

www.first-school.ws/theme/places.htm

Lots of easy craft ideas, with printable pages, for preschool storytimes.

Family Crafts

http://familycrafts.about.com/od/craftprojectsbytheme

Large selection of free craft projects sorted by theme. Make crafts related to everything from animals to transportation.

A to Z Kids Stuff

www.atozkidsstuff.com

The site has free activities for toddlers, preschoolers, and older children. It also includes links to reviews of children's music, movies, and books.

Child Fun

http://childfun.com/

Provides craft ideas, printable coloring pages, and other activities parents can do with young children.

Coloring Pages

www.coloringpages.net

Choose from hundreds of printable coloring pages for kids. Disney coloring pages include characters like Winnie the Pooh; other characters like Scooby Doo are favorites. They include a large selection of Bible and Christian pages, and many holiday pages.

Crayola Crayons

www.crayola.com
Find rich, hands-on learning experiences that can be searched by subject, theme, grade, media, and completion time.

DLTK Kids

www.dltk-kids.com
Features a variety of fun, printable children's crafts, coloring pages and more including projects for holidays, educational themes, and many children's favorite cartoon characters.

Spoonful

www.familyfun.go.com
Lots of activities and crafts sorted by theme or age group, Spoonful is a website sponsored by Disney.

Pop Goes the Page

http://blogs.princeton.edu/popgoesthepage
Need ideas for arts and crafts activities for storytime? Check out the blog "Pop Goes the Page," from Dana Sheridan, the Education and Outreach Coordinator of the Cotsen Children's Library at Princeton University.

Learning 4 Kids Science Activities

www.learning4kids.net/category/science-play/
Photos and simple instructions describe science hands-on activities that even a toddler can do!

Thinking Fountain

www.thinkingfountain.org/
From the Science Museum of Minnesota comes this great collection of easy science activities you can do with preschoolers.

Toys, Puppets, and other supplies

Lakeshore Learning

www.lakeshorelearning.com
A resource for a wide variety of storytime props, including puppets, Big Books, flannelboards, storytelling aprons and figures, musical instruments and shakers, and more.

Folkmanis Puppets

www.folkmanis.com
This small company carries the finest puppets sold commercially; check out its selection of realistic animal puppets.

Melissa and Doug

www.melissaanddoug.com
Melissa and Doug sell traditional toys such as wooden blocks and puzzles that are great for a stay and play storytime.

Read! Build! Play!

http://readbuildplay.com/

The American Library Association has a special initiative called Read! Build! Play! which encourages libraries to incorporate play into their storytimes and other services for young children. Check this website for a free downloadable toolkit.

Campaign for a Commercial-Free Childhood

www.commercialfreechildhood.org/

The CCFC is an advocacy group with the goal of eliminating corporate influences in educational environments (such as schools and libraries); they suggest libraries use noncommercial toys and puppets at storytime.

Beyond the Book Storytimes

http://btbstorytimes.blogspot.com/search/label/Program%20Summary

Children's librarian Steven Englefried offers tips on using puppets and music at library programs.

Mid-Hudson Library System Resource Page

http://midhudson.org/program/support/Flannel_kits.htm

A comprehensive listing by a public library in New York, describing sources for purchasing flannelboards and other storytelling props.

Kimbo Education

www.kimboed.com/

Kimbo Education is well known for its award-winning music recordings for children. They also sell accessories such as scarves and beanbags to go along with some of the dance CDs for young children.

Fat Brain Toys

www.fatbraintoys.com/special_needs/

There are several great resources for toys for children, but Fat Brain offers adaptive toys for children with special needs.

Parent Education and Special Programs

Every Child Ready to Read @ Your Library

http://everychildreadytoread.org/

Every Child Ready to Read is a program sponsored by the American Library Association. The website lists suggestions on incorporating preliteracy tips for parents into your storytimes, and has printable handouts including booklists for different age groups.

Born to Read

www.ala.org/alsc/issuesadv/borntoread

Another program sponsored by the American Library Association, Born to Read offers free materials to motivate parents to read to their children.

Storytime Share

www.earlylit.net/storytimeshare

If you would like to add simple advice for parents on how a book relates to literacy, the Storytime Share blog is a great resource. Saroj Ghoting is a noted expert on early literacy, and her blog shares songs and books, with tips on how they can help children acquire preliteracy skills.

Kent Library District—Five Early Literacy Practices

www.kdl.org/kids/go/pgr_five_practices

Kent Library has a clear explanation of the five literacy practices you can encourage parents to do at home by demonstrating them in your storytimes.

Linda Lucas Walling Collection

http://faculty.libsci.sc.edu/walling/bestfolder.htm

Linda Lucas Walling was a professor of Library and Information Science at the University of South Carolina. Walling's website offers guidelines for evaluating children's books that depict disabilities, and contains lists of recommended children's books that show the disabled.

Sensory Storytime Program Plan

www.ala.org/alsc/sensory-story-tots

Barbara Klipper of the Ferguson Library in Stamford, Connecticut, offers detailed plans on constructing a sensory storytime, on the website of the Association of Library Service to Children.

Zero to Three

www.zerotothree.org/site/PageServer?pagename=homepage

Zero to Three is a national nonprofit organization that promotes education for babies and toddlers. Their website has a wealth of printable handouts on a variety of topics, including brain development in babies and building bridges to literacy.

National Association for the Education of Young Children

www.naeyc.org/

From knowing what toys are recommended for which age groups, to advice on using singing as a teaching tool, to brain research in young children, this website has a wealth of concise and clear information for parents, caregivers, and preschool teachers.

Using Volunteers for Storytimes

Reach Out and Read

www.reachoutandread.com

Reach Out and Read was developed in 1989 by two doctors in Boston. Doctors and other healthcare practitioners encourage parents to read aloud to their young children, distribute free children's books, and create literacy-rich environments in their waiting rooms.

1,000 Books before Kindergarten

www.cde.state.co.us/cdelib/LibraryDevelopment/YouthServices/1000Books.htm

For more on starting this program, check out the materials offered by its originator Sandy Krost of the Bremen Public Library, Indiana.

1,000 Books Bloom

www.pinterest.com/lochwouters/let-1000-books-bloom/
Another great resource for starting a 1,000 Books before Kindergarten program is this Pinterest site
maintained by librarian Marge Loch-Wouters of La Crosse, Wisconsin.

Intermountain Therapy Animals

www.therapyanimals.org
Therapy Animals is the organization that promotes the use of animals for several different therapy
causes, including literacy. The site includes lots of helpful information including a training
guide.

Youth Service America

http://ysa.org/
Youth Service America is a nonprofit organization dedicated to helping youth contribute volunteer
service. This website has great tip sheets on working with teen volunteers, and information on
grants and other partnerships.

INDEX

ABOUT THE AUTHOR

PENNY PECK is a part-time instructor at San Jose State University, specializing in classes on youth services and programming. She was a children's librarian for more than 25 years. Her published works include Libraries Unlimited's *Crash Course in Children's Services: Second Edition* and *Readers' Advisory for Children and 'Tweens*. She received her master of library science degree from San Jose State University.